Malaysia, Southeast Asia
and the
Emerging China:
*Political, Economic and
Cultural Perspectives*

Malaysia, Southeast Asia and the
Emerging China:
Political, Economic and Cultural Perspectives

Edited by

Hou Kok Chung   Yeoh Kok-Kheng

Institute of China Studies
University of Malaya

Institute of China Studies
University of Malaya
50603 Kuala Lumpur
Malaysia
Tel: 603-79565663 Fax: 603-79565114

COPYRIGHT

Perpustakaan Negara Malaysia Cataloguing-in-Publication Data

Malaysia, Southeast Asia and the Emerging China : Political, Economic
    and Cultural Perspectives / editors Hou Kok Chung, Yeoh Kok-
    Kheng.
    ISBN 983-3602-90-8
    1. China–Foreign relations–Malaysia–Congresses. 2. Malaysia–
    Foreign relations–China–Congresses. 3. China–Foreign relations–
    Asia, Southeastern–Congresses. 4. Asia, Southeastern–Foreign
    relations–China–Congresses. I. Hou, Kok Chung. II Yeoh, Kok
    Kheng.
    327.510595

Printed by Herald Printers Sdn. Bhd. (19965-V)

CONTENTS

III   China and Southeast Asia: Regional Perspectives

Editors

Contributors

Professor **Lee** Poh Ping, Institute of Malaysian and International Studies (IKMAS), Universiti Kebangsaan Malaysia, Bangi, Malaysia.

Professor **Lee** Kam Hing, fromerly at the University of Malaya, is now the research editor of the Malaysian daily *The Star*.

Dr **Hou** Kok Chung, Associate Professor and Director of the Institute of China Studies, University of Malaya, Kuala Lumpur, Malaysia.

Dr **Qu** Hong, Assistant Professor of Religious Studies at the Agnes Scott College, Georgia, USA.

Professor **Kong** Yuanzhi was formerly at the Institute of Southeast Asian Culture Studies, Peking University, Beijing, China.

Professor George T. **Yu**, Director of the Center for East Asian and Pacific Studies, University of Illinois, Urbana-Campaign, USA.

Professor **Zheng** Yongnian, Director of research at the China Policy Institute, University of Nottingham, United Kingdom.

Lye Liang Fook, Research Officer at the East Asian Institute, National University of Singapore.

Dr Edmund Terence **Gomez**, Associate Professor at the Department of Administrative Studies and Politics, Faculty of Economics and Administration, University of Malaya, Kuala Lumpur, Malaysia.

Professor **Wang** Hailiang, Deputy Director of the International Programs Office, Shanghai Academy of Social Sciences, China.

Professor Leo **Suryadinata**, Senior Research Fellow at the Institute of Southeast Asian Studies, Singapore.

Professor **You** Anshan, Director of the Department of Regional Economic Cooperation Studies, Institute of World Economy, Shanghai Academy of Social Science, China.

Professor Yoshihide **Soeya**, Faculty of Law, Keio University, Tokyo, Japan.

Professor **Tan** Chee-Beng, Department of Anthropology, Chinese University of Hong Kong.

FOREWORD

This volume has its origin in the international conference "Emerging China: Implications and Challenges for Southeast Asia" organized by the Institute of China Studies (ICS), University of Malaya, in July 2004. Included here are eleven of the papers presented and one of the roundtable presentations on China Studies and Southeast Asia. As ICS's inaugural conference, the gathering of international scholars on China Studies was highly significant as it presented an opportune platform for dialogue in the light of the many challenges faced by Southeast Asian nations due to the materialization of China as an emerging economic powerhouse and her ever growing political influence in the world. The conference marked the birth of ICS as a new institution within the University of Malaya dedicated towards building comprehensive dialogue, enabling regular exchanges of views and perspectives, and coordinating action on matters of mutual concerns not only between China and Malaysia but also with the rest of Southeast Asia. It is, therefore, our hope that the publication of this volume would contribute towards a deeper understanding, from perspectives ranging from the political, economic to the cultural, of the present phenomenal rise of China and the country's relations with Malaysia and ASEAN.

Dr Hou Kok Chung
Director
Institute of China Studies
University of Malaya

I

Malaysia and China:
Bilateral Relations, Culture
and Identity

Chapter 1

Malaysia-China Relations: A Review

Lee Poh Ping and Lee Kam Hing

Introduction

The last time China stepped out into the international scene as a world power was some 600 years ago. China in the early 15th century was probably the most powerful country in the world and for the first time ever, sent out huge expeditions to show off its naval might. Of the great fleets sent out the most famous were those under the command of Admiral Zheng He. Zheng He commanded seven expeditions. Just at about this time, a new port-polity was emerging in the Straits of Malacca. This was the Malacca Sultanate, and it was to feature importantly in Ming China's overseas policy.

The new sultanate of Malacca was one place Zheng He visited in his first expedition. Earlier in 1403 Ying Li had commanded a fleet that visited Malacca. Some historians argue that China and Malacca developed common strategic and economic interests.[1] Consolidation of the China-Malacca link came in 1405 when the Ming Emperor assigned an engraved inscription to Malacca for the "mountain protecting the country". This could be Bukit China. Zheng He and others traveled to Malacca again in

1408, and in 1411 the ruler of Malacca himself went to China on the returning ships of Zheng He's third expedition.

However by the middle of the 15th century, China ended all overseas expeditions and did not engage in further maritime ventures beyond its own shores. Chinese merchants continued to trade in Southeast Asia including the Malay Peninsula. The next five hundred years then witnessed a gradual decline of Malay political power and a withdrawal of China from the Malaysian area. Western powers came to dominate the region. It is only in the post-Second World War period of nationalism and revolution that it is possible to talk of a re-emergence of Malaysia-China relations.

It is fitting therefore that this conference on China and Southeast Asia, including Malaysia should be held at around the time of the commemoration of the 600th year (2005) of Zheng He's first expedition to Malaysia and at the 30th year anniversary (2004) of the establishment of Malaysian diplomatic relations with China. The former marks an important historical event of long ago while the latter commemorates the beginning of the development of modern diplomatic relations between the two nations in the post-war era.[2] A review of Malaysian relations with China is thus appropriate. There is also another reason for such a review apart from the historical commemoration, and that is to consider the growing impact of China, which has been a rising power in recent times, on Malaysia.

The Rise of China

There is no doubt the rise of China constitutes one of the most striking developments of the last quarter of the twentieth century. There is no general agreement as to what this rise means for the international system. There are those who think that China's emergence has no parallel in history. Certainly, the former Prime Minister of Singapore, Lee Kuan Yew, subscribes to this view when he argues that one could not turn to history for any guidance of China's rise. China will emerge as no ordinary player but as the biggest player in the history of mankind! (Quoted in Huntington, 1996:231) The respected London weekly *Economist*[3] some years ago suggested that the most impressive aspect of the economic rise of China lies not so much in the achievements that have been made since the Chinese open door policy of 1978 such as the massive growth of China's Gross National Product (GNP), increase in Chinese personal income, and a great reduction of poverty but rather on what this rise reveals about the potential the developments of the past quarter century have for the creation of a unified continental Chinese economy. By that is meant the integration of the various provinces of China, which hitherto in many cases have each acted as though they were autonomous economic units, into a truly national economy. The impact of such a unified, modern Chinese economy on the international economy will be enormous. The comparable example is the unification of the continental economy of America in the nineteenth century. This unified American economy, as it emerged into the twentieth century, had as we know a tremendous impact on the global economy. And only recently, a former foreign editor of Time Magazine, after spending some time in China, not only agrees that China is a continent on the move but suggests it could prove to be a model for those countries not enamored with the approach of those who subscribe to the Washington consensus.[4]

There are however those who hold a more modest expectation of this rise of China. They argue that for all the hype about China, that country is still only the sixth largest economy in the world measured by GNP. And measured by GNP per capita, it is way behind not only the industrial economies but also the newly industrializing Asian economies.[5] There are also those who believe that this Chinese economy is hobbled by problems already evident such as a vast sector of uncompetitive state-owned enterprises and a shaky banking system. At the same time China's economic rise has led to growing social inequality and to divisions between the prosperous coastal regions and the poorer interior areas. These could cause China problems in the future. Finally, it remains to be seen, in the eyes of those with a critical view of China, whether an authoritarian communist regime such as is found in China is compatible with the management of a modern economy.[6] Nonetheless, whether China will become a superpower or not, this emerging China will have a tremendous impact on Southeast Asia, including Malaysia. As it is, this impact is already felt and will likely increase greatly in the future.

This chapter will review briefly the history of Malaysia-China relations since 1949. This review will touch on the part which domestic politics and the Malaysian communists had upon early bilateral relations. It will then be followed by a discussion of the state-to-state relations, particularly from the perspective of how Malaysia views an emergent China.

Background to Malaysia's Relations with China

The most recent historical perspective of bilateral Malaysia-China relations is relevant for an appreciation of the contemporary situation. This is because the establishment of normal diplomatic relations between China and Malaysia and indeed between China and with many other Southeast Asian nations had been complicated by two factors. One had been Beijing's policy towards Malaysians of Chinese origin and the other is its policy towards the Communist Party of Malaya. Unlike the establishment of diplomatic relations of China with many other countries such as for example with the African countries where communities of Chinese origin and African communist parties linked closely to China were not present in any significant degree to complicate matters, these two issues featured prominently in the establishment of diplomatic relations between China and Malaysia.

China and Malaysians of Chinese Origin

When the communists took power in China in 1949, they had not thought out clearly a policy towards Southeast Asians of Chinese origin. What they then did was to continue with the policy of the previous

Kuomintang government which was to consider as Chinese those who had a grandfather who was a Chinese citizen.[7] This, of course, created difficulties with many Southeast Asian nations which had just obtained independence from colonial rule. These newly independent nations would not tolerate large communities living in their midst who were citizens of another country, especially of a big nearby communist power such as China. The Chinese communists, meanwhile, were keen to establish diplomatic relations with these new Southeast Asian states, particularly those that were then not seen as Western allied. Yet at the same time they could not renounce their claims on those Southeast Asians of Chinese descent without some reciprocity from these Southeast Asian states. Eventually China, in the process of establishing diplomatic relations with Indonesia in 1955, came out with a policy that subsequently formed the basis for its relations with other Southeast Asian states that have Chinese minorities. The Chinese communists, in the Indonesian case, in exchange for diplomatic recognition, would relinquish their claims to those of Chinese origin who had become Indonesian citizens of their own free will. For those Chinese residing in Indonesia who for one reason or other could not be Indonesian citizens, Beijing urged them to respect the law and the customs of Indonesia.

When in 1974 Tun Razak visited China to establish diplomatic relations, the situation in Malaysia however was different from that of Indonesia. In the Malaysian case most of the Malaysians of Chinese origin had, by 1974, already embraced Malaysian citizenship and were integrated into the Malaysian polity, unlike the Chinese in Indonesia in 1955 and even after.[8] In fact it has been suggested that one reason for Razak's opening to China was an attempt on the part of the Barisan Nasional to win Malaysian Chinese votes for a general election that was expected to be declared after the Razak visit to China. UMNO leaders had become sufficiently confident of Malaysian Chinese loyalty to use the China card. Still, there was the problem of the many Chinese residing in Malaysia who even as late as 1974, for one reason or the other, had yet to obtain Malaysian citizenship. They were the so-called stateless Chinese. Their number was estimated to be around 200,000.[9] It was feared that these stateless Chinese could cause complications in the negotiations between Malaysia and the Chinese communist authorities. The Chinese communist government could not openly abandon them. But so keen were both sides to establish diplomatic relations that in the joint communiqué in 1974 between Razak and the Chinese premier Zhou En-lai, there was no mention of this group of Chinese beyond the usual urging by the Chinese premier that Chinese residents in Malaysia should respect Malaysian laws and customs.[10]

Tun Razak's visit to China marked a departure from that of the Tengku in terms of the governmental view of the linkage between relations with China and the domestic inter-ethnic situation. Under the Tengku, Kuala Lumpur had no diplomatic relations with China. Malaysians were also not allowed to visit China. This was despite growing trade between the two countries, particularly in rubber. China was then one of the largest markets for Malaysia's rubber.

One reason was the then evolving ethnic political balance. This shaped the nature and extent of Malaysia's dealings with China. On one hand, the Malays then were not totally confident of their grip on political power. Thus, the government of the day had to be sensitive to Malay concerns, especially at a time when there were still those who contended that too many political concessions had been given to the Chinese and to open up ties with China at that stage might not be acceptable to most Malays. On the other hand, it was also thought unwise to risk exposing the Chinese to possible competing loyalties at a time when many had just become citizens, and when adjustments were still being made to the new format of inter ethnic cooperation.

A second reason was the negative attitude of the Tengku regarding official relations with China. This attitude was greatly shaped by his experience of the Malaysian communist insurgency which he saw as being greatly influenced by communist China. Given the fact that a majority of the Malaysian communists were of Chinese origin, the Tengku feared that recognition of communist China would not only be a morale booster to the insurgents but might give occasion for China to interfere in the internal affairs of Malaysia. Also the Tengku was very pro-West. He seriously regarded China as a threat to regional security. He saw for example the Sino-Indian border conflict in 1962 as a Chinese attack on democracy and launched a "Save Democracy Fund" in support of India. He also believed that China threatened Malaysia when in the 1963-65 period, China aligned itself with Indonesia's confrontation against Malaysia. Thus, given his pro-West policy and in an environment of the Cold War and the containment of China it was unlikely that the Tengku, even if he wanted to, if only to gain Malaysian Chinese votes, could make any radical move towards China.[11]

Third, there were a number of leaders in the Malaysian Chinese Association, the Chinese coalition partner of the Tengku's party, UMNO, in the Alliance who had previous links with the Kuomintang. Furthermore, many of the founders of the MCA in 1949 were business groups who were strongly anti-communist. A number of them were developing business ties with Taiwan. A few of them were close to the Tengku and had influence over his China policy. Not surprisingly, the government allowed travel to Taiwan for business and education. Several hundred Malaysian students, mainly from Chinese-language schools enrolled each year in Taiwanese universities. A trade mission was sent to Taiwan in November 1965 and in 1966 a Malaysian consulate was established in Taiwan.

Thus, the Razak visit marked the diplomatic resolution of the status of the Malaysian Chinese from the point of view of both countries. With a reputation as a Malay nationalist, the Malays generally trusted Razak's China initiative.[12] This did not mean however that controversial issues pertaining to the Malaysian Chinese connection with China might not crop up every now and then. For example, not so long ago, a prominent Malay politician criticized investments in China by Malaysian Chinese businessmen. Such investments, he argued, should be directed to Malaysia instead. However, this criticism did not seriously affect relations between China and Malaysia nor did it escalate into a major domestic political issue. One reason is simply that many of the Malaysian investments in China come from Malaysian business groups with Malay participation. There is now a broader appreciation of Malaysia-China relations to which the local communal factor, while significant, does not predominate.

China and Communism in Malaysia

While it can be argued that the Chinese communists did not inspire the Communist Party of Malaya to take up arms in 1948 the Chinese origins of the party and the moral support given to it by the Chinese communist party until 1989 make it understandable as to why the Malaysian government, even after the establishment diplomatic relations in 1974, believed that its bilateral relations with China would not be entirely normal until Beijing dropped its support of the Malaysian communists or until some settlement had been achieved between the Malaysian government and the Malaysian communists. The establishment of diplomatic relations did not resolve this problem. While Tun Razak's visit resulted in the Chinese acknowledging the legitimacy of the Malaysian government, the Chinese did not disavow their party's relations with the Communist Party of Malaya. This, the Chinese argue, was consistent with the manner in which they conducted their foreign policy. This policy was in three directions: that of state-to-state relations, party to party relations, and people to people relations. The Chinese suggested that the relations of the Chinese communist party with that of the Communist Party of Malaysia came within the ambit of party-to-party relations and should not affect government-to-government relations. The Malaysians saw this as sophistry in semantics simply because they knew that the Chinese government was controlled by the Chinese Communist Party. The Foreign Minister of Malaysia during the early years after the Malaysian recognition of China, Tan Sri Ghazali Shafie, once used a piscine metaphor to describe this, calling this the equivalent to serving sweet and sour fish i.e. the Chinese communists were playing some kind of a double game.

Thus it was that while the Malaysian Chinese no longer constituted an issue in bilateral relations the problem of the party to party relations was to plague bilateral Sino-Malaysian relations until 1989 when the Communist Party of Malaya in meetings with the Malaysian government agreed to end their armed struggle.

State-to-State Relations – 1974 to the Mid-1980s – Obstacle to Good Relations

While 1974 marked the beginning of a new relationship between Malaysia and China, it cannot be said that bilateral state to state relations in the decade or so following the Tun Razak visit was of the most desirable or ideal kind. This was because the Chinese Communist Party did not give up its support of the Communist Party of Malaya. And even if the issue of the Malaysians of Chinese origin had been settled, their presence in such large numbers, however integrated they might be, could not help but influence the Malaysian government's attitude towards China. Hence, Malaysians until the late 1980s were not allowed to freely visit China. Still, the momentum developed from the 1974 diplomatic recognition could have led to a reasonable period of good relations. That this did not happen could largely be due to the demise in 1976, soon after diplomatic relations were established, of Zhou En-Lai and Tun Razak. Zhou, despite being a Chinese revolutionary, and Razak, a Malay aristocrat, had achieved a certain chemistry between them that went some way to building trust between the two nations.[13] Their successors had no such chemistry.

The successor to Razak, Hussein Onn, continued with the policy of diplomatic recognition. But because of continued Beijing support for the Malaysian communists, the Hussein Onn government veered towards the perception of China as a long-term threat to the region. This became evident in the aftermath of the Vietnamese invasion of Cambodia in 1978 and the Chinese limited invasion of Vietnam in 1979. Thus in the process of forging a common ASEAN position towards the Vietnamese invaders, Malaysia, under Tun Hussein Onn, and Indonesia, under President Suharto, were seen as wanting a soft line towards the Vietnamese as both considered China to be the long term threat to the region. A weakened Vietnam would enable China to exert its influence in Southeast Asia. Singapore and Thailand (the frontline state as it bordered the invaded country, Cambodia) on the other hand saw the

Soviet Union as the long-term threat. The USSR was presumed to be using Vietnam as a proxy to dominate Southeast Asia and hence Vietnam had to be resisted.

The Changed Malaysian Perception of China

The perception of China as a threat to Malaysia began to undergo a change from the mid-1980s onwards (the threat perception was dropped altogether in the early 1990s). This was a result of various factors. One was the increasing acceptance by the Malaysian government that the Malaysian Chinese were well integrated into the Malaysian polity. Any further opening towards China such as allowing Malaysians to visit China with the same degree of freedom they were permitted to travel to any other friendly country and the encouragement of business ties between Malaysian and Chinese, would not have negative domestic political consequences. Indeed it was suggested that Malaysian Chinese were likely to regard themselves as being better off in Malaysia (and thus more loyal) after they see and experience for themselves prevailing conditions in China.[14] Second, China, as mentioned, had begun to distance itself further from the Communist Party of Malaya. The Sino-Soviet competition for the allegiance of communist parties worldwide and in Southeast Asia in particular, was running out of steam, given the changes in both the USSR and in China. Thus, the Chinese saw the continued armed resistance of the Communist Party of Malaya based in southern Thailand to be a real impediment to good relations between Malaysia and China. They began to exert pressure on the Malaysian communists to come to terms with the Malaysian government.[15] Given this pressure and the apparent futility of their continued resistance, the Communist Party of Malaya in 1989 under Chin Peng, finally gave up the armed struggle they had first started in 1948. This removed the last remaining major internal obstacle to normal state-to-state relations between both countries.

A third reason is the changed situation in China. Since the decision by the central committee of the Chinese Communist Party in 1978 to implement an open door policy, China has increasingly been behaving like a normal state in the sense that it was no longer encouraging communist revolution worldwide and was doing everything it could to integrate itself to the international market economy. Such integration was to culminate in China's admission to the World Trade Organization (WTO) in 2001. At the same time the Chinese economy was developing at such a rapid pace that its impact was beginning to be felt by Southeast Asia, not least Malaysia. There was also the possibility that an economically strong China could have a corresponding military and political impact on the region. Under such circumstances, it does not make good sense for Malaysian and Southeast Asian leaders to continue with the China threat perception. The perception had either to be changed or has to be more nuanced. If any event were to mark a turning point in this connection it would be Dr Mahathir's official visit to China in November 1985. That visit when Dr Mahathir was accompanied by a large entourage of Malaysian businessmen signified that whatever lingering problems there were that existed over the Chinese support of the Communist party of Malaya, it was more important for Malaysia to consider the changed circumstances in China and the international environment. This would allow for Malaysia to greatly benefit from enhanced economic relations with China.

If Razak can be considered as having laid the foundation for Malaysian-Chinese relations, Dr Mahathir should be given credit for the normalization of relations between the two countries when, among other things, he abandoned the Chinese threat perception. While it can be argued that any other Prime Minister might eventually have dropped this threat perception given the changed circumstances, it cannot be denied that Dr Mahathir hastened this. He overcame any lingering bureaucratic and military resistance to a more benign view of China and as was reported gave his backing to efforts to a negotiated settlement of the Malaysian communist insurgency.[16] In addition he created a climate of opinion in Malaysia and indeed elsewhere for a more positive view of China. The essence of his argument was that the assumption of a Chinese threat could be self-fulfilling in that China would really become a threat if one kept regarding it as a threat. Dr Mahathir made the observation that, unlike that of the West, the history of China's relations with Southeast Asia had not been marked by territorial hegemony or economic colonialism.[17]

Hence, under Dr Mahathir, Malaysia enhanced ties with China. The 1985 visit resulted in the signing of four major trade agreements. Since then relations between Malaysia and China continued to improve with the exchange of official visits. The growing congruence in interest of the two countries was highlighted during the first Malaysia-China Forum held in Kuala Lumpur in January 1995. Dr Mahathir, in his keynote address, indicated that Malaysia did not regard China as a military threat, noting that China's military spending was not large when compared with those of other major powers. And, President Jiang Zemin, during his official visit to Malaysia in November 1995, declared China's support of the EAEC (East Asian Economic Caucus) proposal by Malaysia.

The Economic Impact

Since the Razak visit, and particularly from the 1990s onwards, there has been a great increase in economic exchange between the two countries. Indeed the most salient aspect of the rise of China has been the Chinese impact on the Malaysian economy and it is thus appropriate that an evaluation of this impact be made. In essence, China poses both an opportunity and a challenge to the Malaysian economy. The opportunity lies in the areas of trade and services. China has been one of the largest buyers of Malaysian commodities like rubber and palm oil. And if one looks at the statistics of the past two decades or so (Table 1) Chinese imports of Malaysian products has been growing, particularly from the year 2000 onwards.

Table 1: Trade between Malaysia and China (in 100 million US dollars), 1985 to July 2003

Year	Total	Malaysian exports to China	Malaysian imports from China
1985	3.68	1.86	1.86
1986	4.58	2.55	2.03
1987	5.57	3.02	2.55
1988	8.76	5.68	3.08
1989	10.44	6.92	3.52
1990	11.76	8.35	3.41
1991	13.32	8.04	5.28
1992	14.75	8.30	6.45
1993	17.88	10.84	7.04
1994	27.40	16.20	11.20
1995	33.46	20.65	12.81
1996	36.14	22.43	13.71
1997	44.15	24.95	19.20
1998	42.94	26.98	15.96
1999	52.79	36.06	16.73
2000	80.45	54.80	25.65
2001	94.25	62.05	32.30
2002	142.71	73.64	49.75
2003 (Jan-Jul)	104.39	71.62	32.77

Source: Chinese Customs (taken from *Sin Chew Jit Poh*, Malaysia), Sept 9, 2003.

The increase is even more astonishing if one were to make a comparison with the figures ten years before 2002. In 1992, Malaysian exports to China amounted to only 830 million US dollars while total trade came to 1.475 billion US dollars. In 2002, the Malaysian exports came to 7.36 billion US dollars and total trade reached 14.27 billion US dollars! (The trade figures from the Malaysian side are different because of a different method of compilation but nonetheless they also show a big increase in Malaysian exports to China). Table 2 below (for the three years of 1995, 2000 and 200) shows the major items of Malaysian exports to consist primarily of palm oil, wood, petroleum, and electrical and electronic products.

Table 2: Top Malaysian Exports to China

1995	2000	2002
Palm Oil	Electrical & Electronics	Electrical & Electronics
Wood	Palm Oil	Palm Oil
Electrical & Electronics	Wood	Petroleum
Petroleum	Petroleum	Chemical

Source: Department of Statistics (Malaysia): External Trade Statistics for various years.

Malaysian imports from China (primarily electrical and electronic products, agricultural produce and textiles for the three years of 1995, 2000 and 2002 as seen in Table 3) have also expanded greatly and Chinese goods are competing aggressively with Malaysian goods, particularly those from the small and medium industries, in the local Malaysian market. Data on this score in the textile and shoe industry suggest Chinese products are threatening Malaysian-made goods in the Malaysian market.[18] Nevertheless as far as the balance of trade is concerned, Malaysia, as the above figures indicate, has consistently enjoyed a surplus throughout the years.

Table 3:   Top Malaysian Imports from China

1995	2000	2002
Electrical & Electronics	Electrical & Electronics	Electrical & Electronics
Machinery, appliances & parts	Maize	Maize
Vegetables	Vegetables	Vegetables
Textiles		Petroleum

Source: Department of Statistics (Malaysia): External Trade Statistics for various years.

There are also opportunities in Malaysia-China trade in the area of services. There has been for example, a flourishing of tourism both ways. Malaysia, for its part, has shown great interest in welcoming an increasingly affluent Chinese middle class, many of whom have a great yen to travel. Educational development and exchange is another promising area for future China-Malaysia business partnership. The Malaysian government is keen to develop Malaysia as a regional center for education. There are programmes in Malaysian institutions of higher learning which students from China may want to enroll in. There are courses in China where Malaysian students could pursue. Universities in the two countries are also beginning to collaborate to develop undergraduate and post-graduate studies that are relevant to the developmental needs of both countries.

But it is in the area of investment that China poses a great challenge to Malaysia. The rise of China as a manufacturing center of the world is increasingly attracting a vast amount of foreign direct investment. There is the real possibility that multinationals might divert investment intended for Malaysia and indeed ASEAN to China. There is also the possibility of the relocation by multinationals of enterprises in Malaysia to China. If all these should happen, they could severely affect the Malaysian economy. The Malaysian economy is very dependent on foreign investment for technological diffusion and for other benefits such investment might bring. The case of a very important investor in both Malaysia and China, that of Japan, is very instructive. While the statistics of Japanese direct investment in China and Malaysia are not conclusive for a determination of whether there has been a diversion to China of Japanese investment meant for Malaysia, nevertheless the statements of the intentions of foreign and in this case, Japanese investors, to invest and to relocate in China at the expense of Malaysia and ASEAN are many. Three examples will suffice. One is a survey of Japanese transnational (TNCs) by JETRO (Japan External Trade Organization), an institution under the Japanese Ministry of Economics, Trade and Industry (METI) about their relocation plans to China when China joins the World Trade Organization (WTO) Table 4.

Slightly more than 21 per cent of the 465 TNCs which responded to the JETRO survey plan to relocate to China. The bulk of these (67.5 percent) are from Japan but 7.8 per cent are from the ASEAN countries. Malaysia has the highest percentage (3 per cent) of the five ASEAN countries! Though 3 percent may appear small, the possibility is that this could increase to a bigger percentage.

Another survey, this time by the Japanese Bank for International Cooperation shows the 10 most promising destinations for manufacturing foreign direct investment FDI by Japanese firms for the years 1996, 2000 and 2001 (Table 5). In 1996, 68 per cent of respondents identified China and 20 per cent identified Malaysia. In 2002, the figures came to 82 per cent for China and 8 per cent for Malaysia! And third, there is a survey by the Japanese Chambers of Commerce in Malaysia of Japanese firms already in Malaysia planning to relocate in China (Table 6). Again, many Japanese firms expressed an intention to relocate to China. Thus if these intentions of Japanese enterprises are reflective of global multinationals in general, then the omens are not good for Malaysia.

Table 4: **Planned Relocation of Production Sites of Japanese TNCs to China as a Result of China's Accession to the WTO (percentage of TNCs responding)**

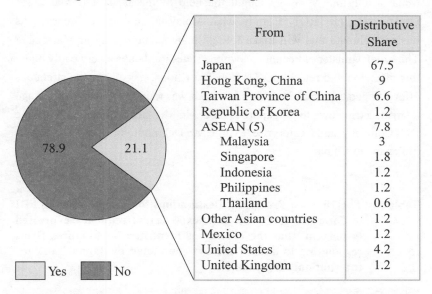

From	Distributive Share
Japan	67.5
Hong Kong, China	9
Taiwan Province of China	6.6
Republic of Korea	1.2
ASEAN (5)	7.8
Malaysia	3
Singapore	1.8
Indonesia	1.2
Philippines	1.2
Thailand	0.6
Other Asian countries	1.2
Mexico	1.2
United States	4.2
United Kingdom	1.2

a. Based on 645 responses among the 720 Japanese TNCs surveyed by JETRO in October 2001.

b. Based on 136 of the 645 responses (21.1%) from TNCs planning to relocate their production to China. Multiple replies apply.

Source: JETRO, International Economic Research Division; UNCTAD press release tad/inf/2850, http://www.unctad.org/en/Press/pr0236en.htm

On the Malaysian side, there is also a strong awareness that diversion and relocation have started and could represent a trend. We need only to quote a leading Malaysian think-tank, ASLI, which stated, in a study of the impact of China's accession to the WTO, that its accession can 'result in a hollowing-out of low cost, assembly-line and labour intensive industries from ASEAN, including Malaysia.'[19] Indeed, in order to forestall such diversion, leading politicians in Malaysia have resorted to personally persuading the multinationals to remain in Malaysia. The Singapore Business Times has an item to the effect that Dr Mahathir in 2003, then Malaysian Prime Minister, sought the help of the Japan External Trade Organization (JETRO) to study what Malaysia must do to improve its business climate that will make foreign manufacturers stay in Malaysia.[20] The Chief Minister of Penang, one of the states in Malaysia very badly hit by this diversion and relocation, Dr Koh Tsu Khoon, has also made strenuous efforts to persuade multinationals to stay. It was reported that some time ago he made a trip down to Singapore to meet Mr. Michael Dell, the owner of the Dell Company, an IT enterprise, to urge Mr. Dell not to move the Dell plants in Penang to China.[21]

Table 5:   The 10 Most Promising Destinations for Manufacturing FDI by Japanese TNCs over the Next 3 Years (frequency, expressed in percent, that the country is identified by Japanese firms responding to annual surveys conducted by Japan Bank for International Cooperation)

Rank	1996 survey	Ratio	2000 survey	Ratio	2001 survey	Ratio
1	China	68	China	65	China	82
2	Thailand	36	United States	41	United States	32
3	Indonesia	34	Thailand	24	Thailand	25
4	United States	32	Indonesia	15	Indonesia	14
5	Vietnam	27	Malaysia	12	India	13
6	Malaysia	20	Taiwan province	11	Vietnam	12
7	India	18	India	10	Taiwan province	11
8	Philippines	13	Vietnam	9	Rep of Korea	8
9	Singapore	10	Rep of Korea	9	Malaysia	8
10	United Kingdom & Taiwan	7	Philippines	8	Singapore	6

Source: Taken from "Meeting the China Challenge: Malaysia's Economic and Business Response", lecture by Woo Wing Thye to ISIS Malaysia, 2 July 2004.

Table 6: Japanese Companies Look beyond Malaysia: Future Investment Strategy of Japanese Companies in Malaysia

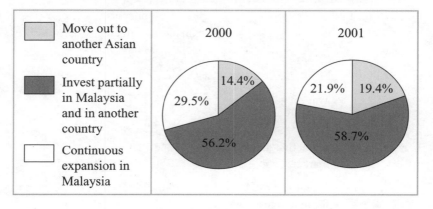

Where they are going

Country	% of Respondents with Plans to Invest Outside Malaysia*	
	2000	2001
China	62.4	n/a
South China	n/a	65.0
East China	n/a	25.2
Around Beijing	n/a	6.5
Other regions in China	n/a	12.2
Thailand	27.7	30.9
Indonesia	26.7	17.1
Philippines	8.9	4.9
Vietnam	24.8	30.1
India	14.9	6.5
Myanmar	1.0	1.6
Others	3.0	6.5

* Numbers add up to more than 100% as respondents may have chosen more than one location for 2001; China was broken up into regions, but not for 2000.

What's attracting them to these countries?

	% of Respondents with plans to invest outside Malaysia in 2001*
Wages	75.2
Labour Force	74.4
Attractive domestic market	42.1
Incentives for foreign investment	14.0

* Numbers add up to more than 100% as respondents may have chosen more than one factor.

Source: *The Edge Malaysia*, 13 May 2002.

Ultimately whether Malaysia can still keep multinationals from going to China depends on the continuing attractiveness of China and Malaysia's success in retaining its attraction to the multinationals.

There is another dimension to this investment issue, that of Malaysian investment in China and Chinese investment in Malaysia. There have been reports of increasing Malaysian investor interest in China. This involves mostly Malaysian private investment though recently there have been reports of state companies like Petronas and Proton having plans to invest there. On the other hand, China's manufacturing investment in Malaysia is very small, at least in the decade of the 1990s (Table 7). Certainly this is nothing compared to the amount of Japanese investment which total in the billions of US dollars for the same period.

Table 7: **Investment from China (paid-up) in Companies in production in Malaysia**

Year	Amount
1990	1.4
1991	3.8
1992	6.4
1993	7
1994	8.7
1995	23.0
1996	21.5
1997	32.5
1998	22.5
	126.8

Source: Figures compiled from Statistics of Malaysian Industrial Development Authority (MIDA) by Tham Siew Yean in "Can Malaysian Manufacturing Compete with China in the WTO?" in *Asia-Pacific Developmental Journal*, Vol. 8, No. 2, December 2001, pp. 19-20.

Bilateral and Regional Political Relations

On the political level, China has shown a conciliatory attitude towards Malaysia and indeed the rest of ASEAN. China has agreed to sign the Treaty of Amity and Cooperation (TAC) of ASEAN which obliges both sides not to use force in the resolution of disputes. This, together with the Chinese agreement to declare a code of conduct in 2002 in the resolution of the Spratlys, have eased the tension between Malaysia and China over their competing claims to this chain of islands.

Malaysia, on its part, is also doing what it can to encourage the peaceful integration of China into the international system. Malaysia is a strong supporter of the ASEAN Regional Forum (ARF) which has China as a member. Despite some critics deriding the ARF as nothing more than a talk shop, the fact that Malaysia and the rest of ASEAN have some influence over the ARF agenda and the belief by China that ASEAN would not allow the ARF to be an instrument for the containment of China have made China well disposed towards the ARF. In addition, Malaysia is keen for China to participate in an Asian regional grouping, more specifically the East Asian Economic Grouping (EAEG) which had been an important foreign policy objective of Malaysia. Chinese participation in the EAEG is seen as crucial.

Conclusion

Relations between China and Malaysia since 1949, have been complicated by the issue of Beijing's policy towards Southeast Asians of Chinese descent and in particular by its support of the Communist Party of Malaya. But these did not prevent diplomatic relations between both countries from being established in 1974. A strong reason for such establishment had been the policy and the political personality of Tun Razak. However, from the mid 1980s onwards, the two long-standing issues had begun to matter less and less as a result of the integration of the Malaysian Chinese into the Malaysian polity and the decision of the Communist Party of Malaya to give up its armed struggle in 1989. These, together with the evolution of China into a normal state and the forward attitude of Dr Mahathir, enabled bilateral relations to take on a normal state-to-state character.

Even as relation normalized, the economic rise of China has posed both a threat and an opportunity to Malaysia. China's economic expansion threatens to divert foreign investments away from Malaysia. And Chinese goods are more competitive in the international market in pricing and quality compared to those made in Malaysia. On the other hand, the gathering pace of development in China offers tremendous market and investment opportunities to Malaysia. On balance, it is more likely that China presents itself more of an opportunity to Malaysia than that of a threat.

Notes

1 Geoff Wade, "Voyages of the Ming Admirals", *Heritage Asia*, Vol. 1, September-November 2003, pp 20-25.

2 On his first visit as prime minister to China in May 2004, Abdullah Badawi in a speech on May 29, 2004 in Beijing traced the bond between both countries which started 600 years ago with the arrival of Admiral Zheng He in Malacca and in recent times with the beginning of diplomatic relations in 1974. He then urged China and Malaysia to strengthen relations at all levels. "Ties at new high – Malaysia and China must build on achievement, says PM" *The Star* (Kuala Lumpur), 30 May 2004.

3 In a subsequent survey on China entitled "Ready to face the World", The Economist emphasized more the problems China had to face in the new century. *The Economist*, (London), March 8, 1997.

4 See "China has discovered its own economic consensus" by Joshua Cooper Ramo in the *Financial Times* (London) in an op-ed article May 8, 2004. Cooper Ramo calls this new model the "Beijing Consensus", the fundamental of which is equitable, high-quality growth.

5 One scholar, T.J. Pempel, in a lecture in 2003 to an ISEAS-organized conference mentioned that Japan's economy, for example is ten times larger than China's economy. "The changing character of Japan's Economic Linkages with Southeast Asia" by T.J. Pempel in *Trends in Southeast Asia Series: 13 (2003)*: ISEAS, Singapore.

6 See Orville Schell, "Enigma of China's Economic 'Miracle'". *The Edge Malaysia* (Kuala Lumpur), Nov 10-Nov 17, 2003.

7 See Barnett (1968).

8 The implementation of the Indonesian citizenship policy after 1955 towards the Chinese residents was plagued with difficulties. Not all the Chinese residents in Indonesia were necessarily citizens of People's Republic of China. Some had Dutch citizenship. Others had citizenship of the Republic of China. Sukarno had to intervene to try to settle the issue in 1961 by having another accord signed known as the Implementation of the Sino-Indonesian Dual Nationality.

9 In an interview Lee Poh Ping had with T.H. Tan, former Secretary General of the Alliance party under Tengku Abdul Rahman, sometime after the Razak visit, T.H. Tan gave this figure of 200,000. Tan was highly critical of the Razak

visit suggesting that the issue of the stateless Chinese should have been settled before the visit.

10 See the joint communiqué between the two governments (signed by Zhou En-Lai and Abdul Razak) in 1974. See also Abdul Razak Baginda (2002) for some mention of the issue of Malaysian Chinese in the bilateral relations. Tan Sri Michael Chen, a former President of the Malaysian Senate and a close confidante of Razak during the 1974 visit, in a series of discussions with the writers of this paper from April-June, 2004, mentioned that Razak was very worried that these stateless Chinese could cause trouble after the establishment of diplomatic relations. Tan Sri Chen told us that he reassured Razak by suggesting that none of these stateless Chinese would go to the newly established Chinese Embassy to register themselves as Chinese citizens and hence expose themselves. In all probability they would lie low and not cause trouble. He was right.

11 The Western constraint was a powerful one. If Nixon had not visited China in 1972, it would have been doubtful whether Tun Razak could have made the 1974 visit.

12 Tan Sri Chen emphasized to the writers of this paper that the critical importance of Tun Razak's standing with the nationalist Malays, who were quite suspicions of China. Tan Sri Chen also mentioned that there was some preparatory building of trust between the Chinese from China and the Malay nationalists. He mentioned as an important example, the Malaysian authorities organizing a meeting between a visiting Chinese Sports delegation and Harun Idris, then a powerful Malay leader, in 1973.

13 Tan Sri Chen pointed to us the existence and the importance of this chemistry in the bilateral relations.

14 The former Prime Minister of Singapore, Lee Kuan Yew, in his autobiography wrote of a similar situation in Singapore. He stated that Singaporean Chinese after visiting China became more aware of how much better conditions in Singapore were. See Lee Kuan Yew, *From Third World to First, The Singapore Story 1965-2000.* (Times Media Pte Ltd., Singapore) pp. 655-656.

15 For an interesting account of the pressure the Chinese put on the Communist Party of Malaya especially after Deng came into power in 1978, not to use China for its confrontation with the Malaysian government, see Chin Peng (2003:456-459). We have in this paper used Malaysian communists and Malayan communists interchangeably, even though the Malayan communists had not recognized the existence of Malaysia. The party was first known as the Malayan Communist Party and subsequently as the Communist Party of Malaya.

16 There was some speculation that Dr Mahathir, had he continued his premiership, could have approved the return of Chin Peng to Malaysia when the issue of the return arose in 2003.

17 One of his latest statements of China not having a history of colonizing Southeast Asia was made in a speech to a World Chinese Entrepreneur Conference in Kuala Lumpur in July, 2003.

18 See "The Dragon Awakes" in *The Edge Malaysia* (Kuala Lumpur) May 13, 2002.

19 "China's WTO Accession – Likely Impact on Malaysian Companies "Paper

presented by ASLI to the Malaysian National Economic Council's Consultation on globalization on 5th December, 2001. (http://www.asli.com.my/China.htm).

20 "Mahathir seeks JETRO aid to keep manufacturers" in the *Business Times* Singapore on February 27, 2003.

21 In an interview with Dato Dr Toh Kin Woon, State councilor in Penang in charge of planning, on 27 February, 2003.

References

Abdul Razak Baginda, "Malaysian Perceptions of China: From Hostility to Cordiality", in Herbert Yee and Ian Story (eds), *The China Threat: Perceptions, Myths and Realty*, London: Routledge and Curzon, 2002.

Barnett, Doak, *Communist China and Asia*, New York, Council of Foreign Relations, 1968.

Buzan, Barry and Foot, Rosemary (eds), *Does China Matter? A Reassessment:Essays in Memory of Gerald Siegel*, London: Routledge, 2004.

Chin Peng, *My Side of History as told to Ian Ward and Norma Miraflor*, Singapore: Media Masters, 2003.

Ho Khai Leong and Samuel C.Y. Ku (eds), *China and Southeast Asia, Global Changes and Regional Challenges*, Singapore: ISEAS, 2005.

Huntington, Samuel P., *The Clash of Civilizations and the Remaking of the World Order*, New York: Simon and Schuster, 1996.

Mahathir Mohamad, "A China That Cannot Be Ignored", in *Achieving Globalisation*, Kuala Lumpur: Pelanduk Publications, 2004.

Mahathir Mohamad, "China: A Challenge or An Opportuinity for ASEAN", in *Reflections on ASEAN*, Kuala Lumpur: Pelanduk Publications, 2004.

Suryadinata, Leo (ed.), *Southeast Asian Chinese and China: The Politico-economic Dimension*, Singapore: Times Academic Press, 1997.

Wade, Geoff, "Voyages of the Ming Admirals", *Heritage Asia*, Vol. 1, September-November, 2003.

Wang Gung Wu, *China and Southeast Asia: Myths, Threats and Culture, East Asian* Institute Contemporary China Series No.13, Singapore: NUS, May, 1999.

Wang Jisi and Kokubun Ryosei (eds), *The Rise of China and A Changing East Asian Order*, Tokyo: Japan Centre for International Exchange.

Chapter 2

Mahua Writers:
"China" and Malaysia

Hou Kok Chung

Introduction

Ma means Malaysia. *Hua* means Chinese and can be understood as referring to either the Chinese ethnic group or the Chinese language. Literally, Mahua writers are Malaysian Chinese writing in Chinese, Malay, or English (Malaysia's three major languages), or Malaysians who write in Chinese. The term Mahua writers therefore requires clarification. It simply refers to Malaysian Chinese writers writing in Chinese. This understanding of the term is generally accepted in the literary scene not only because it is originated from Chinese writing circle in Malaysia, but more importantly, only those writing in Chinese have identified themselves as Mahua writers.[1]

This chapter tries to study the relationship of Mahua writers vis-à-vis various issues surrounding "China." The word "China" is culturally sensitive to Mahua writers and should be handled with care because their forefathers and culture originated from China. However, they are disparate from the nation and have no real ties to it. In addressing the China issue, this chapter will be divided into four parts: The first will discuss the shaping of Mahua literature. The second discusses the sensitivity of China or Chinese culture in Malaysian politics and its implication to Mahua writers after independence. The third explores Mahua writers in relation to China's literary world before concluding with the final section.

From China Setting to Malayan Features

Millions of Chinese migrated to Malaya in search of work in the nineteenth century. Most of them did not think that they would be staying in Malaya for good. Although many did not return to their country of origin, national identity was not a problem to them as the period's concept of "nation" (even amongst countries with long histories such as China) was ambiguous at best. Many Chinese came to Malaya for the sole purpose of eking out a living before eventually returning to their own motherland. This was pointed out by Yen Ching-hwang, an expert on the history of early migrants to Malaya and Singapore, "Early Chinese immigrants had little or no time to worry about their identity." (Yen, 1986:284) In concerning themselves with China's affairs, writers, like other immigrants, perceived themselves as temporary settlers.

Nevertheless, after a long stay in Malaya, these Chinese immigrants began to have some sentiment towards Malaya. In January 1927, *New Citizen Daily*'s (Xin Guomin Ribao) supplementary entitled "Deserted island" (Huang dao) remarked upon authors' desires to include South Sea (Nanyang) elements in the literary world. On 1 April 1927, its editor, Zhang Jinyan (pen name Yan), encouraged local writers "to frequently write about South Sea literature in the literary world to promote South Sea literature...as this was more meaningful than writing something pointless." (Zhang, in Fang Xiu, 1972:1:121) Zhang was one of the few who wanted to segregate China and South Sea literature. A few years later, Fei Ming wrote in *Nanyang Siang*

Pau, "Malayan writers should get rid of Shanghai styles. Malayan writers should unify the local associations as they are responsible for the further promotion of Malaya literature."(Fei, in Fang Xiu, 1972:10:260) This is probably the first reference to "Malayan literature" in the Chinese circle. Yi Qiao suggested that "Malayan literature" should be replaced with *Malaiya huaqiao wenxue* (Malaya's Overseas Chinese Literature) in 1936 (Quoted in Yang 2001:17). The term *Mahua Wenxue* was widely used at the end of 1930s making it evident that the term Mahua is the abbreviated form of *Malaiya huaqiao*.

During the 1930s, many articles were published to inspire and encourage writing about Malaya. However, this aspiration was not strongly supported because it was difficult for writers from China to change their personal sentiment towards China. Well-known writers from China were reluctant to recognize themselves as Malayan writers. During that time, reading materials, including textbooks used in Chinese schools were printed and sent from China. In 1929, Chen Lianqing, editor of "Coconut trees" (Ye lin), a supplementary of Chinese daily *Ri bao*, disclosed that ninety percent of Malaya's Chinese newspaper supplements consisted of newspaper cuttings from China (Chen, in Fang Xiu, 1972:10:127-128). Under such circumstances, it is not surprising that the identity of Malayan Chinese writers was similar to that of any other Chinese writers in Mainland China. In this light, it is clear that their main concern was the well being of China. Li Liwen, for example, expressed this sentiment in 1936, "The Chinese will eventually go back to China and will be more comfortable to die in China."(Quoted in Miao, 1968:311)

This situation, however, changed after the Second World War. Since the Japanese occupation in Malaya, the Chinese community had fought for both China and Malaya. Chinese community leaders called on the Chinese and other ethnic groups in Malaya to unite against the Japanese threat. The confrontation with the Japanese, which continued for three years and eight months, evinces the growing gratefulness of the Chinese community towards Malaya. At that time, the many changes in Malaya enabled the Chinese community to realize that the British could not protect Malaya. This burgeoning sense of affection towards Malaya steadily grew during their continued resistance against Japan. In 1946, Qu Zefu pointed out that the Chinese was no longer seen as a visitor but as a host in Malaya. As such, the Chinese community became actively involved in politics so as to protect themselves and the future generation. He said, "Here is our country; no other place will be our country." (Quoted in Cui, 1990:168)

By the close of 1947, a heated and lengthy debate arose as to whether writers ought to focus on China or Malaya. On one hand, writers supporting China had promulgated overseas Chinese literature. On the other hand, writers affectionate towards the local community stressed the importance of understanding and appreciating the local customs of a new country. These writers often sought to promulgate literature with the local context. Ling Zuo, a writer, caught the attention of the public with the following views:

> Mahua literature at the time of confrontation with Japan and anti-Fascism, ...had grown to a new level. ... The war had brought a new notion to Mahua community, i.e. their own fate as well as that of Malaya's multi-ethnic communities. At the same time, the campaign to unify cultural movements and multi-societies became part of the war effort. These changes were responsible for denying the Chinese community the meaning of overseas literature. Mahua literature therefore used the bloody struggles against Japan for Malayan sovereignty and its efforts to realize the liberalization and independence of Malaya as its source and contents (Ling in Miao Xiu, 1972:201).

Our attention should be drawn to the fact that this so-called argument was not centred on writings about China or Malaya. In fact, the consensus to write about local community had never been disputed by writers supporting overseas literature. The debate chiefly focused on whether writers ought to be concerned about Mainland China. In other words, writing about China has. evolved from a longstanding presupposed fact to a mootpoint. Basically, writers promulgating awareness for overseas nationals were put on the defensive, while writers promulgating localism took the offensive. The crux of the dispute was whether awareness for overseas nationals was allowed to exist. Li Xuan, a writer disseminating overseas Chinese literature, had the following appeal, "the existence of overseas Chinese literature does not hinder development of Mahua literature." (Li in Miao Xiu, 1972:206)

As a result of this debate, it was stated in a report that the Malayan Chinese had come to realize that participation in local politics would benefit their community; and therefore the tendency to over-emphasize China's background and subjects in literature must be corrected. This, according to the report, means that writers must identify themselves with local realities so as to serve the goals of local politics (Wong, 1989:110-126).

This debate clearly indicates that Malayan Chinese literature had been established in the true sense of the word and the status of Mahua writers had taken its shape. Mahua literature has entered a new era since then. More noticeably, the literary scene was no longer manipulated solely by the writers and literati from China. This was made apparent in the 1950s where many mainland writers, particularly those who fled China for political reasons, returned to China. Meanwhile, the number of locally born writers rose due to the expansion of Chinese education in Malaya, and the increasing number of locally born Chinese. Thus, locally born writers started having a fair share of contribution in shaping the future of Mahua literature.

De-Chinalizing Mahua Literature

Malayan independence has enabled the Chinese to settle down in the country and proudly declare themselves citizens. Since then, they have been actively involved in local politics and came to possess a deep understanding of issues in Malaysia. Most Chinese did not find giving up their Chinese nationality to become a Malaysian a problem; they were more concerned with adapting themselves to develop their culture in this country.

"The non-Malay communities have accepted 'Malay domination' as the price to be paid for security and the opportunity to maintain their own identities." Harold Crouch made this observation when he commented on the impacts of Malaysia's affirmative action policy; a policy that seems to have captured the other "bargain" between Malay and non-Malay communities

(Crouch, 2001:225-262). If that was really the "price", then the Chinese community would expect to get what they desire - that is, the maintenance of their cultural identities. Unfortunately, such a transaction seems to be incomplete because the Chinese community is preoccupied with the thought that Chinese cultural identities are under threat.[2]

This is especially true in the area of Mahua literature. Mahua literature has been either misinterpreted or belittled since it came into existence. The colonial reign did not pay attention to Mahua literature and the writers worked independently without any encouragement. Nevertheless, prior to independence, the writers did not have to solve their problems on political identity; works produced were matters of personal choice. The situation changed after Malaya achieved independence. Other ethnic groups repeatedly questioned the loyalty of the Chinese. The pressure to display loyalty to their adopted country prompted Mahua writers to emphasise local values in their literary works. They believed that in doing so, the other ethnicities would be convinced of their dedication to the socio-political issues in this country; furthermore, such effort did not differ from that of the Malay writers.

The declaration of the National Cultural Policy in August 1971 highlighted the Government's reluctance to accept Mahua literature as a component of national literature. The Government could not accept Mahua literature as a national literature because its medium of writing is Chinese. The leaders, especially those from the Malay community, are ignorant about Mahua literature and to the aggravation of Chinese writers, Malaysian leaders are not interested in taking heed of their problems. To upgrade the status of Malay literature, the Government not only has set up Dewan Bahasa dan Pustaka (Institute of Language and Literature Malaysia), but has also came up with various literary awards. Apart from sharing a common view that Malay literature has been heading towards a bright direction, the Chinese writers generally feel marginalized.[3]

How then, can Mahua literature be justifiably acceptable as a national literature? Mahua writers believe that one of the best ways is to show that the contents of Mahua literature are loaded with local values. This shows that Mahua writers are fettered by politics. The rationale behind this method is clear: Their emphasis is more on the content than the "literature" itself. Given that Malaysian identity is an important factor differentiating literary works from Mainland China or Taiwan and Mahua literature, the logic behind this is understandable. According to them, Mahua literature is replete with Malaysian contents and its own identity; as such, they see no reason why the Government should reject something thus imbued with local values. If this Malaysian identity is taken seriously, the Government ought to share a role in developing this literature. In so doing, Mahua literature would be able to flourish like Malay literature.

Nevertheless, this proposal is foolproof. What is meant by Chinese culture? What are the characteristics of Chinese culture in Malaysia? It is easy to espouse a notion such as "The Chinese in Malaysia should have their own cultural identity," but in practice, problems lie in the practicability of listing these components in a clear manner. When it is mentioned that the Chinese should inherit their cultural traditions, what are they inheriting and could these elements be listed? Given their cultural similarity, how can Chinese culture in Malaysia be differentiated from that of Mainland China? Where should we add with Malaysian identity? From the cultural aspect, there are many things that are beyond political explanations. For instance, if a writer came from China and eventually stayed in Malaysia, or if a Malaysian resided in Malaysia for an extended period but eventually migrated to other country. How should we fix his cultural orientation? If cultural problems are viewed from a political aspect, it might be easy to solve this problem. The question here is whether cultural development occurs without people's awareness. There are many ambiguous areas between the Chinese culture of Malaysia and China, where we could not pinpoint clearly the effect of human cultural awareness. In the tradition of creative literature, we would usually study the produced work before deciding whether they fulfil a certain set of criteria. It would be strange if we were to instruct a writer to choose from Chinese and Malaysian elements before a literary work is created.

Despite the fact that the country has been independent for over 40 years, it seems that the Government has no thought of supporting Mahua literature. However, this does not jeopardize the ambitions of the Chinese writers striving for recognition of Mahua literature as a national literature. In this process, Malaysian awareness of its identity has been repeatedly raised. Fang Beifang, president of the Writers' Association of Chinese Medium of Malaysia from 1980 to 1984, had reiterated the same view in a speech:

> Apart from the medium of expression being the Chinese language, other materials constructing Mahua literature including the contents, thoughts and issues touched have no relevancy with the Mainland China where Mahua literature originated (Fang, 1995:10).

This excerpt from a speech is not a mere personal view. Meng Sa, president of The Writers' Association of Chinese Medium of Malaysia from 1988-1990, shared the same view. He said,

> Mahua literature has released itself from being a branch of literature of Mainland China since 1930s and 1940s. It is a literature truly belonging to the country (Meng, 1986:26).

The above statements show the close links between literature and politics. The Chinese literary writers from other places including China are also sensitive to the situation in Malaysia, and they avoid categorizing Mahua literature as a branch of literature in China. At a Chinese literary conference on "Chinese literature outside the Mainland China" in 1986, most of the participants agreed that though Chinese literature in Southeast Asian countries, especially Mahua literature and Xinhua literature (Chinese literature in Singapore) inherit modern Chinese literature germinated in the May Fourth Movement in 1919, Chinese literature in these countries are not part of the Chinese literature scene in the Mainland China. Instead, these literatures are based on local values, and are part of the national literature of the particular countries concerned (Yue, 1988: 402-404).

The same definition of Mahua literature has been raised repeatedly almost at every meeting held between Mahua Chinese writers and their counterparts from Mainland China. One of the stereotyped explanations is:

> Ever since Mahua Literature started, it is concerned with the "now and here" as it depicts the lives of various ethnic groups, thereby displaying local identity. It has further developed into a

literary tradition with its unique characteristics. This individuality can be gleaned from its exposition of the daily lives and experiences of the Chinese via their interaction with other ethnicities. This local value is also closely linked to the patriotic characteristics based on anti-imperialism, anti-colonialism, anti-feudalism and nationalism that strive for independence, democracy and racial strengths. It is also closely related to Chinese cultural upbringing. This literature is therefore a new literature. Apart from fulfilling the needs of Malaysian Chinese by characterizing their lives after migration, it contributes to enrich Malaysian cultures (Ma, 1998:19-20).

While it is clear that Mahua literature has been accepted widely at the international level, it must stressed there is a strong political motivation behind its definition. Apparently, the issues raised by the definition of this literature are not meant to assess the works of Mahua writers from the aspects of strengths and weaknesses; rather, it is a deflection to other ambitions. In other words, literary writers are constantly reminded of local values. The philosophy behind this lies in the belief that it is of vital importance for a writer to produce something as proof that he/she is a current witness for the happenings occurring in the vicinity of his/her residence. As a result, Mahua literature's emphasis on local value has given rise to many problems.

A case in point is Li Yongping's novel *Jiling Chronicles* (Jilin chunqiu), which was widely acclaimed. Li was originated from Sarawak, spending his undergraduate years in Taiwan and finally settling down in Taiwan after finishing his Ph.D. at Washington University. While literary critics were drawn to the manner in which the language was used and presented, as well as the structure and symbolic of the novel, they were more concerned with locating the fictional place of Jiling. In Li's novel, Jiling is meant to be symbolic for it resembles both tropical and temperate areas. Critics have been split as to whether it represents Malaysia, Taiwan or the Mainland China.

Although there were speculations, it remains that the place in *Jiling Chronicles* is purely symbolic. Li Yongping's novel is an extraordinary case because the debate engendered did not affect its local value as a Mahua literature component. One can go so far as to say that Li used his novel to express the displacement of his youth. When Li confessed in an interview that his other masterpiece, *Mrs Lazi* (Lazi fu), was also a Mahua literary work, he shocked Malaysian students studying in Taiwan who aspired to be writers by telling them the following:

> Don't follow my footprints. My journey is too languishing...I hope they can go back to Malaysia and continue to write. They should write about the life of Chinese in Malaysia...Don't follow me writing something about Taiwan.   A writer should not write about Taiwan like I did. A writer should write about something he/she is most familiar with. Otherwise, they are laying themselves up for trouble, so to speak. (*Guanghua zazhi*, August 1998:110)

Could it be that Li decided to break away from tradition by not writing about life in Malaysia after *Mrs Lazi*? While this appears to be a seemingly unimportant question, we are still confounded as to why Li chooses not to write about life in Malaysia. Since Mahua literature came into being, Mahua writers have felt marginalized. Li Yongping's experience has proven that in order to enter mainstream Chinese literature, the characteristics of Mahua can be avoided. Yet doing so is an odd-and-lonesome way in which Li had to "work doubly hard" to succeed (*Guanghua zazhi*, August 1998:110).

In the 1990s Huang Jingshu (Ng Kim Chew) and Lin Jianguo (Lim Kien Ket), both teaching at universities in Taiwan, proposed that the definition of Mahua literature be extended to the writings of all Chinese people in Malaysia and not be confined to the Chinese language medium. Huang's reason is that "in so doing, the development of Mahua literature will be in concordance with the history of Chinese in Malaysia." (Huang, 1996:26) Lin, on the other hand, argued that such as move could "enable Mahua literature to become a more liberal and dynamic concept." (Lin, 1993:109) It is evident that they wish to make Mahua more acceptable to the people of other ethnic groups. Nevertheless, this proposal might meet with some resistance from the other Chinese writers. Although writers of the Chinese medium and their non-Chinese medium counterparts face different problems, there is no denying that both parties feel sidelined by the Government's policies in favour of Malay literature. These writers, however, are unable to unite because they have very different intellectual orientations.

The writers of Chinese medium normally confine their writings to one language. For instance, many Chinese writers writing in non-Chinese medium do not understand the Chinese language. In terms of influence from Chinese culture, they are not as strong as those writing in Chinese. The awareness to safeguard Chinese culture among Chinese medium writers is stronger than non-Chinese medium Chinese writers. Both groups are neither close nor do they care to understand each other. If we define Mahua literature as a literature for the Chinese people regardless of the languages of transmission, it becomes clear that a new term must be found to categorize the majority of Chinese writers writing in Chinese, so that their problems can be attended to effectively.

Mahua Writers and Chinese Literature

In 1972, Lai Ruihe (Lai Swee Fo), published an essay in Taipei asking why some students from Malaysia chose to stay in Taiwan after they finished their studies there. One repercussion of this essay among some writers was the issue of identity. Students from Malaysia residing in Taiwan as well as students from other areas such as Hong Kong, most notably Ao Ao and Liu Shaoming also took part in the discussion. Lin Lu's essay in response to Lai Swee Fo is most interesting. At that time, Lin Lu had already finished his first degree in Taiwan and was pursuing his Ph.D. at the University of Washington. After reading Lai's essay, Lin responded by illustrating his own personal experience. According to Lin, he lacked maturity and direction when he left for Taiwan. His experience in Taiwan had made him a new person, from an "overseas Chinese" to a "pure Chinese." Lin claimed that given this transformation, it was not surprising that he gradually forgot Mahua literature. Lin made it clear that he perceived Mahua literature as a branch literature of China (Lin, 1975:57-61).

Lai, who had never been to Taiwan, indeed sympathized with these students who never returned. After reading the response, he lamented,

> I have this opinion. A writer, if he is really involved in Chinese literature or writing with strong Chinese knowledge, will finally realize that Malaysia is not a good place to stay. The reason is that this is not a pure Chinese society (Lai, 1974:154).

Both Lai and Lin's opinions were certainly not isolated. Wen Rui'an, another young writer strongly felt the same. He was more forthright in his opinion as to whether Mahua literature was a part of literature from China. He argued that Mahua literature would not have existed if Chinese literature did not exist. Since both Mahua writers and Chinese writers used the same language, "overemphasizing local features in Mahua literature would only result in losing Chinese culture that belonged to them whilst destroying the ability to create a new one" (Wen, 1977:12-15).

Wen's article, unlike Lai's essay, was widely circulated amongst writers in Malaysia. Many writers disagreed with Wen's logic. Ye Xiao, a writer three years younger than Wen argued,

> The future of Mahua literature depends on Mahua writers themselves. If Mahua writers believe that they are working for Mahua literature and not a branch literature of China or exile works, then the works created by Mahua writers will always be Mahua literature. If we do not surrender, we will not live under the shadow of Chinese literature. We must have enough confidence to make Mahua literature ingrained in our motherland (Ye, 1978:38).

Indeed, the responses against Wen expressed the perpetuation of the same argument on the localization process experienced by the locally born Mahua writers. However localized the Mahua writers sought to be, they could not fully escape the influences from China and Taiwan in the process of writing. This is especially so whenever the Chinese feared that the smooth development of Mahua culture would be hampered by conflicts in the local ethnic communities. The upshot of this is the emergence of writings where strong ties for Chinese tradition are expressed amidst a desire to find one's roots. This phenomenon can be deemed a societal reaction.

It has, however, raised grievances among some writers. In 1992, Wu An, vice president of The Writers' Association of Chinese Medium of

Malaysia, reminded writers that Mahua writers would be taken seriously internationally if they threw off China's influence and ceased imitating Chinese literature (*Nanyang Siang Pau*, 6 July 1992). By the phrase "throwing off China's influence," it is clear that Wu believes localism to be an intrinsic part of Mahua literature. It is hinted that writers outside Malaysia would not be able to accurately capture the sentiments and scenarios within the country. Moreover, learning from writers of China would not make Mahua literature unique. Wu wanted Mahua literature to come into its own.

While it is desirable for Mahua literature to possess its own characteristics, a few other points require clarification. Firstly, is it possible not to be influenced by literary work published in China or Taiwan? It is clear that if Malaysian Chinese want to retain their culture, they cannot escape learning from the various Chinese classics considered compulsory books in Chinese intellectual history. The classics include philosophical works in the pre-Qin era, Confucian Classics, historical texts and Chinese poetry. Since there are only a select group of scholars in Chinese studies in Malaysia, most of these classics are still interpreted by China scholars. Thus, China still plays an important role in shaping the interpretation of the classics.

Secondly, there are not many literary works published in Malaysia. The reading list of Mahua writers, as evinced by the books available in Malaysian bookshops, still comprises of mainly literary works from China. Over ninety percent of literary works in the bookshop are books published in China or Taiwan. The small circulation of Mahua literary works has resulted in publishers' reluctance to publish local literary works. At present, Mahua literature have no foreign market. Locally, the publishers are well aware that they have to compete against literary works from China and Taiwan; as such, Mahua literary works are in a constant losing battle.

In this light, it is interesting to study the attitude of younger generation towards Mahua literature. In May 1991, Xian Sulai (Silvia Sian Suk Lai) a student from University of Malaya who did her M.A. in Japan, wrote an essay entitled "The Trial." This essay was based on a seminar on Mahua literature she attended. The seminar was presented by one of her course mates. The immediate question from the floor after the presentation was whether there was a so-called "Mahua literature." Almost everybody except the speaker and Xuan herself thought that the term of "Mahua literature" was indeed a mistake. The audience argued unanimously that it was China (Zhongguo) literature in Malaysia. Xuan, of course, did not agree with the statement. While Xuan was disturbed by the discussion, she realised too late that her knowledge on Mahua literature was so limited. She was unable to adequately defend her opinion, as she had never paid any real attention to Mahua literary works (Xian, 1991).

Given that Xuan is a Mahua writer, why does she seldom read literary works by other Mahua writers? Is this unusual among Mahua writers? What are the reasons behind this? Why is she only interested in literature from China or Taiwan?

As a matter of fact, the readers choose the works they enjoy and do not really bother about the background of the works. To many readers, Mahua writers neither have the skill to render their work interesting nor the ability to highlight the beauty of the language. Mahua writers do not generally read the works of other Mahua writers.

The fact that "The Trial" drew the attention of so many writers has nothing to do with the existence of Mahua literature. It was another issue. As mentioned by Xuan after great contemplation, "If a Mahua writer wins Nobel Prize one day, will the audience still insist that the works do not belong to Malaysia?" (Xian, 1991) This statement was made under an assumption that if there were some good literary works produced, then only the literary works from a particular place might be taken seriously.

Huang Jinshu, another writer near Xuan's age, echoed her opinion with his essay entitled "No Classics in Mahua literature". In his essay, he teased Mahua writers for attempting to "classicise" their own works.

In order to shape new Malaysians, the Ministry of Education has encouraged more literary works with local features, to be written as reading texts for primary and secondary school. In this context then, Huang can be taken to mean that the works of many writers could be chosen as school texts because of "local features" rather than the quality of the text. Huang was suspicious whether the works chosen would be accepted in general. He was afraid that this would send a wrong message and was very uncomfortable with the trend. By criticizing Mahua literary works, he further expressed his opinion by outlining what he knew of books on the history of Mahua literature,

> Various books on the history of Mahua literature are attempts to "classicise the works of Mahua literature." These are only books that put all the materials together for decorative purposes. What is the point of doing so? Why should these books be written? Works mentioned in the books on history of Mahua literature are works in the experimental stage. I feel that such books are not worth publishing. In a nutshell, Mahua literature is still in the experimental period (Huang, 1992a).

Such a provoking statement received protests from many writers. Chen Xuefung questioned Huang as to number of Mahua literary works he read (Chen, 1992). Huang replied in another article that he did not reject Mahua literature as a whole, rather he used a higher yardstick to access its quality. In fact, he claims to be "expecting a better literary work in the future." (Huang, 1992b)

It is not easy to conclude whether Mahua literature has come into its own or if it is of an acceptable standard. Some may argue that it is not fair to compare Malaysian writers with China's writers because China has more writers than Malaysia and it is easier for readers to find a favourite among China writers than local ones. Whatever the reason, the problems remain the same: Mahua writers are still not well known among the readers or critics.

Mahua writers are both ethnic Chinese and Malaysians. Due to their experience of localization, the Chinese in Malaysia do see themselves as Malaysian Chinese rather than part of the wider Chinese Diaspora. In other words, as ethnic Chinese, they need not be territorially bound. Mahua writers argue that the characteristics of Mahua literature are of local features, but in reality, as they also well understand, comparison with literary works of other places is inevitable.

The relationship between Mahua writers and the rest of the world is close especially after Malaysians were permitted to travel to China in 1989. Likewise, China writers were also invited to Malaysia. The fact that they hold frequent meetings and dialogues proves that there are many things worth discussing in modern Chinese medium literature.

Mahua writers think that it is important to go beyond Malaysia and enter the international arena to serve the dual purpose of exposing Mahua literary works to outside world and to serve as a catalyst for motivation to continue writing. To Mahua writers long marginalized in Malaysia, as described by Yun Lifeng, president of The Writers' Association of Chinese Medium of Malaysia from 1990 to 2002, acknowledgment by counterparts in China is a real encouragement (Yun, 1992:2). Yun's view is not surprising. In Malaysia, Chinese medium writers only gain recognition from the Malaysian Chinese, not the Malays. Their counterparts from China are considered as outsiders, and getting recognition from outsiders is considered extraordinary.

From 1980s to 1990s, a number of Mahua literary works was reviewed by writers from China. Most of these reviews were published in Malaysian newspapers. The editors were unconcerned with the quality of the critiques because they probably believed that more attention should be paid to foreign critics. Most of these reviews were nothing more than praises and as such, gave rise to many murmurs of dissatisfaction.

Both Mahua and China writers criticised this trend. Gu Yuanqing, a scholar working on modern Chinese literature, could not abide by the panegyric of these works. He claimed that the critics of China did not have enough knowledge about Malaysia or Mahua literature to see its flaws. They wrote the reviews based on the materials provided by Mahua writers themselves. He said that materials provided by Mahua writers to the China critics affected the resultant review. According to him, it is difficult to get materials on Mahua literature in China. Papers presented by Mahua writers or scholars at conferences in China are the main references for them. This has resulted the unprofessional critique of Mahua literature (Gu, 1998: 108-117). It is evident that most critics are friends of Mahua writers, and at the end of the day, friendship was more important than the review itself. The reviews have also misled other readers in China as well. On the other hand, the pleasing remarks could be seen as encouragement in the face of the difficulty in the development of Mahua literature.

Zhong Yiwen is a writer dissatisfied with this phenomenon. In the preface of *A Collection of Contemporary Mahua Prose Writings*, Zhong Yiwen, the writer and the editor of the book, said,

> We do not want lenient criticisms. Mahua prose writings must be examined and reviewed by the same yardstick as Chinese literary works from China and Taiwan. This is the only way to promote Mahua literature in the fastest way.
>
> (Zhong, 1996:7-12)

There is rationale in Zhong's remarks. When examined in the context of the entire canon of Chinese literature, the embarrassing status of Mahua writers is made apparent. For example, in the selection of the best one hundred Chinese novels organized by *Yazhou Zhoukan* (Chinese Asiaweek), a magazine well known in Chinese world, only *Jiling Chronicles* was the only Mahua work chosen and was ranked 40 (*Yazhou zhoukan*, 13 June 1999). Whether its writer Li Yongping can be considered a Mahua writer is debatable. After the announcement, many Mahua writers were asked to respond. Most writers felt bitter and said that the members of the board did not have any opportunity to read the Chinese literary works of South East Asia." (*Lianhe zhaopao*, 20 June 1999)

While these comments could be seen as slights on the members of the board such as David Wang Der-wei, Wang Meng, and Yu Qiuyu, who are all highly influential contemporary writers or critics. The fact remains that Mahua writers' bitter remarks prove that Mahua Literature is not really relevant in the international level. Having an impact on the international scene still remains as a dream and not a reality for Mahua writers.

Conclusion

When Malaysian Chinese were permitted to visit China in 1989, a clear distinction can be drawn between the Malaysian Chinese and Mainland Chinese. This feeling was captured in an article of Dai Xiaohua, the present president of the Writers' Association of Chinese Medium of Malaysia, published in mid 1990s in which she stated, "China is a place that gives me affection but there is a gap... I went to China because I wanted to be better acquainted with people of the same ethnicity as mine and to understand a culture I believe is similar to mine." (Dai, 1996:77) This so-called gap indicates that there are differences in the lifestyle of Malaysian Chinese and Mainland Chinese. Apart from the difference in nationality, "Malaysian Chinese Culture" has become increasingly obvious in the display of its unique identity. This identity may include the daily phrases used in communication, food and thought; in fact, going to China is no longer akin to their ancestors' desire of "returning to the motherland." Such differences, coupled with other factors, prompted the recognition of Malaysian Chinese as a separate entity from Mainland Chinese and Huang Jingshu captures this sentiment with these words,

> Born in a place other than the land of my ancestors, I am a *Huaqiao* (overseas Chinese); I was labelled as an overseas student when studying at the university; as a foreigner when applying for visa; as an illegal worker when working; and as the first batch of 'fujian' immigrants applying for citizenship....
>
> (Huang, 1994:3-4)

So long as no changes are exacted to the current political situation in Malaysia, the development of Chinese culture would remain stagnant. However, with the rapid changes taking place in Mainland China's political and economic scenes, as well as the spread of localism from Taiwanese literature influencing the Mahua literary field, the awareness of Mahua identity is expected to grow in the years to come. Though the future Mahua writers may find it difficult to do away with their cultural homesickness or feelings of discontentment against Malaysian politics, they use these sentiments to take "Mahua" seriously. They will use it either as a point for contemplation or as a landmark to position themselves. As such, the name of Mahua literature will inevitably come into its own as a literary concept.

Literally, the Chinese writers have been moving forwards since they left China. Their precarious future will depend on how they choose to move forwards. The latest developments in China have undeniably contributed to the interest in the study of the Chinese language, but the fact remains that they are Malaysian writers, not China writers. Mahua writers must learn to grasp their destiny in their own hands.

Notes

1   Mahua literature is considered a field of studies in Malaysia. For example, the term, instead of Malaysian Chinese Literature, has been used by all Ph. D. or M.A. theses related to the field. Department of Chinese Studies, University of Malaya, has offered a course entitled Mahua Literary Texts. A Malay book by Yang Quee Yee also used the term (see Yang, 2000).

2   For a discussion on the perceptions and responses of the Malaysian Chinese towards "Malay domination," see also Ho (2003: 239-262).

3   For example, see Nian Hong's comments [Nian (1986:62-72)].

References

Chen Lianqing, "Ye lin bianhou ti hua" (Postscript by the editor of Coconut trees), reprinted in Fang Xiu, *Mahua xin wenxue daxi* (An anthology of Malayan Chinese new literature), Singapore: Shijie shuju, 1972, vol. 10.

Chen Xuefeng (pen name Xia Mei), "Xuan Sulai, Huang Jinshu he mahua wenxue" (Xuan Sulai, Huang Jinshu and Mahua literature), *Nanyang Siang Pau*, 15 July. 1992.

Crouch, Harold, "Managing Ethnic Tensions through Affirmative Action: The Malaysian Experience," in Nat J. Colletta, et al. (ed.), *Social Cohesion and Conflict Prevention in Asia*, Washington, D.C.: The World Bank, 2001.

Cui Guiqiang, *Xin ma huaren guojia rentong de zhuanxiang 1945-1959* (A change of national identity of Chinese in Singapore and Malaysia 1945-1959), Singapore: Nanyang Xuehui, 1990.

Dai Xiaohua, *Shenqing kan shijie* (Looking at the world affectionately), Hebei: Hebei Jiaoyu Chubanshe, 1996.

Fang Beifang, *Kan mahua wenxue shengji fuhuo* (A high-spirited Mahua literature), Kajang: Xuelan'er wulu lengyue xing'an huiguan, 1995.

Fang Xiu, *Mahua xin wenxue daxi* (An anthology of Malayan Chinese new literature), Singapore: Shijie shuju, 1972, 10 vols.

Fei Ming, "Difang zuojia tan" (On local writers), reprinted in Fang Xiu, *Mahua xin wenxue daxi* (An anthology of Malayan Chinese new literature), Singapore: Shijie shuju, 1972, vol. 1.

Gu Yuanqing, "Mahua wenxue yanjiu zai zhongguo" (Mahua literary studies in China), in Dai Xiaohua and You Chuotao (eds), *Zhagen Bentu, Wangxiang Shijie* (Rooted in motherland, looking at the outside world), Kuala Lumpur: Malaixiya huawen zuojia xiehui ji malaya daxue zhongwenxi, 1998.

Ho Khai Leong, "Imagined Communion, Irreconcilable Differences? Perceptions and Responses of the Malaysian towards Malay Political Hegemony," in Ding Choo Ming and Ooi Kee Beng (eds), *Chinese Studies of the Malay World: A Comparative Approach*, Kuala Lumpur: Eastern Universities Press, 2003.

Huang Jinshu, "Mahua wenxue jindian quexi" (No Classics in Mahua literature), *Sin Chew Jit Poh*, 28 May 1992(a).

Huang Jinshu, "Dui wenxue de waihang yu dui lishi de wuzhi: jiu mahua wenxue da Xia Mei" (Ignorance of literature and unawareness of history: An answer to Xia Mei on Mahua literature), *Sin Chew Jit Poh*, 11 August 1992(b).

Huang Jinshu, *Meng yu zhu yu liming* (Dreams, pigs and sunrise), Taipei: Jiuge chubanshe, 1994.

Huang Jinshu, *Mahua wenxue: neizai zhongguo, yuyan yu wenxueshi* (Mahua literature: internalized China, language and literary history), Kuala Lumpur: Huazi Resource & Research Centre Berhad, 1996.

Lai Ruihe, " 'Wenhua huigui' he 'ziwo fangzu'" (Cultural home and self-exile) in Wen Wen Renping et al., *Mahua wenxue* (Mahua literature), Hong Kong: Wenyi shuwu, 1974.

Lin Lu, *Lin Lu zixuanji* (Selected works of Lin Lu), Taipei: Liming wenhua shiye gufen youxian gongsi, 1975.

Li Xuan , "Lun qiaomin wenyi" (On overseas Chinese literature), reprinted in Miao Xiu (ed.), *Xin ma huawen wenxue daxi: lilun* (An anthology of Chinese literature in Singapore and Malaysia: criticism and theory), Singapore: Jiaoyu chubanshe, 1972.

Lin, Jianguo, "Wei shenme mahua wenxue?" (Why Mahua literature?), *Zhongwai Wenxue* (Chungwai Literary Monthly), 21:10 (Mac 1993).

Ling, Zuo, "Mahua wenyi de dutexing ji qita" (On the distinctive features of Mahua literature and art as well as other related issues), reprinted in Miao Xiu (ed.), *Xin ma huawen wenxue daxi: lilun* (An anthology of Chinese literature in Singapore and Malaysia: criticism and theory), Singapore: Jiaoyu chubanshe, 1972.

Ma Xiangwu, "Dangdai mahua xiaoshuo de zhuti jiangou" (Theme constructions in contemporary Mahua fictions), Dai Xiaohua and You Chuotao (eds), *Zhagen Bentu, Wangxiang Shijie* (Rooted in motherland, looking at the outside world), Kuala Lumpur: Malaixiya huawen zuojia xiehui ji malaya daxue zhongwenxi, 1998.

Meng Sha, *Mahua wenxue zacui* (On the various issues of Mahua literature), Petaling Jaya: Xueren chubanshe, 1986.

Miao Xiu, *Mahua wenxue shihua* (History of Mahua new literature), Singapore: Qinnian shuju, 1968.

Miao Xiu (ed.), *Xin ma huawen wenxue daxi: lilun* (An anthology of Chinese literature in Singapore and Malaysia: criticism and theory), Singapore: Jiaoyu chubanshe, 1972.

Nian Hong, *Wei xinyidai kachuang xin tiandi* (Exploring a new world for the new generation), Muar: Nanma wenyi yanjiuhui, 1986.

Wen Rui'an, *Weishuo muyun yuan* (Looking back), Taipei: Siji chubanshe, 1977.

Wong Seng-tong, "The Identity of Malaysian-Chinese Writers," in Wong Yoon Wah and Horst Pastoors (eds), *Chinese Literature in Southeast Asia*, Singapore: Goehter-Institut and Singapore Association of Writers, 1989.

Xuan Sulai, "Kaiting shenxun" (The trial), *Sin Chew Jit Poh*, 1 May 1991.

Yang Quee Yee, *Perkembangan Kesusasteraan Mahua Moden 1919 -1965* (The development of Mahua new literature 1919-1965), Kuala Lumpur: Dewan Bahasa dan Pustaka, 2000

Yang Songnian, *Zhanqian xinma wenxue bendi yishi de xingcheng yu fazhan* (The formation and development of localism of literature in Singapore and Malaya in the pre-war era), Singapore: Department of Chinese Studies, National University of Singapore, 2001.

Ye Xiao, "Jueze yitiao yao zou de lu: mahua xiezuozhe suoyao renqing de chujing he guixiang" (A road to follow: Current state of Mahua writers and their future direction, *Chao Foon Monthly*, No.303 (May 1978)

Yen Ching-hwang, *A Social History of the Chinese in Singapore and Malaysia 1800-1911*, Singapore: Oxford University Press, 1986.

Yue Daiyun, "Cong shijie wenhua jiaoliu kan huawen wenxue yanjiu" (A review of Chinese literary studies from the aspect of world cultural exchanges), *Taiwan xianggang yu haiwai huawen wenxue lunwenxuan* (A collection of papers on literature in Taiwan, Hong Kong and Chinese Overseas), Fuzhou: Haixia wenyishe, 1998.

Yun Lifeng, "Jiushi niandai mahua wenxue zhanwang" (Prospects of Mahua literature in the 1990s), *Chao Foon Monthly*, No. 448 (May/June 1992).

Zhang Jinyan (pen name Yan), "Nanyang yu wenyi" (Nanyang and literature), reprinted in Fang Xiu, *Mahua xin wenxue daxi* (An anthology of Malayan Chinese new literature), Singapore: Shijie shuju, 1972, vol.1.

Zhong Yiwen, *Mahua dangdai sanwen xuan, 1990-1995* (A collection of contemporary Mahua prose writings, 1990-1995), Taipei: Wen shi zhe chubanshe, 1996.

Chapter 3

Islam in China and Malaysia: Similarities and Differences

Qu Hong

Both China and Malaysia are multi-racial and multi-religious countries. China is a big nation with 56 ethnic groups. Apart from the majority Han Chinese (94%), minority ethnic groups constitute a significant part of its population (6%). Among the 55 minorities, 10 are classified as Muslim ethnic groups. Malaysia, by contrast, has 178 ethnic groups, consisting of Malays (55%), Chinese (32%), Indians (10%), and other indigenous peoples (3%). To understand China and Malaysia in this era of globalization, one has to understand, first of all, the peoples and their different cultures, different religious beliefs and different life-styles. Such an understanding will be a sound basis for mutual cooperation in various fields.

Historical Overview

Islam and Muslims Came into Malaysia and China

According to the historical records, Islam's first arrival in these two countries, coincidently, can be traced back to the seventh century. In Malaysia, it is dated as far back as 674 C.E. when the Umayyad Caliph Muawiyah was in power, but most scholars argue for a date nearer the 13th century. With regard to China, it was one of the earliest missionary fields for Islam. When Chinese Islamic scholars search their historical sources, they find the earliest records of Islam and Muslims in China focused on seven different dates. Five of them are in the Tang dynasty (618-907 C.E.), which are as follows: (1) 618-626 in Tang under the first emperor Li Yuan's rule; (2) 628 the second year of Tang Zhenguan; (3) 651 the second year of Tang Yonghui; (4) 710-711 Tang Jingyuan; and (5) 757 the second year of Tang Zhide. The other two dates in the Sui dynasty are not regarded as credible. But based on critical research, 651 or 757 are most commonly accepted as the year that Islam first arrived in China. From these dates the Muslims in both countries started their existence respectively. Their history has lasted more than 1300 years.

Basically, Islam came to Malaysia in two ways: (a) from India to the west coastal area, especially in the ports and trading centers, where Islam was embraced in the late ninth century around 878 C.E.; and (b) from China to the east coast, though this is debatable. However, a stone dating back to 1386 or 1326 C. E., inscribed with Arabic letters, served as the first physical evidence of the arrival of Islam in the Malay Peninsula. It was found at a spot up the Terengganu River and supports the theory that Islam could have come to the Malay Peninsula through China. Similarly, Islam and Muslims entered the Tang Dynasty via two main routes: (a) the Silk Road, overland across Central Asia, to the Northwestern part of China, now called Xinjiang Autonomous Region; and (b) the Spice Road, by sea from the Persian Gulf, into the Indian Ocean, along the sub-continental coast, down through the Straits of Malacca, and on up to southeastern China.

Islam's Spreading and Muslims' Development in China and Malaysia

The spread of Islam in the two countries was not the result of any organized missionary movements; rather, it appears to have been a gradual and perhaps unconscious process of religious and cultural assimilation. This process took a long time probably several centuries which allowed Islam in China and Malaysia to be shaped in each place with its own characteristics and made them similar and different, as well as particular and general.

I would like to give a brief history of Islam and Muslims in China. It can be divided into the five periods: (a) from the Tang to Song dynasties (618-1279); (b) the Yuan dynasty (1271-1368); (c) the Ming dynasty (1368-1644); (d) the Qing dynasty (1644-1911); and (e) the Republic of China and P. R. China period (1911-present).

It must be kept in mind that China's Muslims generally are not ethnic Chinese converts but are descendants of Muslims from the Middle East and Central Asia who migrated to China at various times and for various reasons. Some were soldiers, some were merchants, some were voluntary migrants, and some were taken to Tang as slaves or bondsmen. During the Tang (618-907) and Song (960-1279) dynasties, many Arabic and Persian merchants came to the Southeastern part of China, and settled down in port cities along the coast like Quanzhou, Changzhou and Guangzhou (Canton). Originally, Han Chinese called these Muslim merchants "*fan ke*", (*fan* meaning "foreign", *ke* meaning "guest"). Their living places were called "*fan fang*", (*fang* meaning "house"). Apparently, they were just guests! These were the first source of the present Muslim population of China, as the temporary trading outposts changed into permanent settlements. In the later Song dynasty, those Muslims were called "*tu sheng fan ke*", means "China-born foreign guests". They began to have some economic impact or influence upon the import and export business. For instance, the office of Director General of Shipping was consistently held by a Muslim during this time. Meanwhile, there was no record whatsoever of anti-Muslim sentiment on the part of Han Chinese for "*tu sheng fan ke*" were recognized as being fair, law-abiding, and self-disciplined.

The Yuan dynasty (1271-1368), established by the Mongols, provided another opportunity for China's Muslims to spread their faith and to increase their population rapidly. There are two reasons that profoundly affected the composition of China's population. (1) During the Mongol conquests, Genghis Khan's army conquered Baghdad, and ended the great Islamic Empire the Abbasid Dynasty in 1258. The army also took other major Islamic centers in Central Asia, including Bukhara and Samarkand. As a result of their westward expeditions, the Mongols transported sections of the population eastward, and lots of Muslim people such as army-men, craftsmen, women and children thus were brought to China, where they were settled to serve the Mongol rulers. (2) The Yuan's political and social policies recognized four social classes in the Yuan dynasty; they were: (a) Mongols, the ruling class; (b) *Se-mu ren* (colored-eyes), means "foreigners, generally Central Asians", the second class; (c) *Han ren*, Han people, the third class; and (d) *Nan ren*, the fourth class, native people living in the southern China. Clearly, Muslims had full citizenship and enjoyed a high social position in this society. Many of them were appointed as high-ranked officials and served the emperors. Moreover, it is worth mentioning that quite a few native Chinese converted to Islam at this time. It was a good time for Chinese Muslims to develop themselves in every respect. We may say that the Mongol conquest was the single most important factor in spreading Islam and creating the Muslim communities in China.

The Ming and Qing dynasties are also important times in the history of Islam in China, but for very different reasons. These were hard times for Chinese Muslims. The Han Chinese Ming (1368-1644) took back the political power from the Mongols. Being a minority, the Muslims went back to a lower position. Also, there are two points to be made: (1) The creation of Hui Muslim ethnic group: Muslims during this period, even with their Central Asian origins, first became a permanently settled community in China and began to identify themselves as Chinese. Thus a new Muslim ethnic group was created i.e. the Hui. The Han Chinese call them "Hui Hui" and Islam as "Huihui *Jiao*" (literally, Huihui religion). "Huihui" thus is used both as the name of an ethnic group and as a description of a religion, Islam, simply denoting Muslim. Though both uses of the term are evident from sources dating to the later years of the Yuan dynasty, an identifiable and independent ethnic group is evident only from the early years of the Ming dynasty. (2) Political factors involved in shaping the geographical distribution of Muslims in China: Since the Hui Muslim people were politically and socially looked down upon by the Han, the Ming government sent them to garrison the distant frontiers. For this reason most of the Hui Muslim communities today can be found in Gansu and Ningxia provinces in the northwest and Yunnan province in the southwest.

The Qing dynasty (1644-1911) was founded by another minority, the Manchu. The Emperors and their nobles progressively became more Chinese and accepted both the Han culture and outlook. Even so, most Han Chinese still think of them as alien conquerors. During the Qing dynasty, China's Muslims started getting a reputation as a fierce and rebellious minority. Many rebellions and uprisings continually broke out from the 17th century to the 19th century, and the Qing eventually put them down with military force. As a result the Muslim population, especially for the Hui, was largely reduced and faced the possibility of extinction. These insurrections devastated the border regions of China and left behind a legacy of mutual suspicion between Muslims and Han Chinese. This is the reason why Chinese officials have remained vigilant about Muslim separatism ever since.

Since 1911, great changes have taken place in China. The May Fourth Movement in 1919 and the Cultural Revolution from 1966 to 1976 had a strong impact upon Chinese society and people. Islam and Muslims were surely affected. Since the opening of the era of reform in the early 1980s, the government has put serious effort into implementing the Constitution's policy on freedom of religious belief. Islam has become one of the five officially recognized religions in China.

The development of Islam and Muslim people in Malaysia provides us with a different picture. Its history can be divided into the four periods: (a) the Hindu Kingdom period (674-1400); (b) the golden age of Malacca (1400-1511); (c) the colonial period (1511-1957); and (d) the current period (1957-

present).

The Hindu Kingdom actually existed in the Malay Peninsula for about 1500 years from 100 B.C. to 1400 A.D. As mentioned earlier the historical record of Islam in this part of world dates from as early as 674 C.E. That is why the first period starts from that date. Having been ruled under the Hindu tradition for such a long time, Malaysia was heavily influenced by the Indian culture. This is the context in which Islam was spread, in actual fact, and it helps explain how the Arabic Islam was modified by Indian ideas as it was practiced by Indian Muslims and introduced to their trading partners. The first converts in Malaysia were from the aristocratic class. Once Islam had established a foothold among the rulers and chiefs of the coastal commercial areas and these rulers had set their seal of authority on the new faith, immediately it became acceptable to the common local people. The faith was greatly enhanced partly by social contact as a consequence of trade, but more important still, by marriages. Diplomatic marriages among aristocratic families in and across many kingdoms spread the faith further. For instance, the Malacca sultans arranged many such marriages with Pahang, Kedah, Borneo etc. The common people down the social scale gradually followed such practices.

At the close of the 14th century when Islam was spreading in conjunction with the prospering Indian trade, the nucleus of a new and powerful Malay Kingdom and empire took shape with the emergence of Malacca. Malacca was in an ideal location, thus attributing to its great success. It was founded in 1400 and within 50 years it was a major port, actually the most influential in Southeast Asia. With alliances being built with other tribes and ports, Malacca was able to "police" the waters and provide an escort for vessels that needed it. With its rapid rise, Malacca quickly became the power in control of all of Malaysia's west coast. Thus, Islam acquired a firm hold in the region, and the single most important factor was when the Hindu ruler of the powerful city-state Malacca, Parameswara Dewa Shah, converted to Islam. This event is equal in significance for Islam in Malaysian history to the Yuan's rule in Chinese history. Furthermore, Malacca became the spearhead of the further advance of Islam. Sultan

Muzaffar Shah around 1450 declared Islam to be the official religion in the Malacca Kingdom,[1] Muslim scholars enjoyed high status at the time. Meanwhile, the Muslim scholars or ulama played a very important role in spreading Islam from one place to another. Their formal practice was to open a religious training center called *pondok* (Islamic boarding school). After graduation the students would go back to their hometown, often in some remote corner of the country, and start their own *pondok*. Or they would teach at a surau, and link these schools in a chain, thus making a network of teacher-student-teacher between one ulama and another as well as between *pondok* schools.[2] *Ulamas*, in addition to giving lectures in the school, house, surau or mosque, also served as advisors for the village families and communities as well as worked in the *padi* fields, gardening and craftwork, etc.

The colonial period started in the year of 1511 when Malacca's power and success was extinguished by the Portuguese. The Portuguese were overthrown by the Dutch in 1641, and the British took the turn in 1795 and formally established protectorates in Malaysia in the 1880s. For 130 years from 1511, Portuguese policy in Malacca — the religio-political center of the peninsula, was characterized by the desire to check the spread of Islam and Muslim trading enterprises. They failed in these tasks because their occupation was continuously resisted by Malays. The Dutch's policy was to tolerate traditional Malay rulers who were divided at this time because of competing state rivalries. The British policy, under the Pangkor Treaty in 1874, was not to interfere in matters affecting Malay custom and religion. For about 150 years, however, the British occupation was of a great significance in shaping the course of Islam in Malay society. Its administration and regulation affected the society and religion on at least three important issues.[3]

(1) The introduction of a multi-ethnic society: This was one of the major outcomes of British rule. Non-Malays, predominantly Chinese and Indians, had been brought into Malay Peninsula in large numbers to serve British economic interests. Based on the "divide and rule policy", the British colonial government did not make any integrative effort to bring the different ethnic groups together.

(2) The policy toward Malay and Islamic education: Formal education for Malay children at that time was religious, beginning in the mosques, particularly at *surau* in the rural areas. It was also conducted at the *pondok*. The colonial administration did not help develop Islamic education in any respect. Christian missionaries, however, were allowed to open Christian or Christian-oriented schools and encouraged Chinese, Indians, and others to be educated in the western way. On the one hand, Malay families seldom sent their children to the Islamic schools; on the other hand, Malays were marginalized by the colonizers, who disparaged them because they were said to be unskilled in fulfilling basic human needs. The significance of colonial educational policy to Islam in Malaya was twofold: first, it contributed to the relative passivity of the Islamic factor in the life of Malays, and thus strict adherence to Islam was not so firm or so uniform throughout peninsular Malaya; second, it produced a generation of Muslim bureaucrats who were "westernized" and "secularized", thus creating a cultural split among the Malays.

(3) The administration of Islamic law: The extent of British control in Malay-Muslim affairs can be seen from the way the influence of the Islamic *shari'ah* on Malay life was curtailed. For instance, important rulings affecting the Islamic courts and Islamic law were subject to British sanction; the *kadhi's* (the Islamic judge's) powers were limited by the provisions of British-influenced state legislation. Moreover, civil magistrates tended to refer to the precedents of British statutory law rather than to those of *shari'ah* law; and Islamic courts had their role subordinated to the civil courts.

Objectively, however, it should be noted that British rule did assist the development of Islam and the Malays in some ways, for example, co-ordination and regulation of Muslim institutions such as the *zakat* and *wakaf* collections, the Islamic court system, and pilgrimage procedures.

Doubtlessly, Islam has been flowering in Malaysia since independence in 1957. The Constitution stipulates: "Islam is the religion of the Federation" (article 3). I will not go into details about this period as it is still going on.

Islamization in Malaysia and Cultural Accommodation in China

As mentioned above, Muslims in Malaysia are mainly local converts. This is so because Islamization took place in the Malay society from the ruling class down to the common people, giving content to the definition of "Malayness" and to Malay values, and reformulating the concept of the Malay, Melayu, and its connection with Islam over the past three hundred years.

The term "Melayu" was initially associated more closely with ideas of stratification or rank and hierarchy than with ethnicity or social boundaries. It was first used in connection with a myth of origin for the royal rulers.[4] The common people had been considered of low caste, who could acquire Malay status only through connection with a true "Malay", that is, one of royal descent. This was achieved by affiliation as fictive "children" of the *rajah*.[5] The coming of Islam contributed a new dimension to Malay identity undoubtedly. At the political level, while the royal rulers and the heads of the state in most parts of Malay world embraced the Islam religion, the people were impressed and attracted by the assertions in the Qur'an and the Hadith of an interpersonal equality, that no longer defined people's lives within a social class or a religious caste system. Many common people converted to Islam, particularly during the Malacca Kingdom period. Any outsider who converted to Islam was automatically eligible for a Malay status following the adage that to "enter Islam" was to "become a Malay". In local speech being a Malay and becoming a Malay are synonymous with being a Muslim and converting to Islam. Thus a linkage between religious and ethnic identity is enforced. This is even enshrined in the Constitution. Legally, a major prerequisite to be Malay, as defined in the Constitution, is that one must be Muslim and one automatically loses one's "Malayness" if one relinquishes Islam. Thus it has come to be generally accepted that Islam is an integral and significant factor in Malay culture. This can be seen through the nature of traditional Malay political leadership (the sultanate) and the Malay "Islamic-based" educational system.

Islamization also created the Malay written language. In the pre-Islamic period, the Malay language had many indigenous and Hindu writing scripts. However, the coming of Islam provided the Arab script, the Jawi spelling system,[6] which was a necessary precondition for the development of an effective religious and educational tradition and the foundation of an ulama-guru class. Thus began a long and rich tradition of written religious literature in Malay Jawi script. It encompassed both translations from Arabic originals as well as local Malay commentaries and texts, known as the *Kitab Jawi* (Malay/Jawi books), many of which are still used in the *surau*, mosques, and religious schools throughout Muslim Southeast Asia. In the early 19th century, Malay Jawi was the only version of the language formally taught and used largely as the medium of religious instruction. Meanwhile, Jawi was probably the regional trading lingua franca, and many of the first Muslim visitors to Southeast Asia came on missions of trade first and religion second. A common linguistic medium thus assisted both. This literary tradition established through Islam thus became the vessel of Islam and in return, further spread the faith, especially across political boundaries. Today it has become the largest "Muslim" language.

Islamization in the early times dramatically transformed Malay society. Islam thus is viewed as the ultimate source of Malay cultural unity, ethics, morality, and value.   However, from the beginning, the religion had to wrestle with traditional norms, practices, and conventions already well established in Malay culture, commonly referred to as *adat*, which still exist and even now are privately practiced.[7] Here a little discussion on the pre- or non-Islamic elements in Malay culture seems needed. Clearly, the *adat* shows their origins in Hindu, Buddhist, and other pre-Islamic religions or traditions. Most of these customs are an assortment of agricultural and fishing rituals designed to appease spirits, some magical curing rites, and many practices attached to rites of passage. For example, the known ritual feast of *puja pantai*, or offerings on the beach to the sea spirit used to be performed by various fishing communities in Malaysia. Another adat still practiced in the both Islamic and traditional Malay wedding is the tradition of *bersanding*, which is the climax of the wedding ritual. The bride and the groom are made to sit on a platform for some time receiving in audience the relatives and guests. The couple should try to remain apparently unmoved during this act, staring in front of them with their hands placed on their laps. This ritual is derived from court traditions and is strongly Hindu influenced. The intention of this ritual is to protect the new couple from forces in the surroundings and to strengthen their ties. It therefore becomes a hallmark of Malay identity and tradition. But the ritual is obviously associated with an unIslamic propitiation of spirits, and in theory is not proper for a true Muslim though the Malays adopt it. In the past few decades, the government has tried to ban those traditional unIslamic *adats*, with the result that the rituals have become more individual and private. Public rituals with a big audience are hardly found anymore, though they may still be quietly performed. Malay *adat*, being integral to Malay life, cannot be neglected without misgivings from the community. Its complementarities with Islamic principles can be acknowledged. Malay culture is a part of Islamic culture in a broad sense, for it is not possible to be Islamic without retaining one's own cultural characteristics. *Adat* make Malay culture distinct from other cultures.

In contrast to Malaysia, Islam in China developed quite differently. When Islam came into China, the biggest problem it faced was how to adapt itself to the Chinese cultural environment with Confucianism and Daoism at its base. As Muslims in China are minorities, under the shadow of the majority Han prejudices against them, they remain united and try to establish their own religious and educational system with Chinese characteristics. The best option in such a context is to learn to accommodate Islamic faith and practice to Chinese culture. Muslims in China did this generally in three ways.

The first is to develop religious education in mosque-attached schools for Muslim children, which started at the end of the Ming Dynasty. When the new schools called *"Jingwen Xiaoxue"* or *"Jingwen Xuexiao"* (Islamic elementary school) were opened, they needed textbooks. In most cases these were Islamic classics in Arabic or Persian loosely translated into Chinese language. This new practice created a foundation for religious education in Chinese language, which in turn helped the spread of Chinese among the Muslims, especially among the Hui Muslims. As a result, a number of good Muslim scholars who were well versed both in Chinese and Islamic cultures appeared. As teachers they tried to interpret Islamic doctrines in terms of Confucianism and at the same time they tended to understand Confucianism in accordance with Islamic views. Thus a common language became the first factor in a critical synthesis between Islam and traditional Chinese cultures. This new style of giving religious instruction in Chinese is later called the Chinese school of Islam.

The second is a reinterpretation of Islamic views of the Universe and the Creation in terms of Taoism. Many are the Muslim scholars who have made remarkable contributions in this area, of which Wang Daiyu (1584-1670) and Liu Zhi (1655-1745) are the best known. Wang Daiyu, the most influential Chinese Islamic scholar of all time, wrote a most influential work titled *Zheng Jiao Zhen Quan* ("Righteous Commentary on the True Religion") and other religious treatises, which became the basis of *Hanxuepai* (Han studies order) of Islam in China. Liu Zhi was author of many books on Islam, of which two works called "Theories of the Human Nature and the World of Arabia" and "Rites and Ceremonies of Arabia" are most important. The former attempts to interpret Allah's creation of the Universe in terms of Daoism so as to harmonize the traditional Chinese worldview with the Islamic worldview as expounded by Sufism. According to Daoism, everything existing in the world originates from the Dao or *Tai/Dai Ji* which is the primary *"qi"* (air). *Tai/Dai Ji* has two forms: *Yang* and *Yin* (positive and negative), which interact with each other. The universe is made of four primary elements: water, fire, air and mud. I do not need to go any further here. Indeed, the traditional Chinese worldview is different from that of Islam. Nevertheless, Liu Zhi created three basic concepts that are both agreeable with Islam and acceptable to Daoism. They are "true oneness", "oneness in manyness", and "the experience of oneness".[8] Of the three, "true oneness" refers to God who is higher and pre-exists *Dai Ji*, thus affirming

God's primordial role in creation; "oneness in manyness" refers to the unity of all beings created by God, united, namely, in their common status as reflections of God's will; "experience of oneness" refers to apprehending the existence of God by experiencing God's creation in the world.

The third is the harmonization of Islamic ethics with Confucian moral norms. This is done in two forms. One is to create and elaborate the idea of "double loyalties", which is easy for Muslims in China. A typical interpretation is to reinterpret God's command of "Obey God, obey his Prophet and those in authority". They say "those in authority" refers to the emperors on earth. So there is no contradiction between believing in God and obeying the emperor or loving one's motherland in modern terminology. The other is to reinterpret Islamic ethics, the basic way being for Chinese Muslims to add the five moral relationships honored in Confucianism to the five pillars of Islam. This means in practice that the five moral norms are accepted as complements to the five duties of Muslims.[9] They are called ways of fidelity, namely, the observance of a proper relationship between the emperor and his subjects, the intimacy between father and his sons, the differentiation between husband and his wife, the correct ordering of the old and the young, and cultivation of sincerity between oneself and one's friends.

This general trend of cultural development in Islam in China is termed by scholars as Sinicization. As a result, Islam in China is both Islamic and Chinese in character. It is Islamic, for the basic tenets of Islam remain unchanged. It is Chinese, for Islam becomes harmonized with traditional Chinese culture. This paves the way for the modern development of Islam in China today.

In summary, in the course of Islamization, intermarriage and acculturation, Islam successfully rooted itself in Malaysia and survived in China. Over long periods of time, Malays fully became Muslims and thus today Islam enjoys a majority status in the country; and in China, a large number of Chinese minority people who embraced Islam at various times and localities became what we call Muslims in China or simply Chinese Muslims.

Religious Traditions and Customs

As one can observe in the Islamic world, Muslims are divided into different religious sects. Malaysian Muslims and most Chinese Muslims regard themselves as orthodox Sunni Muslims, standing firmly in the mainstream tradition of Islam. With regard to the *Mazhab* (Islamic law school), Malaysian Muslims follow the Shafiyi School of Islamic law. However, there are many Muslims in Malaysia who do not follow any law school, for instance, the Perlis state constitution specifies that Perlis follow the Qur'an and Sunnah and not a particular *mazhab*.[10] By contrast, a majority of Chinese Muslims follows the Hanafi School of Islamic law, which is the largest of the four *mazhabs*. But there are also small groups of Shiite Muslims living in Xinjiang who follow the Jafari School of Islamic law.[11]

Sufism, which gives more emphasis to the disciplines of spiritual cultivation practiced by individual believers, in general has had a tremendous influence upon Islam. Many Sufis arrived in the Malay Archipelago and in China's deeply Muslim northwest. Sufism was introduced into the Malay world in the 17th century. There are three great Sufi scholars to be noted.[12] The first was al-Raniri who was not only a Sufi, but also a theologian and *fiqih*. He insisted on the importance of *shari'ah* in mystical practices and clarified the distinction between the true and false interpretation and understanding of Sufi doctrine and practice when he initiated the religious reform in the Malay world. The other two Sufi scholars were al-Sinkili and al-Maqassari. Al-Sinkili's teachings indicate that what he transmitted to the Malay Muslims was the harmony between the orthodoxy Islam and Sufism. Thus he affirmed that Islamic mysticism should go hand in hand with the *shari'ah*. Whilst the central concept of al-Maqassari's Sufism was purification of the faith in the Unity of Allah, he reserved Sufi practice for an elite only. Malay scholars mushroomed in the 18th century, among them, Muhammad Nafis al-Banjari was very prominent.[13] Inheriting the three great scholars' teachings in the 17th century, he maintained and further elaborated that it was vital for every Sufi on the mystical path to fulfill the *shari'ah* rules. There is not, however, much information on the Sufi orders in

Malaysia.

Sufism was brought into China's Northwest in the 14th century. The Sufi order or brotherhood in China, particularly in Gansu, Ningxia, and Qinghai where they are strongest, is usually known as *menhuan* (hereditary Sufi or other mystical orders among the Hui people). Sufi masters have their own "*Daohao*" (special name for the Saint, often in Arabic), live in their own "*Daotang*" (the saint's residence, also becomes a Sufi teaching and ritual center) and are buried at their "*Gongbei*" (tombs in the northwest China, the object of veneration by Sufi and other orders) or "*Mazar*" (the Uyghur equivalent of the gongbei tombs) after they die. There have been four main groups of menhuan: they are the Khufiyya, tracing its origin back to Abu Bakr; the Kubrawiyya, to Omar; the Jahriyya, to Osman, and the Qadariyya to Ali. The Khufiyya and the Jahriyya, both of them branches of the Naqshbandiyya, the most fundamentalist Sufi brotherhood in the Islamic world, find their origins in Yemen. The Kubrawiyya and the Qadariyya, by contrast, originated in Central Asia.

With regard to ethnicity and race among Muslims in both countries, most Malaysian Muslims are Malays, and a small number are Indian and Chinese Muslims, whilst Chinese Muslims consist of Turks, Aryans, and Mongols who form 10 ethnic groups — the Hui, the Uyghurs, the Kazakhs, the Kyrgyz, the Uzbeks, the Tatars, the Salars, the Bao'an, the Dongxiang, and the Tajiks.

By language use, Malaysian Muslims generally speak Malay for it is the national language (Cantonese, Mandarin, and Tamil are also in use within each community). For Chinese Muslims, basically, there are four different languages known to have been spoken and written. (1) The Chinese-speaking: the Hui is the largest group, who comprise over half of China's Muslim population, and are scattered throughout all of the country. But, there are still two big significant concentrations of Hui people in northwest China, in Gansu and Ningxia provinces. Hui Muslim people also have their own special language, the "*Huihui hua*" or "*Jingtang yu*" (Hui speech that incorporates Islamic Arabic and Persian terms), which is used in their religious life and activities. The Huihui are regarded in China as native

Muslims, for they are the only Muslim group who have Chinese facial features, speak Chinese language and intend to blend into the Chinese majority. (2) The Turkic-speaking: It includes the Uyghurs, the Kazakh, the Kyrgyz, the Uzbeks, the Tatars and the Salars, a total of 6 ethnic groups. Nearly all of the Turkic Muslims are found in the western part of Xinjiang province, though some are in Gansu. The largest of them are the Uyghurs who make up some 60% of the total population in Xinjiang and enjoy their majority privileges. (3) The Mongolian-speaking: the Bao'an and Dongxiang. The Bao'an once was a part of Hui, known as the Bao'an Hui. They were accepted as a separate ethnic group only in 1952. Dongxiang means "eastern village" because most live in the mountains east of Linxia. Both trace their origins to groups of Mongolian and Central Asian Muslims brought into China in the Yuan dynasty. (4) The Persian-speaking: the Tajik. It is a small group, largely confined to Tashkorgan region in southwestern Xinjiang. Their language is related to Persian, which is also spoken among their kindred in Tajikistan and Northern Afghanistan.

Regarding attire, food and eating habits, Malaysian Muslim men usually wear shirt and trousers in the workplace and a sarong at home whilst women wear their national dress *baju kurong* and *baju kebaya* with *tdung* covering their hair, eat only *halal* (permissible to Islam) food, often using only the fingers of the right hand. Chinese Muslims again differ from group to group. The Turkic Muslims normally wear their ethnic clothes, both men and women have a colorful cap on their head, and eat mainly beef and mutton with their hands. The Hui dress like Chinese Han but keep certain distinctive customs, like the distinctive beards and white caps worn by their menfolk and the colored head-covers worn by their women, and their own dietary restriction. Their halal food is called "*Qingzhen Shipin*" (pure and clean food); they eat it by using Chinese chopsticks.

In names, Chinese Muslims, particularly the Hui, have both surnames and given names. This may be an example of acculturation. In that process Muslim names changed. Many who married Han women simply took on the family name of the wife, like Liu, Yang, Ding, etc. Others took the Chinese surnames of Mo, Ma, and Mu, which were adapted from Mosoud,

Muhammad and Mustafa. Those who could not find a Chinese surname similar to their own, simply created their surnames from their Arabic names such as Ha from Hassan, Hanifa, or Harun, Sha from Shafiyi, Hu from Hussin, Sai from Sayd, Da from Dawoud, An from Anshari, Ai from Ahmad, or Amin, etc. Compared to Chinese Muslims, Malay Muslim names come more frequently from Arabic, such as Abdullah bin Hamid, Amina binti Abbas, and there is no surname needed, only the father's name followed by "bin or binti" (son or daughter).

Both Malaysian and Chinese Muslims celebrate the great festivals Id al-Fitri and Id al-Adha though they also celebrate many other festivals or holidays in their home country. For instance, Chinese Muslims put emphasis on the holidays Ashura and Fatima, the former to memorialize the prophets Adam and Ibrahim, and the latter, called in Chinese *"Gu-tai Jie"* (the Grandaunt Festival), to show respect to the daughter of the Prophet Muhammad. As for the Prophet's birthday and death-day, both were on the same date. In Malaysia, the Prophet's birthday (Islamic calendar March 12 / *Rabiulawwal* 12) is one of most significant celebrations, however, in China, the Prophet's death day is stressed, not particularly on March 12 of the Islamic calendar, but it could be any day in this month. The memorial service is conducted as Han Chinese do for their ancestors on death anniversaries.[14]

In terms of religious organizations and education, the most important organization in charge of religious affairs for Chinese Muslims is the Chinese Islamic Association at the national level, established in 1953, which had 25 branches at provincial and municipal levels, 491 at city and county levels by the end of 1995. Developing religious education is an important function played by the Association, whose general aim is to develop Islamic learning by training high-level Islamic scholars. In 1955 the first Chinese Academy of Islamic Learning was founded, which was auspicious for the systematic development of Islamic higher education in China. Since the eighties when China entered the new stage of reform and openness to the outside world, eight more such academies have been founded in the different provinces of China and a new network of Islamic higher education has been created throughout the country.[15]

In Malaysia, there are large numbers of Islamic and Muslim associations such as the Federation of the Organization of Islamic Societies (FOSIS), the Islamic Representative Council (IRC), the Muslim Youth Movement of Malaysia (ABIM), the Muslim Students Associations (MSAs), the Malaysian National Association of Muslim Students (PKPIM), the Muslim Students Society of University of Malaya (PMIUM), the Society for Islamic Reform in Malaysia (JIM), Darul Arqam, etc. They all play roles in pushing Islamic norms and principles and education in the country. Malaysian Muslims demand that Islamic religious knowledge should be included as a subject in the government elementary and secondary schools. Currently, this subject has been given 180 minutes per week to the Muslim students at primary level and 120 minutes at the secondary level. The Malay Muslims have also been concerned with establishing independent religious schools. From 1977 to 1995, there were 39 secondary religious schools founded and administered by the government.[16] Moreover, the Islamic or Muslim associations started their own religious schools. ABIM, for example, opening its kindergartens in 1979, had 409 such pre-schools all over the country by 1992. Its primary school, started in 1989, had established 8 branches throughout Malaysia by 1995. It continues establishing its secondary schools and pre-university colleges.[17]

Finally, some information about mosques and imams in China should be noted. Currently, there are more than 34,000 mosques in the entire P. R. China, most of them in Xinjiang, Gansu and Ningxia, and 45,000 imams are available to lead the Muslim communities and their religious activities.[18] In addition, Islamic literature is easily accessed and there are some 8 different translations of the Qur'an in Chinese and in Uyghur and the other Turkic languages as well.

In conclusion, Islam in both Malaysia and China developed with its own characteristics, and thus displays a lot of similarities as well as differences. Similarities lie in the truth that Islam is a universal faith, which emphasizes the Oneness of God, and the role of *shari'ah* law in regulating a Muslim's five duties to Allah. Differences arose out of the varying patterns of historical development that Islam experienced and their resulting differences in status that Muslims enjoyed in the two countries. Beyond these, I would like to say that Malay Muslims who want to do business in China will not feel like strangers, because the Muslim brotherhood and mosques can be found everywhere in China.

Notes

1 Sultan Muzaffar Shah ruled from 1445 to 1459. At this time, the Malacca state was managed well with two legal digests known as the *Hukum Kanun Melaka* and *Undang-undang Islam*. Please See Hussin Mutalib, *Islam and Ethnicity in Malay Politics*, Singapore: Oxford University Press, 1990, p. 37, note 5.

2 Ahmad Kamar, "Islam in Malaysia", *www. geocities.com/westhollywood/park/ 6443/malaysia/*, p. 1.

3 See Hussin Mutalib, pp. 15-17.

4 Judith Nagata, *The Reflowering of Malaysian Islam*, Vancouver: University of British Columbia Press, 1984, p. 2.

5 *Ibid.*

6 *Ibid.*, p. 8. Also see Mohd. Taib Osman (ed.), *Islamic Civilization in the Malay World*, published by Dewan Bahasa Dan Pustaka, Kuala Lumpur, Malaysia and the Research Center for Islamic History, Art, and Culture, Istanbul, Turkey, 1997, chapter 5.

7 See Hussin Mutalib, pp. 13-14; and Anne Katherine Larsen, "The Impact of the Islamic Resurgence on the Belief System of Rural Malays", Temenos, 32, 1996, pp. 143-147.

8 Liu Zhi, *Theories of the Human Nature and the World of Arabia*, printed by Chinese Islamic Association.

9 Liu Zhi, *Rites and Ceremony of Arabia*, printed by Chinese Islamic Association.

10 See Ahmad Kamar, p. 2.

11 Mi Shoujiang and You Jia, *The Concise History of Islam in China*, Beijing: Religious Culture Publishing House, 2000, p. 135.

12 See Mohd. Taib Osman, pp. 172-175.

13 *Ibid.*, pp. 176-177.

14 See Mi Shoujiang and You Jia, p. 146.

15 The Government White Paper on Freedom of Religious Beliefs in P .R. China in 1997.

16 M. Kamal Hassan, *Towards Actualizing Islamic Ethical and Educational Principles in Malaysian Society*, Kuala Lumpur: published by Muslim Youth Movement of Malaysia, 1996, p. 109.

17 *Ibid.*, p. 113.
18 *China's Religions*, No. 4, 2004, the last page.

References

Department of Statistics, *www.statistics.gov.my*

Dillon, Michael, *China's Muslims*, Oxford University Press, 1996.

Gladney, Dru C., *Muslim Chinese: Ethnic Nationalism in the People's Republic*, New York: Harvard University Press, 1991.

Hassan, M. Kamal, *Towards Actualizing Islamic Ethical and Educational Principles in Malaysian Society*, Kuala Lumpur: Muslim Youth Movement of Malaysia, 1996.

Kamar, Ahmad, "Islam in Malaysia", *http://www.geocities.com/malaysia/ismy.html*

Larsen, Anne Katherine, iThe Impact of the Islamic Resurgence on the Belief System of Rural Malays", *Temenos*, 32, 1996, pp. 137-154.

Lipman, Jonathan Neaman, *Familiar Strangers: A History of Muslims in Northwest China*, Seattle: University of Washington Press, c1997.

Liu Zhi, *Theories of the Human Nature and the World of Arabia and Rites and Ceremony of Arabia*, printed by Chinese Islamic Association.

Mutalib, Hussin, *Islam and Ethnicity in Malay Politics*, Singapore: Oxford University Press, 1990.

Nagata, Judith, *The Reflowering of Malaysian Islam*, Vancouver: University of British Columbia Press, 1984.

Osman, Mohd. Taib (ed.), *Islamic Civilization in the Malay World*, Kuala Lumpur: Dewan Bahasa Dan Pustaka, and Istanbul: Research Center for Islamic History, Art, and Culture, 1997.

Qin Huibin and Li Xinghua, *The History of Islam in China*, Beijing: Chinese Social Sciences Publishing House, 1998.

The Government White Paper on Freedom of Religious Beliefs in P.R. China in 1997, and *China's Religions*, No. 4. 2004.

Wang Daiyu, *Zheng Jiao Zhen Quan*, Chinese Islamic Association.

Chapter 4

Bab 4

China-Malaysia Relations: Retrospect and Prospect

Hubungan China-Malaysia: Retrospek dan Prospek

Kong Yuanzhi

In retrospect, the contact between the people in China and in Malaysia in the past 2000 years can be summarized by five characteristics: long history, mutual support, complementarities, culture exchange and peace and friendship promoting. The cooperation between the two countries has developed rapidly ever since the establishment of diplomatic relations in 1974, and has proven to be increasingly beneficial to the people of both countries. Sino-Malaysia relations at the present time are the most favourable of the last thirty years. Politically, China and Malaysia are expected to establish further cooperation in both regional and international issues. China's remarkable economic development has created more opportunities than challenges to the Malaysian economy. Specifically, in terms of bilateral trade, competition and complementarities are present; and improving international competitiveness has become the key to realizing the potentials. In addition, culture exchange and education cooperation between China and Malaysia are likely to continue to grow.

Tiga puluh tahun yang lalu, 31 Mei 1974, pertemuan antara PM Malaysia, Tun Abdul Razak dengan PM China Zhou Enlai di Beijing memulakan secara rasmi hubungna diplomatik China-Malaysia. Dalam hal ini ada baiknya kita mengadakan retrospek dan prospek terhadap hubungan kedua-dua bangsa: China dan Malaysia.

Retrospek Hubungan China-Malaysia

Sekurang-kurangnya terdapat lima ciri yang nyata apabila kita meninjau kembali hubungan kedua-dua bangsa kita selama lebih daripada 2000 tahun.

Bersejarah Panjang

Dalam *Han Shui* (Buku Dinasti Han) Vol. 28, karya tulis Ban Gu (32 - 92) pada abad ke-1 sudah tercatat jalur maritim antara China dengan India. Ketika utusan Dinasti Han (China) balik dari India, Semenanjung Tanah Melayu dan Selat Melaka merupakan tempat persinggahan bagi mereka. (Zhu, 1984:77) Di sepanjang maritim itu terdapat nama tempat "Duyuan" dalam tulisan China, yang sebenarnya ditujukan kepada Duyun di Terengganu kini.(Hsu,1961:10) *Han Shui* tersebut merupakan catatan yang paling awal dalam buku China kuno mengenai hubungan China dengan India dan Alam Melayu.

K.G.Tregonning dalam bukunya *Malaysiaan Historical Sources* (Tregonning, 1965:2)dan *The Encyclopedia Americana* (edisi 8, 1965:164) pun menunjukkan bahawa Semenanjung Tanah Melayu meruakan suatu relay station bagi usaha perdagangan China-India sekitar abad ke-1.

Penemuan arkeologi yang berupa banyak pecahan seramik Dinasti Qin (221 SM - 206 SM) dan Dinasti Han (206 SM - 220 M) China di lembah Sungai Johor (Jian, 1960:58) merupakan suatu bukti pula yang membenarkan bahawa sudah ada hubungan dagang China-Malaysia 2000 tahun yang lalu.

Hubungan politik antara China dengan Malaysia dimulai pada awal abad ke-3. Empayar Wu (222-280) pernah mengirim Kang Tai dan Zhu Ying sebagai utusan muhibah ke puluhan empayar dan kawasan di Asia Tenggara, antara lain ke Tantalam, Johor dan tempat-tempat lainnya di Semenanjung Tanah Melayu.

Selama Dinasti Song (420-479) yang termasuk Dinasti Nanbei (420-589) dan Dinasti Liang (502-557) ada utusan muhibah empayar-empayar Dan-dan, Ban-ban (menurut ejaan bahasa China) dan Langkasuka dari Semenanjung Tanah Melayu, yang dikirim ke China.

Pada awal abad ke-7 kaisar China Dinasti Sui mengirim Chang Jun dan Wang Junzheng sebagai utusan persahabatan ke Empayar Chi Tu (di bagian timur laut Semenanjung Tanah Melayu). Ketika Chang Jun bersedia kembali, raja Chi Tu mengutus putra mahkotanya turut ke China untuk mengadakan kunjungan balasan. Sang putra mahkota mendapat sambutan meriah pula di China.

Dari Dinasti Tang (618-907), Dinasti Song (960-1279) sampai Dinasti Yuan (1206-1368), hubungan persahabatan antara China dengan empayar-empayar di Semenanjung Tanah Melayu berkembang terus melalui kunjungan timbal balik dari utusan kedua-dua belah pihak. Misalnya pada tahun 1001, empayar Tambralinga mengirim 9 utusan muhibah ke China dan bertukaran cendera mata dengan empayar Song. Demikian catatan *Song Shi* (Sejarah Dinasti Song) Vol.489, bab Tambralingan.

Pada abad ke-15 hubungan China-Empayar Melaka merupakan suatu masa gemilang di sepanjang sejarah China-Melaka.Sepanjang tujuh kali berlayar ke Asia Tenggara, Asia Selatan, Asia Barat dan Afrika Timur, armada Zheng He melawat ke Melaka demi persahabatan antara China-Melaka. Selama tahun 1411-1424 sahaja Melaka telah tigabelas kali mengirim utusannya ke China.Tiga generasi Raja Melaka telah berturut-turut mengadakan kunjungan muhibah ke China sebanyak lima kali. Antara lain pada tahun 1411 Parameswara Iskandar Shah (raja pertama Melaka) bersama permaisuri, puter dan pengiring-pengiringnya yang berjumalh lebih dari 540 orang berkunjung ke China. Rombongan ini merupakan suatu rombongan asing yang terbesar yang melawat ke China pada Dinasti Ming.

Hubungan baik antara kedua-dua bangsa tersebut telah dirosakkan akibat agresi penjajah-penjajah Barat ke Semenanjung Tanah Melayu sejak akhir abad ke-15. Namun tali persahabatan itu dipertahankan dengan ramainya imigran China berturut-turut bermastautin di Semenanjung Tanah Melayu (khasnya sejak akhir abad ke-19) dan lama kelamaan mereka membentukkan diri sebagai kaum Cina di Malaysia.

Hubungan China-Malaysia sejak abad ke-1 sampai awal abad ke-20 betapa eratnya sehingga di antara buku-buku China kuno sekurang-kurangnya terdapat 194 judul yang mencatat hubngan itu. (Lin dan Zhang, 1991:v-xii).

Selepas perjalinan hubungan diplomatik China-Malaysia pada tahun 1974, terbukalah halaman baru di sepanjang sejarah hubungan kedua-dua bangsa : China dan Malaysia.

Sokong-Menyokong

Ensiklopedia Malaysia mencatat, "Sejarah Melaka mula direkodkan sejak zaman pemerintahan Dinasti Ming China (1368-1643). (*Ensiklopedia Malaysia*,8, 307) Pada awal abad ke-15 Melaka terpaksa mempersembahkan 40 tahil emas kepada Siam. Kalau tidak, Melaka akan mengalami ancaman Siam. Dengan kunjungan utusan China Yin Qing ke Melaka pada tahun 1403, Melaka berharap agar dapat memanfaatkan pengaruh China sebagai suatu negara yang terkuat di Asia pada masa itu untuk membela kedaulatannya.

Menurut pengaduan utusan Melaka ke China pada tahun 1407, Siam telah mengirim tentaranya ke Melaka dan telah merebut cap kempar empayarnya. Atas permohonan Melaka, Raja Ming berhasil membantu Melaka menyelesaikan persengketaan tersebut. Pada tahun 1409 Zheng He diutus ke Melaka untuk menegaskan atas nama Raja China bahawa Melaka punya kedaulatannya yang tak boleh diganggu-gugat oleh negara mana pun. Perlu dicatat pula bahawa Melaka telah membantu Zheng He dengan izinnya agar Zheng He dapat menubuhkan gudang besar di Melaka. Hal tersebut sangat penting dalam mensukseskan palayaran-palayaran Zheng He ke banyak kerajaan Asia Afrika (1405-1433).

Kunjuangan Zheng He ke Melaka (1409) begitu besar maknanya baik dalam sejarah Malaysia maupun dalam hubungan Malaysia-China sehingga kini terdapat suatu gambar besar tentang peristiwa tersebut di tembok luar Muzium Negara Kuala Lumpur.

Revolusi 1911 yang dipimpin oleh Dr Sun Yat Sen berjaya menamatkan kemaharajaan China feudal yang telah berlangsung lebih daripada 2000 tahun. Revolusi itu mendapat bantuan pula dari bangsa Malaysia, khasnya penduduk Pulau Pinang. Selama 1905-1911 Dr Sun Yat Sen pernah 5 kali datang ke Pulau Pinang, yang masing-masing pada 1905, 1906, 1908, 1910 dan 1911. Beliau telah menubuhkan The Penang Philomathic Union (1907) dan akhbar Pinang *Kwong Wah Yit Poh* (1910) yang kini telah menjadi akhbar yang terbesar di Malaysia bahagian utara. Dalam pertemuan musim gugur 1910 di The Penang Philomathic Union tersebut Dr Sun Yat Sen dan kawan-kawan seperjuangannya telah menyiapkan Pemberontakan Huang Hua Gang yang terjadi di Guangzhou pada 27 April 1911.

Pemberontakan Huang Hua Gang tersebut gagal, namun telah memberi pukulan besar kepada empayar Qing yang dekaden. Berhubung dengan banyak kaitan antara Dr Sun Yat Sen dengan Pulau Pinang, Pada tahun 1988 PM Malaysia Dr Mahathir menganjurkan agar ditubuhkan batu bersurat Dr Sun Yat Sen di Pinang demi memperingati tokoh besar itu. (*Kwong Wah Yit Poh*, 15 Ogos 1988).

Sejak perjalinan hubungan diplomatik China-Malaysia, kedua-dua bangsa kita ini telah mengembangkan tradisi sokong-menyokong, terutamanya dalam membela kedaulatannya masing-masing. Misalnya pada Majlis Pertubuhan Bangsa-bangsa Bersatu tahun 1971 utusan Malaysia telah memberi suara untuk mendukung pemulihan hak China sebagai anggota organisasi antarabangsa itu. Empayar Malaysia mengaku Dasar Satu-China (One-China Policy), iaitu Republik Rakyat China, manakala Taiwan adalah sebahagian dari wilayah China.

China mengambil kebijaksanaan untuk tidak mendevaluasikan mata wangnya, antara lain buat mendukung pemulihan ekonomi sebahagian negara (termasuk Malaysia) yang tertimpa kegawatan ekonomi sejak Julai tahun 1997. Disediakan pula oleh China AS$ 6 bilion untuk membantu negara-negara yang terjejas dalam krisis Asia.

Di samping itu, kedua-dua negara juga berpendirian sama dalam menentang satu dua negara Barat yang mencari berbagai-bagai dalih untuk mencampuri urusan dalam negara lain.

Saling Melengkapi

"Saling melengkapi" merupakan suatu tradisi baik dalam perniagaan China-Malaysia. Dalam hal ini "seramik" merupakan suatu contoh yang baik. Menurut catatan China kuno, pada abad ke-14 sudah terdapat seramik China di Pahang, Kelatan dan Terengganu. (Wang,1349:96, 99 & 102) Pada tahun 1954 diperoleh 33 buah keramik China yang berhasil tergali daripada tanah Johor. Diantaranya banyak seramik yang berwarna biru dan putih.

Namun peningkatan kwaliti seramik China yang biru dan putih itu tidak terpisahkan dari semacam bahan seramik yang bernama "boqing" (dalam ejaan bahasa Cina) yang justeru diimport dari bahagian utara pulau Kalimantan (termasuk kawasan Sarawak dan Sabah kini). Bahan itu sangat penting untuk membuat seramik yang biru dan putih di China. Dengan kata lain, bangsa Malaysia telah membantu bangsa China untuk meningkatkan kwaliti seramiknya.

Dalam hal herbal ubat-ubatan tradisional pun nampak sifat lengkap-melengkapi antara kedua-dua bangsa. Pada Dinasti Ming sudah ada banyak herbal yang diimport dari Melaka, Johor dan Pahang ke China. Di lain pihak terdapat 456 jenis ramuan tradisional China di Malaysia. (Zhou,1987) Di Malaysia kini sudah terdapat perpaduan pemakaian antara herbal tradisional China dan herbal tradisonal tempatan untuk mengubati orang sakit (Li, 1996).

Adapun karet, bibit karet pertama di pulau Hainan (China selatan) didatangkan dari Malaya pada sekitar tahun 1906. (Wang, 2004:454) Kini bibit karet yang unggul itu telah cukup populer di kebun karet pulau Hainan.

Dari Jadual I di bawah ini tampak keerjasama China-Malaysia di bidang ekonomi yang pesat kemajuannya selama empat tahun (2000-2003) ini.

Jadual I : Statistik Perdagangan China-Malaysia (2000-2003)
Unit:US$ Juta

Perdagangan / Tahun	Total Perdagangan	Perbandingan dengan periode sama sebelumnya	Jumlah Eksport China	Tambahan Tahunan	Jumlah Eksport Malaysia	Tambahan Tahunan
2000	8045	52.4%	565	53.3%	5480	52%
2001	9425	17.2%	3220	25.6%	6205	13.2%
2002	14271	51.4%	4975	54.4%	9296	49.8%
2003	20128	41%	6141	23.5%	13987	50%

Sumber data: Kastam China 2004; *Malaysia-China Business Magazine*, April 2004, p.31& 56.

Jadual I menunjukkan bahawa selama empat tahun (2000-2003) sahaja nilai total perdagangan China-Malaysia bertambah 161 peratus, dan setiap tahun nilai eksport Malaysia ke China tetap lebih besar daripada nilai eksport China ke Malaysia.

Berinteraksi Budaya

China-Malaysia berinteraksi budaya sepanjang sejarah. Misalnya sekurang-kurangnya terdapat 1046 kata pinjaman bahasa Cina (khasnya dialek Hokian) dalam bahasa Melayu (termasuk bahasa Indonesia). Misalnya amoi, apek, bangsat, beca, capgomeh, cat, cuka, ginseng, hongsui, kuih, popia, sampan, tauge, tauhu, takua, teh, teko, tong dan lain sebagainya (Kong, 1993). Manakala dalam bahasa Cina terdapat 233 kata pinjaman bahasa Melayu seperti sarung, pinang, durian, duku, datuk dan lain sebagainya. Di antaranya kata pinjaman Melayu pinang sudah muncul dalam buku sarjana China Yan Shigu (581-645). (Kong, 1992)

Yang tidak kalah pentingnya ialah, pada abad ke-7 Yi Jing pendeta China yang menuntut ilmu Buddha ke India dan Asia Tenggara telah berjaya mencatat bahasa Melayu Kuno dengan nama bahasa Kunlun. Catatannya sangat berharga untuk pengajian sejarah bahasa Melayu. (Kong, 1990)

Dalam pertembungan bahasa, yang patut dicatat pula ialah, pada abad ke-15 sudah lahir kamus Cina-Melayu yang terawal, iaitu Man La Jia Guo Yi Yu (Perkataan Negeri Melaka). Perkataan-perkataan bahasa Melayu yang berjumlah 482 buah itu dikumpulkan oleh keturunan Cina di Melaka selama tahun 1403-1511, dan kemudian disemak dan dipruf oleh Yang Lin, pejawat Tong Shi (penerjemah di istana China) tahun 1549. (Edwards and Blagden, 1930-32; Liang, 1996:90-98) Kamus itu mempunyai makna historis. Disamping kamus Cina-Melayu terawal, ianya merupakan karya penting untuk membahas sejarah Melaka dan hubungan antara China-Melaka pada abad ke-15.

Selama belasan tahun ini telah diterbitkan di China sejumlah buku yang berkaitan dengan sastera, sejarah dan politik Malaysia di satu pihak. Di pihak lain telah bermuculan pula buku yang ditulis oleh sarjana China, yang diterbitkan di Malaysia. Karya-karya itu telah mendorong saling pengertian antara kedua-dua bangsa.

Jadual II: Buku Sastera, Sejarah dan Politik Malaysia
Terbitan China (1985-2004) *

Judul Buku	Penulis	Penerjemah	Penerbit & Tahun Penerbitan	Jenis
Antologi Cerita Pendek Indonesia & Malaysia	Mas, Keris dkk.	Wang Shouyi	Guangzhou: Penerbit Sastera-Seni Selat, edisi ke-1,1985; edisi ke-2,1991	Antologi Cerita Pendek
Sarinah	Said, A Samad	Yu Yu	Taiyuan: Penerbit Beiyue, edisi ke-1, 1985; edisi ke-2, 1991	Novel

Bunga Mawar Dalam Botol- Antologi Cerita Pendek Malaysia	Mas, Keris dkk.	Ai Ma dkk.	Taiyuan: Penerbit Beiyue, 1991	Antologi Cerita Pendek
Sejarah Perantau Malaysia-Singapur	Lin Yuanhui & Zhang Yinlong		Guangzhou: Penerbit Perguruan Tinggi Guangdong, 1991	Buku Sejarah
Antologi Cerita Pendek Pengarang Wanita Malaysia	Amin, Adibah dkk.	Bai Can dkk	Beijing: Penerbit Moden, 1993	Antologi Cerita Pendek
Buku Bahasa Malaysia Untuk Pelajar China	Wang Qing		Beijing: Penerbit Pengajaran & Studi Bahasa Asing, edisi I,1993;edisi II,1998	Buku Pelajaran (2 jilid)
Sejarah Melayu	Lanang, Tun Sri	Huang Yuanhuan	Taiyuan: Penerbit Beiyue, 1999	Novel Klasik
Pilihan Pidato Dr Mahathir Bin Mohamad PM Malaysia	Dr Mahathir Bin Mohamad	Wu Naihua dkk.	Taiyuan: Penerbit Ilmu Dunia, 1999	Pilihan Pidato

Sejarah Hubungan Budaya China-Malaysia	Zhou Weimin & Tang Lingling		Haikou: Penerbit Hainan, 2002	Buku Sejarah
Kaum Cina & Modenisasi Malaysia	Han Fangming		Beijing: Peneribt Sangwu,2002	Buku Keilmuan
Data-data Mengenai Singapur & Malaysia dalam Buku Kuno China	Yu Dingbang dkk. (ed)		Beijing: Penerbit Zhonghua, 2003	Kumpulan Data
Sastra Melayu	Wang Qing		Beijing: Penerbit Pengajaran & Studi Bahasa Asing, 2004	Buku Perkenalan Sastra Melayu Klasik & Moden

*Statistik ini ditujukan kepada karya-karya yang diterbitkan di tanah besar China, belum termasuk Taiwan.

Selama ini Dewan Bahasa & Pustaka Malaysia telah berjaya menerbitkan lebih dari 50 judul karya sastera China yang diterjemahkan ke dalam bahasa Melayu. Buku-buku yang ditulis dalam bahasa Melayu oleh sarjana-sarjana China diterbitkan pula di Malaysia. Misalnya *Lembaran Sejarah Gemilang: Hubungan Empayar Melaka-Dinasti Ming Abad ke-15* dan *Pelayaran Zheng He & Alam Melayu,* yang masing-masing ditulis oleh Liang Liji (1996) dan Kong Yuanzhi (2000) telah diterbitkan oleh Penerbit

Universiti Kebangsaan Malaysia. *Lagu Persahabatan China-Malaysia* sebagai Antologi Puisi Usman Awang (Pengerusi Persatuan Persahabatan Malaysia-China) dan Chen Haosu (Pengerusi Persatuan Persahabatan Rakyat China dengna Negara Luar), yang diselenggarakan oleh Chen Haosu, diterjemahkan oleh Wu Zongyu dan diterbitkan oleh Dewan Bahasa & Pustaka Malaysia (2003). Di samping itu *Semenanjung Tanah Melayu Di Mata Orang China & Orang Arab Zaman Kuno* yang ditulis oleh Gao Weinong dalam bahasa Cina telah diterbitkan oleh Intelligensia Book Statin (Kuala Lumpur) than 1995.

Pengajaran dan pembelajaran bahasa Melayu di institusi pengajian tinggi China sudah berterusan setengah abad lamanya. Pada tahun 1946, jabatan bahasa Melayu ditubuhkan di Institut Bahasa-Bahasa Timur di kota Nanjing, dan kemudian dipindahkan ke Peking University (Beijing). Kini China mempunyai 4 buah universiti di mana tersedia Jabatan Bahasa Melayu, masing-masing ialah Peking University (PU), Beijing Foreign Studies University (BFSU), Guangdong University of Foreign Studies (GUFS) di Guangzhou dan Luoyang Foreign Languages University (LFLU) di Luoyang. Setiap tahun terdapat kurang lebih 60 graduan daripada keempat-empat institusi tersebut.

Di sini patut dicatat pula, cerita Hang Li Po sebagai ode persahabatan kedua-dua bangsa China-Malaysia tersiar luas di Malaysia dan sangat menarik pula bagi rakyat China. Sejak tahun 1960-an, sekurang-kurangnya ada lima pertunjukan yang bertemakan Hang Li Po telah diadakan di Malaysia.(Kong, 2001)

Mengutamakan Perdamaian dan Persahabatan

Sepanjang sejarah perhubungan China-Malaysia tidak pernah terjadi peperangan walau sekali pun. Yang ada ialah banyak peristiwa yang mengharukan. Antara lain, pada bulan ke-6 tahun 1411 Raja Melaka Parameswara bersama permaisuri, putra dan pengiring-pengiringnya yang berjumlah lebih dari 540 orang berkunjung ke China. Ini merupakan suatu rombongan asing yang terbesar yang melawat China pada Dinasti Ming.

Selama lawatan ke China, tamu-tamu agung dari Melaka mendapat sambutan hangat dari empayar Dinasti Ming.

Contoh kedua ialah sambutan rakyat Malaysia terhadap utusan Dinasti Ming, Zheng He yang berjulukan Sam Po. Di Melaka,Terengganu, Pulau Pinang dan Sarawak masing-masing terdapat Tokong Zheng He di samping legenda indah mengenai lawatan Zheng He ke kawasan-kawasan itu pada abad ke-15.

Sejak perjalinan hubungan diplomatik China-Malaysia pada tahun 1974, pemimpin kedua-dua negara ini sering mengadakan kunjungan timbal balik. Antara lain pemimpin-pemimpin China Deng Xiaoping, Jiang Zemin, Li Peng, Zu Rongji dan Hu Jintao masing-masing telah melawat ke Malaysia, manakala empat Perdana Meneri Malaysia telah berturut-turut berkunjung ke China, iaitu Tun Abdul Razak, Hussein Onn, Dr Mahathir dan Abdullah Badawi. Diantaranya Dr Mahathir sudah 7 kali melawat ke China.

Yang patut dicatat pula Persatuan Persahabatan Malaysia-China (PPMC) telah ditubuhkan di Kuala Lumpur dengan PM Malaysia Dr Mahathir sebagai penaung dan Dato' Dr Usman Awang sebagai pengerusinya pada 30 Disember 1992. Tahun berikutnya Persatuan Persahabatan China-Malaysia (PPCM) berjaya ditubuhkan pula di Beijing dengan Hu Gang, bekas duta besar China ke Malaysia sebagai pengerusinya. Baik PPMC maupun PPCM sangat berjasa dalam memajukan persahabatan antara Malaysia dan China.

Prospek Hubungan China-Malaysia

Kerjasama di Bidang Politik Akan Terus Diperkukuhkan

Adalah amat tepat yang dikatakan oleh Dr Mahathir bahawa Malaysia dan China mempunyai banyak persamaan dan berkongsi pendekatan berhubung isu serantau dan antarabangsa. Hubungan kedua-dua negara akan terus diperkukuhkan.(*Berita Harian*, 27 November 1999)

Masa kini adalah masa yang terbaik sepanjang hubungan China-Malaysia, demikian menurut PM Wen Jiabao dan PM Abdullah Badawi.

Sebagai negara yang menjadi pengerusi Pergerakan Negara-negara Berkecuali (NAM) dan Pertubuhan Persidangan Islam (OIC), Malaysia akan memainkan peranan yang semakin penting dalam isu-isu angarabangsa

Mengenai persengketaan mengenai kepulauan Nansha (Spratlys area) di Laut China selatan, yang melibatkan China, Taiwan, Brune, Malaysia, Pilipina dan Vietnam, kedua-dua negara kita, China dan Malaysia, berpendirian bahawa masalahnya harus diselesaikan secara damai demi menjaga stabiliti region itu. Dr Mahathir berkata: "Seperti negara China kami percaya bahawa negara-negara jiran perlu menyelesaikan masalah melalui rundingan." (Mahathir,1994)

Berbicara tentang apa yang disebut "ancaman militer, politik dan ekonomi dari China", Dato' Seri Abdullah berkata, bahawa sejarah China sudah menunjukkan negara itu tidak tertarik untuk menaklukkan negara lain, melainkan berkepentingan menjadi suatu kekuatan stabiliti di region ini.(*Straits Times*, 17 Sep. 2003)

"Saling Melengkapi" dan "Berkompetisi Satu Sama Lain" Berbareng dalam Kerjasama Ekonomi

Amat tepat yang dikatakan oleh Datuk Seri Abdullah Ahmad Badawi di Forum Perniagaaan Malaysia-China (Beijing, 16 September 2003) bahawa kemunculan China di bidang ekonomi tidak harus dianggap sebagai cabaran kepada Malaysia, tetapi sebagai peluang yang perlu direbut oleh Malaysia untuk meningkatkan hubungan perdagangan dan investasi dengan China. Ini kerana sekalipun cabaran ekonomi dari China kuat, kedua-dua negara boleh saling lengkap melengkapi jika kedua-dua negara dapat mencari peluang di sebalik cabaran yang wujud.

Investasi China di Malaysia totalnya US$ 1 bilion (1980-2003), manakala investasi Malaysia di China berjumlah US$ 3.1 bilion. Kini Malaysia adalah rakan dagangan ke-7 terbesar (rakan dagangan terbesar dalam ASEAN) dan investor ke-18 terbesar bagi China, dan China adalah investor terbesar ke-9 bagi Malaysia. (*Utusan*, 1 Jun 2004)

Perdagangan China-Malaysia sangat potensial dan punya prospek cerah mengingat "Malaysia kini adalah negara ke 17 terbesar dalam perdagangan dunia dengan jumlah perdagangan AS$200 bilionî (*Utusan Malaysia*, 16 September 2003). Manakala jumlah perdagangan China (2003) sudah melebihi AS$850 bilion.(Akhbar China *Berita Referensi*,18 Februari 2004) Maka telah dijangkakan oleh para pakar bahawa perdagangan Malaysia-China tahun 2004 akan mencapai US$25 bilion yang bererti bertambah 20 peratus berbanding dengan tahun 2003. Sebagai suatu contoh, China merupakan pembelli terbesar minyak kelapa sawit Malaysia dengan jumlah 2 juta tan metrik setahun. Jumlah itu akan bertambah di tahun-tahun yang akan datang.

Dalam lawatan Abdullah ke China akhir Mei 2004, sebanyak 28 memorandum persefahaman (MOU) telah ditandatangani. Ia meliputi soal pendidikan, pembinaan, penjagaan kesihatan, teknologi maklumat, bioteknologi, perawatan air, pelancongan dan beberapa sektor lain.Selain itu enam memorandum persetujuan (MOA) juga turut ditandatangani, bermakna MOU sebelum ini sudah menjadi kenyataan

Pernyataan Bersama (31 Mei 2004) China-Malaysia menggariskan yang kedua-dua kerajaan meneruskan kerjasama dalam bidang-bidang yang membawa faedah bersama kepada ekonomi kedua-dua negara, terutamanya dalam sektor-sektor seperti pertanian, penerbangan, perkapalan, tenaga, kewangan, buruh, sains dan teknologi, angkasa lepas, kebudayaan, pendidikandan kesihatan umum.

Dalam memajukan proses China-ASEAN Free Trade Area (FTA), pemimpin China mengharapkan agar perdagangan antara China dengan ASEAN hendaknya melampaui nilai US$ 100 bilion pada tahun 2010. Demikian menurut Akhbar China *Ren Min Re Bao* (edisi luar negeri), 24 Februari 2004.

China dan Malaysia berkompetisi baik dalam menarik investasi negara asing, maupun dalam mengeksport sejumlah produk yang sejenis dan hampir seperingkat kwalitinya. Kompetisi itu adalah wajar dan akan mendorong maju daya persaingan Namun sifat saling melengkapi akan memainkan peranan yang lebih penting mengingat China merupakan suatu market yang luar biasa besarnya dengan penduduk 1.3 bilion. Di antara produk yang masing-masing dieksport China dan Malaysia pun terdapat banyak perbezaan sehingga dapat isi-mengisi di bidang ekonomi. Misalnya sekitar 40 peratus dagangan China-Malaysia mempunyai sifat nyata "Saling melengkapi" mengingat yang dieksport dari China adalah bahan makanan, minyak, buah-buahan, sayur-sayuran, ternak, produk tekstil, kapal, semen dan bahan baja, manakala yang diimport dari Malaysia ialah minyak kelapa sawit,bahan kayu dan karet. Di antara 60 peratus dagangan kedua-dua negara ialah produk elektronik mekanikal. Yang diimport oleh Malaysia kebanyakan ialah barangan mekanikal dari China, manakala yang dieksport Malaysia ke China kebanyakan adalah barangan elektrik dan elektronik. (*Malaysia-China Business Magazine*, April 2004, p.26)

Akan Lebih Ramai Aktiviti China-Malaysia di Bidang Kebudayaan

Pengajaran dan Pembelajaran bahasa Melayu di institusi pengajian China sudah berterusan setengah abad lamanya. Kini China mempunyai empat buah universiti di mana tersedia Jabatan Bahasa Melayu. Pusat Pengajian & Pembelajaran Bahasa Melayu RRC ditubuhkan di Beijing pada 1997 dan selama ini telah menyelenggarakan empat kali seminar bahasa Melayu atau budaya Melayu di *Beijing Foreign Studies University* (BFSU). Dengan penubuhan *Institute of China Studies* di Universiti Malaya (2004), interaksi budaya, khasnya kerjasama di bidang pendidikan Malaysia-China pasti akan lebih erat.

Kini pelajar Malaysia yang belajar di China berjumlah sekitar 1.000 orang, manakala pelajar China yang menuntut ilmu di Malaysia telah mecapai 11.000 orang. Anak muda China tertarik pada kolej dan universiti Malaysia yang umumnya lebih mementingkan bahasa Inggris dan lebih banyak bekerjasama dengan kolej dan universiti negara maju. Manakala banyak anak muda Malaysia ingin mempelajari bahasa dan budaya China. Maka dapat dipastikan pertukaran pelajar dan kunjung-mengunjung personil antara kedua-dua negara kita akan meningkat.

Mengenai pelancongan, tahun 2002 Malaysia telah menerima kedatangan 557 ribu pelancong dari China, pertambahan 23 peratus daripada tahun sebelumnya. Ini menjadikan China sebagai pelanggan pelancongan keempat terpenting bagi Malaysia. Pelancong Malaysia ke China sudah mencapai 590 ribu orang tahun 2003. Pada tahun-tahun yang akan datang kedua-dua jumlah tersebut akan bertambah mengingat Malaysia dan China berdekatan, dan kedua-duanya negara yang indah pemandangannya, maju pesat ekonominya, stabil masyarakatnya dan rakyatnya ramah tamah. Aktiviti-aktiviti lain yang berkaitan dengan hubungan budaya China-Malaysia akan lebih ramai pula.

Kesimpulan

Apabila diretrospeksi hubungan antara bangsa China dan bangsa Malaysia selama 2000 tahun, nampak lima ciri nyata, iaitu bersejarah panjang, sokong-menyokong, saling melengkapi, berinteraksi budaya, dan mengutamakan perdamaian serta persahabatan. Sejak perjalinan hubungan diplomatik China-Malaysia (1974), kerjasama kedua-dua negara di pelbagai bidang maju pesat dan telah mendatangkan faedah yang nyata kepada rakyatnya masing-masing. Kini adalah masa terbaik hubungan China-Malaysia selama 30 tahun ini. Kalau diprospeksi masa depan, kerjasama politik China-Malaysia akan lebih erat menghadapi isu-isu serantau dan antarabangsa. Kebangkitan ekonomi China merupakan peluang sekaligus cabaran bagi Malaysia, namun peluang lebih besar daripada cabaran. Kini perdagangan kedua-dua negara belum mencapai potensi sebenar. Perdagangan itu bersifat "Saling melengkapi" disamping "berkompetisi satu sama lain". Adalah penting bagi China dan Malaysia untuk meningkatkan daya kompetisi produknya masing-masing. Dan interaksi budaya kedua-dua belah pihak pasti akan digalakkan pula.

Kepustakaan

Edwards, E.D. and C.O. Blagden, "A Chinese Vocabulary of Malacca Malay Words and Phrases Collected between A.D. 1403 and 1511 (?)", *Bulletin of the School of Oriental and African Studies* (London), 1930-32.

Ensiklopedia Malaysia, Kuala Lumpur: Anzagain, 1995.

Jian Zhai, *Han Tang De Tao Ci Qi* (Seramik Dinasti-dinasti Han dan Tang), Hong Kong: Nan Yang Wen Zhai, No.12, 1960.

Hsu Yun Tsiao, *Ma Lai Ya Cong Tan* (Berbicara Tentang Malaya), Kedai Buku Pemuda Singapur, 1961.

Kong Yuanzhi, "Bahasa Kunlun Dalam Sejarah Perkembangan Bahasa Melayu", *Jurnal Dewan Bahasa & Pustaka*, Februari, 1990.

Kong Yuanzhi, "Ciri Kata Pinjaman Bahasa Melayu Dalam Bahasa Cina:Suatu Studi Permulaan", *Jurnal Dewan Bahasa & Pustaka*, Julai, 1992.

Kong Yuanzhi, "Kata Pinjaman Bahasa Cina Dalam Bahasa Melayu", *Jurnal Dewan Bahasa & Pustaka*, Julai-Ogos dan September, 1993.

Kong Yuanzhi, *Pelayaran Zheng He dan Alam Melayu*, Bangi: Universiti Kebangsaan Malaysia, 2000.

Kong Yuanzhi, "Cerita Hang Li Po: Ode Persahabatan Kedua-dua Bangsa China-Malaysia", *Sari*, 19, Penerbit Universiti Kebangsaan Malaysia, 2001.

Kong Yuanzhi, "Pembelajaran Bahasa Asing dan Interaksi Budaya Tionghoa-Melayu", *Jurnal Pemikir*, Oktober-Disember 2002, No.18,.

Li Jinlong, *Ma Lai Xi Ya Zhong Yi Yao Fa Zhan Shi Lue* (Ikhtisar Sejarah Perkembangan Ilmu Kedokteran & Ubat Tradisional China di Malaysia), Singapura: Penerbit Ubat-ubatan China (Singapora), 1996.

Liang Liji, *Lembaran Sejarah Gemilang : Hubungan Empayar Melaka-Dinasti Ming Abad ke-15*, Bangi: Penerbit Universiti Kebangsaan Malaysia, 1996.

Lin Yuanhui dan Zhang Yinlong, *Xin Jia Po-Ma Lai Xi Ya Hua Qiao Shi* (Sejarah Perantau China Di Singapur-Malaysia), Guangzhou: Penerbit Perguruan Tinggi Guangdong, 1991.

Luo Yuejiong, *Xian Bin Lu* (Rekod Negeri-negeri Tamu), diberi anotai oleh Yu Sili, 1983, Beijing: Zhong Hua Shu Ju (Toko Buku China), sekitar 1585.

Mahathir bin Mohamad, *Pilihan Pidato Dr Mahathir Bin Mohamad PM Malaysia*, diterjemahkan oleh Wu Naihua dkk.Beijing:Penerbit Ilmu Dunia, 1999.

Mahathir bin Mohamad, "Kerjasama Malaysia-China Yang Lebih Kukuh", jurnal *Sahabat*, diterbitkan oleh Persatuan Persahabatan Malaysia-China, Bil.1, 1994.

The Encyclopedia Americana, edisi 8, 1965.

Tregonning, K.G., *Malaysiaan Historical Sources*, Singapore: University of Singapore, 1965.

Wang Dayuan, *Dao Yi Zhi Lue* (Catatan Tentang Pulau-pulau di Luar Negeri), diberi anotasi oleh Su Jiqing, 1981, Beijing, Toko Buku Tionghoa, 1349.

Wang Jienan, *Zhong Wai Wen Hua Jiao Liu Shi* (Sejarah Interaksi China Dengan Dunia Luar), Shanxi: Penerbit Shuhai, 2004.

Zhou Nanjing, *Hui Gu Zhong Guo Yu Ma Lai Xi Ya Wen Lai Wen Hua Jiao Liu De Li Shi* (Meninjau Kembali Sejarah Pertembungan Kebudayaan Antara China dengan Malaysia dan Brunei), lihat Zhou Yiliang (ed.), *Sejarah Hubungan Kebudayaan Antara China Dengan Negara-negara Asing*, Penerbit Rakyat Henan, 1987.

Zhu Jieqin, *Zhong Wai Guan Xi Lun Wen Ji* (*Antologi Sejarah Perhubungan China-Negara-negara Asing*), Zhengzhou: He Nan Ren Min Chu Ban She (Penerbit Rakyat Propinsi Henan), 1984.

II

China in Transition

Chapter 5

Political Change and Reform in China

George T. Yu

China is a society in rapid transition, especially since the introduction of the "open and reform" policies in the late 1970s and early 1980s. To those who have followed the remarkable changes, China today is a distinctively different society from that of the early 1980s, not to mention the 1960s and the 1970s. Admittedly, not all geographical and societal sectors have advanced equally. Economic development and urbanization have progressed especially rapidly along the Eastern and Southern coastal regions; meanwhile, China has become the world's manufacturing center, producing massively and exporting globally both low and high end products. On the other hand, income differentiation has greatly widened, between economic and social classes and rural and urban residents; there is also a growing disparity in levels of economic development between the coastal and interior regions of the Northwest and Southwest.

These and other economic and social developments have been recognized by China's governing elite. For example, both President Hu

Jintao and Premier Wen Jiabao have recognized the urgent need for change and reform with respect to the growing economic inequalities between the rural and urban populations and the coastal/interior development imbalance. Indeed, the new administration has made the correction of these and other inequalities their foremost policy priorities.[1]

One sector which has evidenced less overt reform but no less interested in change has been the political arena. The Leninist political structure and practices of democratic centralism remain in force, in both the Chinese State and the Chinese Communist Party. No nationally organized loyal political opposition is tolerated and the move toward local open political competition has been carefully managed. On other fronts, censorship by the state of the print and visual mass media and the Internet is constant, though irregular, and the Party-State remains the final arbitrate of individual political freedom and rights.

However, there is no denying that political change and reform have been evolving in China, albeit at an uneven pace, with a different style and at different levels of the political system. But neither the Chinese nor we can predict the type and style of political institutions and values most likely to succeed. China, as we mentioned, is a society in transition; there is no question that China politically is moving along the continuum from a hard "totalitarian" to a softer "open" (some would say "democratic") society. This chapter will examine two primary sectors, changes in the national leadership and local and rural reforms, as instances of change and reforms in China's political development since the 1980s.

I

Leadership occupies a central role in political development; this is especially critical in societies where the process of succession is still being institutionalized. How leaders are selected, serve and succeeded constitute a key indicator how a society is governed. It is they who set the broad economic, political and social course of the society at large; in turn, the policies of the political elite set the character and conditions of society.

Since the founding of the People's Republic of China in 1949, a succession of leaders has assumed and held power under different conditions and implemented different policies. To date, Chinese leadership can be divided into four primary generations. The first generation was led by Mao Zedong, who dominated Chinese politics from 1949 until his death in 1976. One dominant characteristic of this generation of leaders was that they were mostly soldiers, peasants and members of the urban lower-middle class, whose "education" mainly came from engaging in revolutionary activities rather that in formal education. Indeed, in 1955, for example, only 5 percent of the top leadership had a junior high school education or above. In 1980, only 51 percent of China's estimated 450,000 leaders at the county level and above had only a junior high school level education and as late as 1982, only 4 percent of the members of the Chinese Communist Party were educated beyond the high school level. Mao was well known for his hostility toward intellectuals, branded the "ninth stinking category". In turn, during this era and beyond China's ruling elite reflected a strong anti-educational and intellectual bias.

During Mao's rule, except for a brief period of economic and social reconstruction in the early to mid-1950s, China experienced a series of extreme political and social movements, including the Great Leap Forward (1958-1959) and the Cultural Revolution period (1966-1976), whose policies, according to former Party general-secretary Hu Yaobang, were an economic, cultural and educational "catastrophe" for China.

Deng Xiaoping represented the "core" of the second generation of Chinese leaders; he was China's paramount leader from 1978 to the early 1990s. It was during this era that we have the beginning of the "open and reform" policies and the introduction of policies that were designed to redirect and regenerate China's economic and social development.

China underwent a major elite transformation during Deng's era, from one based upon "revolutionary" credentials and experiences to that grounded in "science and technology". Contrary to the "red" and "expert" division of the Maoist years, Deng made clear that the Party should oppose divorcing its own leadership from expertise. Indeed, he even went so far as to advocate that all leaders should be trained as specialists; some of his colleagues even went further to suggest that all leaders should hold M.A. and Ph.D. degrees! (Can you imagine a country governed by Ph.D.'s!) Though Deng and the vast majority of the second generation of China's leaders lacked a technical background, they realized that science and technology was the key to China's modernization.

In the early 1980s, beginning with the 12th Party Congress in 1982, a determined effort was made to retire Party veterans, while recruiting "technocrats" into the higher levels of power. It was at the 12th Party Congress that Hu Jintao, Jiang Zemin, Wu Bangguo and other leaders of today were recruited to the Party's Central Committee. Concurrently, this was followed with the retirement of more than a million senior cadres, on the one hand, and the recruitment of half a million college-educated cadres into leadership's positions, on the other, between 1980 and 1986. By the late 1990s, it was reported that the percentage of "technocrats" or college-educated leaders had increased from 23 percent to 92 percent among Politburo members, from 38 to 95 percent among ministers, from 4 to 78 percent among military leaders, and from 2 to 91 percent at the county and municipal levels.[2]

Jiang Zemin represents the core group of the third generation of Chinese leaders and the formal beginning of the "technocratic" leadership era. Jiang assumed the position of President of China in 1993 and remains today the Chairman of the Central Military Commission. Hu Jintao succeeded Jiang as President of the People's Republic of China in 2003 and constitutes the leading figure of the fourth generation of Chinese leaders. Both Jiang and Hu received "technical" education, the former from the Electrical Machinery Department of Shanghai's Jiaotong University in 1947 and the latter from the from the Water Conservancy Engineering Department of Tsinghua University in 1964.

China's leadership transformation to a "technocrats" based elite continues. As mentioned, there was a massive turnover of leader's at all levels beginning in the 1980s, with a majority having received a technical education in engineering and the natural sciences. The "Tsinghua Clique", or graduates of Beijing's Tsinghua University, China's leading engineering and science institution of higher learning, is well represented in China's national leadership. But the rapid increase of "technocrats" was due also to an extensive retraining program, at Party cadre schools. It was reported that between 1992 and 1996, half a million officials above the county level studies at the Central Party School. By the beginning of the 21st century, China's fourth generation of leaders, led by Hu Jintao, had fully ushered in the "technocratic" era.

While the educational character of China's leadership was being transformed, the process of national leadership recruitment and selection remained largely unchanged and unreformed. The distinct lack of transparency in the Chinese decision-making process limits our knowledge and understanding of the inner workings of Chinese politics. However, seminal studies on Chinese leadership recruitment all point to one general conclusion: It is a secretive and very personal top down process, with new leaders identified and recruited by the current ruling elite.[3] An extreme example of the process of leadership succession was the 1976 case of Hua Guofeng's recruitment by Mao Zedong to be China's next leader, based on Mao's reputed famous utterance, "With you (Hua) in charge, I am at ease."

A more "scientific" (but incomplete) model of elite recruitment can be found in studies by Professors Richard Daniel Ewing and Murray Scot Tanner, leading scholars of China's leadership.[4] Drawing upon the example of Hu Jintao's rise to power, Professors Ewing and Tanner offers an insightful case study of Hu's career, especially with regard to his ascension to power by building the support and trust of current leaders, in the absence of clearly defined institutionalized rules of leadership recruitment. Hu began his career in Gansu Province, following graduation from Tsinghua University; it is reported that he won the patronage of the provincial Party Secretary, who sent him for training to the Central Party Central, where he came to the attention of Hu Yaobang and other reform minded national party leaders, who placed Hu in charge of the Communist Youth League. Appointments as the

Party Secretary in Guizhou (1985) and Tibet (1988) followed.

One source reports that it was Hu's economic reforms and political toughness in Tibet that brought him to the attention of China's supreme ruler Deng Xiaoping, convincing "Deng that Hu had what it took to be a successor, and caused Deng to 'personally' mark Hu for promotion."[5] Hu's selection to China's leadership was assured when in 2002 Deng "complimented Hu Jintao in public as a model successor and a 'good man.'" Whatever the reality of these and other incidents, it is evident that Hu rise to leadership was not based upon "popular" or institutional support, Party or otherwise. At the risk of over simplifying a very complex series of events over an extended time period, it is clear that the personal support and trust of current leaders, in Hu's case Deng Xiaoping and other Party leaders, was critical to Hu's rise to national leadership.

China's national leadership has witnessed both a major transformation and a lack of reforming political institutions. Changes and reforms have been especially evident in the educational background and qualifications of China's new leadership; the rise of technocrats turned politicians is well documented. However, to date the new national leadership has demonstrated no interest in the institutionalization of political reforms, with open and mass participation in the recruitment and selection of national leaders. Instead, the national leadership has focused on "efficiency-enhancing reforms rather than democratization"[6], and continues to be highly elitist, informal and personalized.

II

Contrary to the national level, political change and reform at the local level has been introduced and institutionalized in China since the 1980s. Village elections and self-governance have been implemented. Democratization from the bottom up has made a beginning, albeit with mixed results and at an uneven pace.

The introduction of village political change and reforms can be traced to several necessary and special factors. First, the general question of the plight of the farmers and the state of the rural economy. To this day, China remains an agricultural society, with 900 million of its 1.3 billion population classified as farmers living in rural areas. According to Chinese explanations and terminology, "contradictions" abound in rural development.[7] For example, the educational level of the rural populations remained low: 13.3 percent of the village youth were either illiterate or semi-illiterate, while only 38.8 percent of the rural population had attained an elementary level education, 40.2 percent a middle school education and 7.6 percent a high school education. On net farm income, even in 2002 it stood at only US$302.00 per capita (compared to and average of $1000.00 in urban areas). Yet, the state of the farmers and the rural economy were central to China's total development; "if the farmers prospered, the whole nation would prosper."[8]

Second, the implementation of Chinese village democracy was a political necessity to save the ruling elite and the political system. Ann Thurston, who has followed village elections since 1994, provides a useful background summary how the elections were introduced.[9] The process can be traced to the demise of the people's commune system that began in the late 1970s and was completed by the early 1980s. The dissolution of the collective agriculture system was the result of both the Chinese farmers disbanding the collective farms, the bottom up efforts, and the more liberal policies of Deng Xiaoping, a top down endeavour. Meanwhile, entrepreneurial activities were encouraged.

In many rural areas, concurrent with the collapse of the people's commune system witnessed the disintegration of existing political structures, e.g., the Communist Youth League, the People's Militia and other organizations, together with the abandonment of leadership role of village leaders, who left their offices to seek more lucrative pursuits. A rural leadership vacuum followed.

By mid to late 1980s, rural China was in a state of potential chaos. On the one hand, there followed a rise of banditry and lawlessness, a breakdown of social order, on the other, some villages came under the control of self-appointed "little emperors", local leaders who exploited the farmers.

Confronted with the potential for instability and chaos in the rural areas, even peasant revolts, China's national leaders suggested that the best way to restore order was to introduce village elections. "By instituting popular elections, they reasoned, village leaderships would at least fall to the more popular and respected members of the village community. Moreover, if those elected were not party members, perhaps they could be recruited to the party, thus infusing the party at the local levels with a new respect."[10]

In 1987, village elections were institutionalized with the passage of the Organic Law on Village Elections by the National People's Congress. Initially, elections were not mandatory. The Ministry of Civil Affairs was responsible for overseeing overall implementation, but each province was charge with coming up with its own concrete regulations. The village elections were mandated into law in 1998, following several years of successful experimentation. Since 1998, all 930,000 Chinese villages have been required by law to hold competitive elections once every three years.

Third, on a more general level, we must consider also village elections as a form of political decompression. Namely, village elections provide the 900 million farmers with a safety valve to express their concerns to the national and local leaders, they introduced a legal procedure into the governing process and they cultivate a sense of political ownership and rights awareness. In this context, two larger political questions relating to village elections confronted Chinese leaders: How will the process be extended to towns and cities and beyond and how best to administer and manage the elections without undermining the Party's leadership.

Since 1998, elections are supposed to have been held in each of the 930,000 villages. Reports of village elections are available, though highly selective.[11] Indeed, we do not know how widespread they are nor do we know how universally they have been implemented. However, individual accounts do exist, including those of the Carter Center, headed by former president Jimmy Carter.[12]

Ann Thurston, who has followed Chinese village elections for both the Carter Center and the Washington D.C. based International Republican

Institute since 1994, draws the following mixed conclusions regarding the election experience.[13]

> First, the local emperors who came to power with the collapse of the communes still exist in some places. Usually they are able to exert control because they are also very rich, are in control of much a of a village's resources, and are able to influence higher levels in the government and party hierarchies.
> Second, many villages continue to exist in a vacuum of leadership. When, for instances, I have had the opportunity to visit Chinese villages with friends rather than through official sponsorship, it seems I invariably happen upon villages which are suffering crises of leadership, villages where elections, if they have been held at all are only pro forma, and the village leader is generally weak and ineffectual.
> Third, I have seen cases, too, where they local emperors are actually elected, ostensibly democratically. These are instances, for instance, where the second candidate seems to have been put there only for the sake of complying with election regulations and where the village chief who is running for re-election also controls a major portion of the village resources...
> Finally, and most important, I have also seen elections that by any measure anywhere in the world would be recognized as genuinely competitive, fair and democratic...

Voter behavior and concerns follows "the way democratic theory says they should have behaved: they voted in their own self interest."[14] The voters wanted better schools and housing; they wanted improved roads; they wanted lower and fewer taxes and fee; and they wanted leaders who could deliver on their promises.

Clearly, two factors were imperative to the success of the village elections: leadership and economic benefits and conditions, the former linked to the national political orientation of China leader's and the latter tied to economic development. China's leaders admit to a serious income and developmental differential between the rural and the urban sectors.[15] As previously note, according to official data since 1996 the income difference between the urban and rural population had greatly increased; in 2002 the ratio stood at 3.1:1, US$1,000.00 for the urban population versus US$302,00 for the farmers. Concurrently, the levels of economic development between the eastern and southern coastal regions and the interior, especially the northwestern and the southwestern regions, were especially conspicuous. It was estimated that approximately 300 million Chinese farmers remained at the impoverished level, lacking the basic needs of clothing, food and housing, mainly in the interior and border areas. This was very different from the government's economic target of achieving an average income of US$800.00, or beginning "xiaokang (well-off) status", for all Chinese.

The enhancement of the economic status and meeting the demands of the farmers was critical to the success of the village elections. However, the economic and political realities of rural China posed many challenges. A 2004 study of conditions in rural Anhui province, *Zhongguo Nongmin Diaocha* (*An Investigation of the Chinese Farmer*), described the negative environment and policies encountered by farmers (Chen and Chun, 2004). Local emperors ruled abound; villages were governed by bloated bureaucracies; and wasteful spending common. Excessive taxation was a special problem: Local governments were quick to impose countless "new taxes". One example cited was the fourteen required wedding "taxes", including registration, introduction, wedding ceremony, pre-marital examination, single child guarantee, family planning and others. Finally, access to financial resources could determine village elections. "Gifts" were freely distributed by candidates during elections, including cigarettes, wine and cash. In one case, it was reported it took a mere four thousand yuan (US$490.00!) to defeat a slate of candidates to the local assembly and elect a deputy village chief!

Electoral irregularities and rural economic and political conditions aside, village elections are now part of China's rural political landscape. Village elections have been institutionalized through the Organic Law of 1987 and while electoral rights vary across China they have been steadily refined. The Ministry of Civil Affairs, the government agency in charge of elections at the local level, has sought to insure the implementation and improvement of the process, inviting international agencies such as the Ford Foundation, the Carter Center and others to assist with and observe the local elections. China also maintains an official Website *www.chinaelections.org*, posting articles, reports and data relating to village elections.

III

What is the future of political change and reform in China? What is the relationship between political and economic change and reform? And what are the prospects for direct elections beyond the local level?

Much debate exists with regard to political change and reform in China. Clearly, China is in the midst of a major political "contradiction". On the one hand, there was the report that Premier Wen Jiabao noted that direct elections at the national level "are not available", while on the other, the Premier commented in the same breath that democratic village elections were necessary for villages to "improve their capabilities".[16]

Barring a major political shift, a change in economic fortunes or war, China appears committed to the present course of "open and reform" policies. New policies and development have been in the forefront of the rapid transformation of China, with a primary focus on the economic sector. Indeed, in the short period of less than a generation China has become the world's factory floor, affecting not only China but also the surrounding regions, including Southeast Asia, and the world. China's commitment to and becoming a "rich and strong" nation is total; China's goal of becoming a modern society of "xiaokang" is absolute. In a word, China has and continues to undergo a major economic transformation, from that of a failed centralized, command and socialist economy to that of a successful more open, decentralized market oriented economic system.

Similarly, China's political system has experienced change and reform; more can be expected. The greatest political changes have been at the local level; village elections have been institutionalized and instituted. To date, though the record is mixed, accomplishments have been real and there is a sense of forward momentum concerning local democracy. The bottom up movement of the 1980s, impelled upon the national leadership to avoid total system failure, stemming from growing rural instability, made adoption of political change and reform imperative for survival and enhanced local "capabilities".

Students of Chinese politics disagree about the meaning, success and needs of the current local reforms. Ann Thurston, as noted, views the villages elections as "genuinely competitive, fair and democratic", have made governance more transparent and have put in "place the mechanisms for elections of higher level officials", the county, the province and the national level. However, for political changes to succeed the reforms "will have to be instituted from above". In short, the national leaders of China must demonstrate the will and vision for political change and reform to advance and succeed at and beyond the village level.

Other perspectives, while questioning the contributions to political stability of village elections (they increase tensions between the villagers and the officials) and whether local elections signifies the beginning of progression of reforms at the higher levels (questionable), do agree that the future of China's political changes and reform will be determined at "higher levels".[17]

"Higher levels" determined the initiation of village elections, stemming from pressure from the bottom. The economic development of China has resulted in the major restructuring of the economic system; multiple centers of economic decision-making have emerged, with multiple interests. The demands (and inclusion) of new economic interests upon China's governing elite have been already recognized in Jiang Zemin's theory of "The Three Represents", recruiting into the ruling Chinese Communist Party "capitalist" as well as "workers".

Demands stemming from the rapid pace of urbanization of China have also had an impact upon the political system, especially as the electoral process has progressed from the villages to the townships and urban areas. However, unlike the villages, the decision for elections in urban areas came from the "top", not bottom up. In part, this was due to the fact that, cities, unlike the villages, retained their administrative structure, the neighborhood committee and the work unit. However, since the 1980s the role of the traditional administrative structures has greatly eroded with economic decentralization, the introduction of the market economy and with the increasing rural population migration to towns and cities.

With China's declared policy of integrating the cities with the villages, calling upon the villages to look to urban areas for economic salvation and with the prospect that fifty percent or more of China's population will be "urban" by 2020, a major transformation of both the rural and urban sectors can be expected. The new economic and social realities are certain to have an impact upon China's political landscape.

The future of political change in China may well depend upon the demands and pressures of the new forces of economic development and urbanization on China's national leaders, similar to the demands and pressures brought upon the leadership resulting from the failure of the rural economic and political structures in the 1980s. With the successful experimentation of the village elections, China's leaders may yet be compelled to promote and permit political change and reform at the next level.

Notes

1   See Premier Wen's remarks at the March 2004 National People's Congress meeting, *Renmin Ribao* (*People's Daily*, Overseas Edition), March 6, 2004.
2   For data on China's new leaders, see Cheng (2001).
3   See Mary Scot Tanner, "Hu Jintao's Succession: Prospects and Challenges," in David M. Finkelstein and Maryanne Kivlehan (eds.), *China's Leadership in the 21st Century: The Rise of the Fourth Generation*, Armonk: M.E. Sharpe, 2003, pp. 45-65 and Richard Daniel Ewing, "Hu Jintao: The Making of a Chinese General Secretary," *The China Quarterly*, 173, March 2003, pp. 17-34.
4   *Ibid.*
5   *Ibid.*
6   Lowell Dittmer, "Leadership Change and Chinese Political Development", *The China Quarterly*, 176, December 2003, pp. 903-925.
7   Lu Liangshu and Sun Junmao, "Chinese Agricultural Development and Modern Agriculture Building in the Next Period", *Zhongguo Gongcheng Kexue* (English title: *Engineering Science*), Vol. 6, No. 1, January 2004, pp. 22-29.
8   *Ibid.*
9   Ann Thurston, "Village Democracy in China", *http://www.chinaelections.org*
10 *Ibid.*
11 See for example Carter Center (2001).

12 *Ibid.*
13 Ann Thurston, "Village Democracy in China". See also Ogden (2002).
14 Ann Thurston, "Village Democracy in China".
15 Lu Liangshu and Sun Junmao, "Chinese Agriculture Development and Modern Agriculture Building in the Next Period", *op.cit.*
16 "China's development: Wen's to challenge", *www.chinaelections.org*, 2004-5-4.
17 See for example, Ying Shang, "Myth and Reality: The Chinese Village Elections", *www.chinaelections.org*; 2004-2-13.

References

Carter Center, "The Carter Center Report on Chinese Elections: Observation of Village Elections in Fujian and the Conference to Revise *The National Procedures on Villager Committee Elections*", Working Paper Series, Atlanta: Carter Center, Emory University, 2001.

Chen Guidi and Chun Tao, *Zhongguo Nongmin Diaocha (An Investigation of the Chinese Farmer)*, Beijing: Renminwenxue, 2004.

Cheng Li, *China's New Leaders: The New Generation*, Lanham: Rowman & Littlefield Publishers, Inc., 2001.

Dittmer, Lowell, "Leadership Change and Chinese Political Development", *The China Quarterly*, 176, December, 2003.

Ewing, Richard Daniel, "Hu Jintao: The Making of a Chinese General Secretary," *The China Quarterly*, 173, March, 2003.

Lu Liangshu and Sun Junmao, "Chinese Agricultural Development and Modern Agriculture Building in the Next Period", *Zhongguo Gongcheng Kexue* (English title: *Engineering Science*), Vol. 6, No. 1, January, 2004.

Ogden, Suzanne, *Inklings of Democracy in China*, Cambridge: Harvard University Press, 2002.

Tanner, Mary Scot, "Hu Jintao's Succession: Prospects and Challenges," in David M. Finkelstein and Maryanne Kivlehan (eds), *China's Leadership in the 21st Century: The Rise of the Fourth Generation*, Armonk: M.E. Sharpe, 2003.

Chapter 6

Reform, Leadership Change and Institutional Building in Contemporary China

Zheng Yongnian and Lye Liang Fook

Political Reform as Incremental Institutional Building

China's political reform has long puzzled scholars and policy makers outside China since Deng Xiaoping initiated the economic reforms more than two decades ago. In the 1980s, scholars hypothesized that economic reform would go hand-in-hand with political reform, and that marketization would necessarily lead to political democratization. When Mikhail Gorbachev launched his radical political reform and initiated the process of political democratization in the former Soviet Union, scholars in the West argued that Gorbachev must be "right" and China's Deng Xiaoping must be "wrong." The collapse of Communism in the former Soviet Union and Eastern Europe led many scholars to claim that the Western style of democracy had prevailed and human history had come to an end.[1] However, when Gorbachev's reforms eventually led to the collapse of the Soviet Union, Deng Xiaoping was proven "right." Scholars began to refine their hypothesis about the linkage between political reform and economic reform, and since then China has been regarded as a model of "economic reform without political reform" (Shirk, 1993).

As a matter of fact, "political reform" means different things to different persons. To many scholars in the West, "political reform" refers to a political process towards Western style democracy based on popular political participation, which usually refers to an open universal election.[2] Furthermore, from a Western perspective, the notion of political reform in an authoritarian state like China implies the weakening of party control. Nevertheless, this is not the case in China. Political reform is not designed to decrease the power of the Party, but rather to increase it.

From the western perspective, China indeed did not have political reform in the past two decades. To them, democratization is central to political reform. But the question is: How can democratization take place in China? What form of democracy do Chinese political elites believe is "good" for the country?

Chinese political leaders, from Deng Xiaoping, Jiang Zemin to Hu Jintao have strongly opposed introducing a Western style of democracy. They genuinely believe that the Western style of democracy is not suitable for China, either because they have learned from China's modern history and the recent history of the former Soviet Union that it will lead the country nowhere but instead bring chaos to, even breaking up the country, or because they are afraid that Party will lose its dominant position once radical democratization takes place.

Nevertheless, the top leaders have argued that they have continuously taken the need for political reform into account.[3] Like economic reform, China's political reform has no model to follow and the leadership has to define political reform on its own terms and define the goal of political reform in the context of economic development. Political reform thus has been characterized by incrementalism: progress by trial and error. It does not mean that the political process will be suddenly opened to the general public, but rather it refers to a managed process of institutional building, which will enable the Party-state to maintain socio-political stability to further its economic development efforts while strengthening its domination and political legitimacy.

Since political reforms are aimed at maintaining the CCP as the ruling party and strengthening its domination, the leadership has made every effort to lead and direct the country's development. Socioeconomic changes, however, often resulted in unintended consequences. We have witnessed the constant rise of social demands for more radical political reform and the development of challenges to the authority of the CCP. As a result, the CCP had to use coercive measures to cope with spontaneous social forces when the existing institutions were no longer able to accommodate them. Nonetheless, using coercion does not necessarily mean that the CCP has declined to adjust its political institutions. Rather, it means that the CCP does not want social forces to lead the process of China's political development.

In practicing political incrementalism, the leadership placed emphasis on different reform practices rather than theories. The leadership implemented various policy experiments and, once a given policy succeeded, the leadership legitimized it. More importantly, the leadership also allowed government organizations at lower levels and social forces to practice their own ways of reforming old institutions. Once these reform practices were proven to be in alignment with central lines, the leadership was willing to legitimize them. By contrast, if a given spontaneous reform practice was against or posed challenges to the CCP, the leadership was determined to constrain its further development. Consequently, the CCP was sometimes able to initiate reform practices, while at some other times, it merely followed and tried to justify or accommodate these initiatives from below.

Without an understanding of the Chinese way of political reform, it is difficult to make sense of the country's dramatic yet relative stable development over the past two decades. Without continuous institutional building, the Chinese political system would not have been able to embrace such drastic socio-economic changes. Furthermore, we have to understand not only the Chinese way of political reform, but also the rationale why the Chinese leadership implemented their version rather than other kinds of political reform.

Our major arguments are threefold. First, China's political reform can be defined as political incrementalism, aimed at continuously adjusting its institutional framework to guarantee economic reforms and political stability on one hand, and accommodate drastic changes resulting from socio-economic development on the other.

Second, whether the Chinese political system is moving toward democratization or not cannot be judged by whether direct measures of democratization have been initiated alone. Instead, it needs to be measured by whether the political system, through its continuous institutional building, has become more accommodative of the democratic forces resulting from drastic socio-economic changes. Even though what the leadership has done is not aimed at democratizing the country, with continuous institutional building, the Chinese political system has displayed its flexibility by being more accommodating towards social changes and democratic developments.

Third, changes that have occurred to China's political system in the past two decades are not merely by products of rapid economic development. Instead, adjusting the political system was a deliberate effort by the leadership to serve the country's economic growth needs and accommodate the consequent drastic socio-economic changes.

This analysis of political incrementalism focuses on three major areas, i.e., leadership transition at the central level, central-local relations in the mid level, and rural governance at the local level. Needless to say, political incrementalism is not limited to these areas.

Institutionalization of Leadership Transition

Leadership transition or power succession is a major issue in every political system. Different political systems have different rules of the game, and power succession bears different socio-political costs and impacts. In democracies, it is relatively easy to handle the problem of power succession.

The selection of top leaders such as "President" or "Prime Minister" is institutionalized, and it is done in a predictable manner by some "rules of game" in the form of legal regulations and constitutional conventions. In other words, the method of election is prescribed by law.

Nevertheless, it is worth noting that democracy as a means of power succession is played out differently under different political systems. In well-established democracies in Europe and North America, power succession appears as a peaceful process, while in late democratized countries, it is often rather violent.

Although some sort of electoral mechanism exists within the CCP, the Party is undoubtedly undemocratic when it comes to power succession. Without institutionalized methods of power succession as in a democracy, the Chinese leadership has to find other ways to deal with the succession issue. Actually, the succession issue has been affecting the country's political stability since the establishment of the PRC in 1949. Mao Zedong ruled China for several decades. He did not need to worry about power succession. Since he owned ultimate power, he was supposed to be able to appoint anyone of his choice to be his successor. Still, during his time, bitter political struggles that resulted from power succession took place and plunged the country into chaos, as in the cases of his appointed successors Liu Shaoqi and Lin Biao.

After returning to power, Deng Xiaoping realized the importance of power succession. As a victim of Mao's personal dictatorship, Deng called for the reform of China's political and leadership system.[4] However, power succession during Deng's time also did not go smoothly, as evidenced by the ousting of Hu Yaobang and Zhao Ziyang by irregular political means.[5]

With the passing of the old generation of leaders, the issue of power succession has become increasingly important. Since China's new leaders lack the personal and autocratic power that their old counterparts shared based on their revolutionary experience, they have to build up new power bases by discovering new rules and methods. Since Jiang Zemin, the Chinese leadership has made great efforts to cope with the issue of power succession.

Power succession has become an integral part of China's political

reforms. In the context of China's political system, power succession is not just choosing a power successor. In fact, it means several things. Four most important aspects of power succession include:
- Restructuring ideology
- Recruiting new types of elite into the leadership
- Building political "exit" for aging leaders
- Grooming the core of the future generation of leadership.

Restructuring Ideology

Ideology plays a complicated role in Chinese politics. It can be used to justify and to preserve the status quo, or it can be utilized to transcend and transform the status quo. Furthermore, ideology can be used to force Party cadres and government officials to identify with the top leadership, shape their behavior and prevent their deviation from the leadership's guidelines.[6] Restructuring ideology is especially meaningful for power succession. Without it, the political legitimacy of any new leadership could hardly be justified.

In Mao's China, the official ideology consisted of Maoism and orthodox Marxist denunciations of capitalism. Maoism emphasized political correctness and public ownership. Orthodox Marxism upheld economic planning and public ownership and rejected capitalism and private ownership. What Mao Zedong achieved was tight political control, but a backward economy.

The decline of Maoist ideology was inevitable after Deng Xiaoping came back to power in the late 1970s. Guided by pragmatism, Deng downplayed the role of ideology, weakened the ideological controls of Maoism and orthodox Marxism, and encouraged officials and the people to experiment with reform initiatives. In 1978, he oversaw an ideological movement that refuted Maoism. This was the so-called first wave of mind-emancipation that under girded China's economic reforms in the 1980s.

In the aftermath of the crackdown on the pro-democracy movement in 1989, China was caught in a heated debate about whether the country's development should be capitalistic (*Mr. Zi*) or socialistic (*Mr. She*). Economic growth was again constrained by the revival of leftist ideology as well as economic sanctions imposed by the West. The leadership was ineffective in dealing with slower economic growth.

In response, Deng Xiaoping made a high-profile tour to southern China, i.e., his celebrated *nanxun*, and initiated a second wave of mind-emancipation.[7] He put an end to the capitalism versus socialism debate. In order to achieve rapid economic development without being bogged down by ideology, Deng proposed the "no-debate" policy so that the Party could focus on economic reforms. This was accepted by the top leadership.

Deng's de-ideologization in the 1980s and 1990s fostered an atmosphere conducive to economic development. Despite several policy setbacks, including the Tiananmen event, reformists eventually triumphed over conservatives in the Party in the early 1990s. The Party, cadres and the population were free to experiment with reform and embrace the market economy. And, without a public forum, orthodox and liberal ideologies lost their wide appeal, and the CCP was freed of any immediate ideological challenge.

However, the de-ideologization did affect negatively the Party and country. Many Party members no longer accepted the ideological mission of the Party as the vanguard of the working classes. Instead, they began to embrace a variety of alternative ideologies, including materialism, old and new leftism, Western liberalism, nationalism, religions, and cults.

In 1995, Jiang initiated the "talking about politics" (*jiang zhengzhi*) campaign. He called on Party cadres and government officials to be serious about political direction and to exercise political discipline, discretion, and sensitivity. In 1998, Jiang further urged the leading cadres to talk about (or stress) politics, virtue, and political studies, termed the "three talks" (*san jiang*). He criticized the then single-minded attention to economic construction, and tried to correct any misunderstanding about the "three talks" by declaring that they were designed to support, rather than replace, modernization as the core of the Party's politics. Unfortunately, both ideological campaigns received a cool reception. Jiang was not frustrated by such a development, and his efforts continued.

On his tour to Guangdong in February 2000, Jiang proposed the "three represents" (*sange daibiao*), meaning that the CCP represents the most advanced mode of production, the most advanced culture, and the interests of the majority of the people. He asked Party members and leading cadres to use these "three represents" to guide their thought and behavior. While conceding there were many problems plaguing the Party members' outlook, organization, and work attitude, Jiang called on the Party committees at various levels to rebuild the Party.

During the tour, Jiang also began to assert that the rule by virtue and the rule of law should be promoted hand-in-hand in reaffirming the Party's ethos and honest politics. By emphasizing the rule by virtue, he wanted to indoctrinate the Party members and cadres with a new set of proper work styles, such as working hard and behave in a down-to-earth manner, living plainly, maintaining a good reputation, sacrificing self-interests for the public, and serving the people. Through virtue education, he believed that the quality and spirit of the cadres could be improved, and violation of laws and Party discipline could be reduced. By the rule of law, he meant reducing legal loopholes, punishing criminals and violators of the Party's rule, and thereby educating the Party members and the populace of the "right" norms.[8]

At the Party's 16th National Congress, the "Three Represents" theory was written into the Party Constitution. This marks the culmination of years of efforts by Jiang to widen the social base of the Party by admitting capitalists as well as to ensure that the theory stays relevant. The preamble of the Party Constitution was also changed to reflect the Party as the vanguard not only of the working class, but also of the Chinese nation and Chinese people. This is a significant move by the Party to distance itself from any distinct social class and move towards a political entity that represents and coordinates the interests of various social classes.

Central to Jiang's vision to transform the whole of China is the concept of *xiaokang shehui* (comfortable society), which was the title of his political report to the 16th Party Congress. The goal is to lay a firm foundation for achieving full-scale modernization by 2050. According to Jiang, China has already accomplished the first of two steps towards modernization set by Deng twenty years ago. Building on previous successes, Jiang has set the target of quadrupling China's GDP by 2020 with 2000 as base year.[9]

The vision to transform the entire country into a *xiaokang shehui* has significant economic implications. It reflects a need to change the pattern of China's economic growth. The emphasis, hitherto, has largely been on unbridled economic growth with wealth concentrated in the coastal provinces and cities while pockets of poverty remain scattered around the country, especially in the inland provinces and rural areas. Jiang's vision aims to address this lopsided development by re-distributing wealth to a larger proportion of the population. This does not imply that China is turning its back on the market economy but rather that increased attention will be placed on re-distributing wealth through growth and stepping up economic development in the backward hinterland. This is a gradual and long-term strategy.

Apart from its economic implications, the term *xiaokang shehui* is politically significant for two reasons. First, in ideological terms, it is not only a deliberate rejection of the "middle class" concept used by the West but is also a denouncement of the Western notion of liberal democracy. In the West, the development of the middle class is inextricably linked to the development of democracy in these countries. Although detractors may argue that the term *xiaokang shehui* is none other than the communist jargon for the middle class, in reality, the significance is more than putting old wine into a new bottle. The Party is telling the whole country and the rest of the world that it wants to decide its own development path and will not be dictated to by outsiders. It is thus not without coincidence that in the same political report, Jiang categorically rejected the idea of China developing along the path of western liberal democracy. Second, *xiaokang shehui* is not only intellectually appealing to the Chinese people, many of whom still yearn for a better life, but also politically correct because it propounds the notion that everybody could become well-off together. A comfortable society has some egalitarian notion that makes it readily acceptable to virtually all strata of society.

Recruiting New Types of Elite into the Leadership

Elite recruitment is crucial for power succession. First, it can increase the sense of loyalty to the Party among newly recruited Party cadres and government officials. We have seen that when a new leader comes to power, he will usually consolidate his power position by recruiting new elites into the leadership. This leads to the formation of new power networks and the creation of political legitimacy for the new leader.

Second, elite recruitment can also increase the political legitimacy of the Party among people. In democratic states, political leaders gain the legitimacy of their power positions through winning votes. In China, without such a mechanism, the Party has to search for other alternatives for political legitimization. After the post-Mao reform began in the late 1970s, the Party's legitimacy has increasingly depended on the Party's ability to deliver economic goods to the people. In order to do so, the Party needs a new type of elite for effective policy implementation. Certainly, the elite transformation from revolutionaries to technocrats in China has been achieved by elite recruitment.[10]

China's technocratic movement was initiated after Deng Xiaoping came to power in the late 1970s. The movement has spread to government and CCP organizations at different levels and has introduced drastic changes into the composition of the Chinese leadership.[11] In 1982, the CCP held its first post-Mao congress, symbolizing the establishment of the Deng leadership. During this congress, many technocrats such as Li Peng, Hu Qili, and Jiang Zemin, among others, were recruited into the Central Committee (CC). Since then, major leaders rise and fall owing to bitter power politics but the momentum of the technocratic movement remains. At the Fifteenth Party Congress in 1997, the movement reached its peak. In this congress, all seven members of the Standing Committee of the CC's Political Bureau and eighteen of the 24 Political Bureau members were technocrats. This new leadership has thus been called a "full-fledged technocratic leadership."[12]

In China, the technocratic movement meant recruiting younger and better educated party cadres and government officials into the leadership. More importantly, most of the elite had their professional training in engineering and other fields of science and technology. In the technocratic state, technically-trained political leaders rule by virtue of their specialized knowledge and position in dominant political and economic institutions.

The rise of the technocratic leadership is a reaction to the Maoist elite recruitment policy. One major theme in Maoist China was the conflict between "red" and "expert." Mao initiated waves of campaigns against intellectuals and professionals in the first three decades of the People's Republic, particularly during the Cultural Revolution. This elite recruitment policy was reversed after Deng Xiaoping came to power as the previous policy had brought disaster to the country. The leadership began to appreciate the role of the "expert" and downplayed that of the "red." To promote the country's economic development, the "expert" had to be placed at the center of the whole system.

The rise of the technocratic leadership is also the outcome of depoliticization. Political chaos during the pre-reform period resulted from Mao's political campaigns and mass mobilization. Mobilization in turn led to the politicization of social life. Recruiting technocrats into the party and government have helped to depoliticize the decision-making process since, unlike politicians whose aims are power and interests, technocrats are more concerned with rational thinking, task orientation, and problem-solving.[13] Therefore, the technocratic leadership has led to the reduced role of ideology in policy making. With generational changes over the leadership, the basis of authority has to be redefined. The old revolutionaries could appeal to their charisma and ideology for mass mobilization, but new leaders did not have such power resources and had to turn to more secular and pragmatic forms of political authority. For technocrats, ideology cannot be taken as a dogma that provides specific and infallible solutions to immediate political as well as economic issues. Rather, technocrats tend to look at issues on their merits alone and are concerned with the technical details and solutions. In this sense, they hold a pragmatic attitude towards reality.

Because of this pragmatism, technocrats are able to overcome difficulties to reach a consensus.[14] They can "evaluate even political decisions in terms of actual outcome rather than ideological value. In developing a range of policy options, each of which carries only different costs, benefits, and feasibility, this way of thinking inclines the bureaucratic technocrats toward compromise and bargaining."[15]

Building Political "Exits" for Aging Senior Leaders

The retirement system for aged cadres has been further institutionalized. According to the CCP regulations on cadre retirement established in the early 1980s, candidates for ministers, provincial Party secretaries and governors have to be below 65 years of age, and those for deputy ministers, deputy provincial Party secretaries and deputy governors below 60 years of age.[16] An unwritten practice is that candidates for the Premier and Vice Premier positions have to be below 70 years of age. These practices have been increasingly institutionalized in Chinese high politics. What is more important though is to build an "exit" mechanism for aging senior leaders.

To a great degree, political succession is a matter of "exit." Only when the old elites step aside can the new ones assume power. Before Deng Xiaoping, China virtually did not have a system of political "exit." Major officials were able to hold on to their positions until the last day of their lives. The "exit" problem has troubled both the top leadership and the country, since it has often been solved by bitter political struggles. More seriously, when leaders become aged, they are unprepared to give up their power positions. When young leaders "fight" at the front lines, old guards stand behind and watch.

From the onset, the new leadership realized how important it was to build a system of political "exit." To a great degree, Jiang Zemin has been quite successful in this regard. During the Fifteenth Party Congress, one of the most powerful political figures, Qiao Shi, retired gracefully from all power positions. Qiao Shi, number two in the Political Bureau of the Fourteenth Central Committee, was widely regarded as the political challenger to Jiang Zemin.[17] Regardless of whether Qiao retired voluntarily or was pushed out, his retirement was a major step for the CCP to resolve its endemic problem of retiring senior leaders. With Qiao's departure, Jiang has now put in place a procedure for old leaders to "exit" gracefully from their power positions when they become aged.

This is also true in the case of the "exit" of General Liu Huaqing. The departure of General Liu from the Standing Committee of the Political Bureau means that Jiang has secured his control over the military. But the significance of General Liu's departure is more than that. It is the first time in the history of the People's Republic that no representative from the military sits on the Standing Committee. In the pre-reform period, Mao Zedong controlled the military as Chairman of the Central Military Commission for more than 27 years (1949-1976), with support from Zhu De, Lin Biao, Ye Jianying and other generals. Deng Xiaoping was also capable of exerting control over the military owing to his strong military background. When Zhao Ziyang was General Secretary of the Party, there was no military representative in the Standing Committee. Nevertheless, it was Deng Xiaoping, as Chairman of the Central Military Commission, that controlled the military. Among the seven members of the Standing Committee at the Fifteenth Central Committee, no one has a military background. The weakening of the military's presence at the top leadership tends to provide the leadership an opportunity to push the country's transition towards a modern pattern of civilian-military relationship.

The "exit" system has been institutionalized to a great degree, as exemplified by the Sixteenth Party Congress in 2002. At that congress, all six of the previous seven-member Political Bureau Standing Committee, other than Hu, stepped down as they had reached or were beyond the mandatory retirement age limit of 70. Also, no one with a military background currently sits on the Standing Committee of the Political Bureau.

Grooming Younger Leaders

Grooming a younger generation of leaders indeed was one of the most important policy legacies of Deng Xiaoping, who argued that the Party could renew itself by recruiting younger cadres into the leadership. Since the early 1980s, we have seen a consistent process of *nianqinghua* (rejuvenation).

Since then, the leadership has continued to push this process forward. Jiang was quite successful in this regard. With the passing of the Old Guards, Jiang and his third generation were in charge of building the next generation of leadership. In previous Party gatherings, old guards such as Deng Xiaoping, Chen Yun, Ye Jianying and Li Xiannian were powerful enough to choose their own successors. However, even these powerful figures were not able to make sure that power succession could be smooth. The third generation leadership learned from the country's past experience that power succession, especially in an age of much transformation, was vital both for the Party itself and for the country. With the reduced influence of the old guards, the Standing Committee of the Political Bureau as a whole has to play the role of guardians to help groom the next generation of leadership. Such was the political background that led to Hu Jintao assuming the top post in the Party.

Hu was born in 1942 in Anhui province. He graduated from Qinghua University in hydraulic engineering in 1965. Later he served as an instructor of a university art association and several years as a leader of economic work in Gansu Province, taking part in the construction of two hydropower stations on the upper reaches of the Yellow River. In 1982, Hu became the youngest alternate member of the CCP Central Committee at the Twelfth Party Congress. In the same year, Hu was elected as Secretary of the Communist Youth League. In 1985, Hu was appointed as the Secretary of Guizhou Provincial Party Committee. Three years later, he was transferred to Tibet as Secretary of Tibet Autonomous Region Party Committee. As we can see, with all these experiences, Hu indeed was well prepared to ascend to the highest level of leadership in the country.

Hu Jintao was elevated to the center of political power at the CCP's

Fourteenth Congress in 1992 when he became the youngest member of the Standing Committee of the Political Bureau. It was Deng Xiaoping that had played an important role in pushing Hu Jintao's rise. Learning from his previous practice of power succession in connection with Hu Yaobang and Zhao Ziyang, Deng realized that it was important to groom successors when they were still young. The political endorsement from Deng Xiaoping granted Hu Jintao a unique position within the CCP leadership. As a matter of fact, there emerged a political consensus among China's top leaders for Hu to emerge as the core of the future generation of leaders. Hu was thus accorded various opportunities to be groomed as Jiang's successor.

One major measure is to use the State Presidency as a platform to expose Hu Jintao to political life at the top. The State Presidency used to be the titular Head of State under both Mao Zedong and Deng Xiaoping. The Ninth National People's Congress in 1998 elected Hu Jintao as Vice President of the State. Previously, this position of deputy Head of the State was assumed by retired Party cadres (as one of the most important political "exits") or senior non-communist politicians (as a symbol of multi-party cooperation). By doing so, Jiang attempted to expose Hu to the outside world and to provide him with opportunities to gain experience in handling China's international affairs.

Yet another, and perhaps the most important, step was to create opportunities for Hu Jintao to develop his relations with the military. Like Jiang Zemin, Hu Jintao also has no military background. Though Hu has engaged in Party affairs for years, he is rather distant from the military. To be an effective successor, Hu had to be provided with an institutional base to develop his relations with the military. In late 1998, the central government initiated a nationwide movement to wind up the military's business operations. Hu Jintao was appointed Director of the Transfer Office (for transferring business operations from the military to the civilian sector) and was put in charge of policy implementation. Hu Jintao also took part in another task force, known as the "Leading Group to Handle the Businesses of Party and Government Units." The group was chaired by Premier Zhu Rongji, with Hu Jintao and General Zhang Wannian as deputies, and its aim was to accelerate the process of de-linking the military from business. The campaign was rather successful for at least the military was formally de-linked with business. The success of the campaign enabled Hu Jintao to earn some prestige from the military and thus paved the way for him to become Vice Chairman of the Central Military Commission in 1999. Needless to say, all these efforts by the third generation leadership had created an institutional setting for Hu Jintao to smoothly succeed Jiang Zemin as General Secretary in 2002.

Selective Recentralization and Rebuilding Central-Local Relationship

Rebuilding the central-local relationship has become one of the foci of China's political reform since it linked central authorities to local society. Therefore, whether the central government can promote rapid economic growth while maintaining order depends on whether it can solicit local cooperation, which, in turn, depends on how the central government adjusts its relations with localities. Because of the significance of central-local relations, the central government has been extremely cautious in adjusting the old institutions that linked the center and localities.

Scholars have tried to conceptualize China's central-local relations to see what "ism" the central-local relationship can fit in, but with not much success. In the past two decades, what concerned the Chinese leadership was not to build a central-local relationship according to an "ism," but how much power should be kept at the national level of government and how much power should be delegated to localities. The evolution of central-local relationship was very incremental. The leadership's emphasis was not on institutionalizing central-local relations, but on continuously adjusting the relationship to cope with local challenges. Since the third generation leadership, the center has begun to institutionalize its relationship with localities through what we would call "selective centralization" (Zheng,

1999a).

After Deng Xiaoping coming into power in the late 1970s, the government attempted to change China's worsening situation by decentralizing power to society and local government. While political elites in the Soviet Union and East European countries implemented a top-down reform strategy, the reformist leadership in China identified the decentralization of economic decision-making power as a major strategy for reforming the economic system and achieving high economic growth. Rapid decentralization created an unprecedented momentum for local development. It, however, produced enormous problems for central-local relations such as economic localism, ethnic nationalism, and greater regional income disparities.[18] At the end of the 1990s, the central government seemed to have lost control over the localities. China watchers in the West were pessimistic in their assessment and predicted that the old institutions of central-local relations would collapse and China as a nation-state would disintegrate.[19]

The 1990s witnessed the center's efforts to recentralize its power. What the center did was to implement *selective* recentralization, which can be exemplified by Zhu Rongji's two major reforms, i.e., taxation reform and central banking system reform, among others. In 1994, the central government began to implement a new taxation system, i.e., the tax-division system or a federal style taxation system. Before this system, the center did not have its own institutions to collect taxes. All taxes from the provinces were collected by provincial governments first and then were divided between the center and the provinces through bargaining. Provincial governments were regarded only as a part or an extension of central power rather than institutions with their own power base. The new taxation system has had a major impact on the old system and changed the way of interaction between the center and the provinces in the following two ways.

First of all, under the new taxation system, taxes are divided into three categories, namely, central, local, and shared. Central taxes will go to the central coffer, local taxes will go to local budgets, and shared taxes will be divided between the center and the provinces according to previously established agreements.

Second, tax administration is centralized. Instead of authorizing local tax offices to collect virtually all taxes, the center now collects taxes with its own institutions, independent from the provinces. This means that the center has established its own revenue collection agency - the national tax service. Nevertheless, the new system also recognizes independent provincial power, that is, provincial authorities can collect several types of taxes without central interference. In other words, there are now two parallel and independent systems of tax administration, namely, a national system for central taxes and a local one for local taxes. Shared taxes are collected by the central government first, and then divided between the center and the provinces. This is the way a federal taxation system works.

These institutional changes shifted fiscal power from the provinces to the center. As a result, total government revenue increased quite dramatically. Before the new system, the central government tended to rely heavily on coastal provinces such as Shanghai, Shandong, Zhejiang, Jiangsu and Guangdong for revenue contribution. But now this trend has been reversed.[20]

Similar efforts have been made to reform China's central banking system. Before the current reform, China's central banking system was very decentralized. The central bank, People's Bank, established branches in every province and assumed that all provincial branches would take orders from the center since they theoretically were parts or extensions of the central bank. But in reality, local branches were often exposed to the political influence from local government since the personnel of local branches were arranged and their welfare provided by local governments. This frequently led to local branches ignoring orders from the central bank and lending themselves to local influences. Local branches of the central bank often became an effective instrument for local governments to promote local economic growth. But rapid local growth was achieved at the expense of the stability of national economy.[21]

At the end of the 1980s, the central government introduced changes into the central banking system and decided that all directors of local branches should be appointed by the central bank rather than provincial governments previously. To do so, the central government expected all local branches to act in accordance with central directive and be independent from local political influence. Nevertheless, the change did not bring the expected results. Local branches had developed their own independent institutional interests and preferred to use their resources to develop local economies since they could benefit greatly from local growth. This eventually led to the crisis of macro economic management in the mid 1990s. In 1998, the central government declared a most daring measure to reform China's financial system: All provincial branches of the central bank were to be eliminated and major cross-provincial or regional branches to be established in the years to come. Late that year, the central government formally declared that the 31 provincial central bank branches were to be replaced by nine regional branches.[22] The reform measure attempts to follow the American model of federal-state relations, aimed at getting rid of the institutional instruments of provincial governments to intervene in the central banking system.[23]

These institutional initiatives provided the new government with some powerful institutional means to constrain growing localism. It is still hard to tell what central-local relations the Chinese leadership would eventually want to build. It is certain, however, that continuous institutional building has enabled the Chinese government to cope with growing localism. After all these institutional adjustments, a rather clear pattern of the central-local relationship has emerged, i.e., China is moving toward economic federalism. Whether China will develop a federal system would depend on the political innovations that can be introduced into the existing central-local political relationship. Such innovations will be increasingly significant due to increasingly complicated nature of central-local relationship.

Democratizing Rural Governance

At the grassroots level where the majority of the Chinese (peasants) live, the Chinese government has focused on restructuring rural governance by introducing rural democracy. The rural reform initiated in the late 1970s was based on the so-called household responsibility system. Rapid spread of this system soon led to the collapse of the old system of governance, i.e., the production brigade system, and eventually the collapse of the commune system. The central state then decided to re-structure the governance system at the basic level. A more traditional form of governance was immediately established, i.e., the township system, to fill the institutional vacuum left by the breakdown of the commune system. But what is important to note is that this does not mean going back to the old tradition. Instead, it is to restructure the system. State power was withdrawn from the village level and villages became the units of self-governance.

In 1987, the National People's Congress passed the "Village Committee Organic Law of the PRC (Experimental)." According to the law, "village committees should be established in China's rural areas in order to safeguard farmers' opportunities and rights of political participation. The control over village cadres by farmers and the level of villagers' self-government will be improved through direct election of the directors, deputy directors and members of the villagers' committees, thus upgrading the quality of farmers' political participation."[24]

For the central government, the goal of initiating rural direct elections was to restructure the governance system. When Peng Zhen promoted rural elections in 1987, he argued that it could be used to help the Party-state to govern China's countryside and perpetuate CCP's rule. According to Peng, without any constraints on Party cadres and government officials at lower levels, the CCP's authoritarian rule could result in popular complaints, even rebellions against the CCP. Rural elections could play a role in constraining local officials' arbitrary behavior. To a great degree, the Party-state had benefited from this system.

The impact of the election system on China's democratic development can be expected to become more significant in the years ahead. The grass-roots democracy has resulted in a phenomenon that may be called "the lowering of the center's political legitimacy," i.e., the lower level the government is, the higher level of political legitimacy it possesses. Because government officials at the grass roots level are elected by local residents, they can say "no" to higher authorities since their political legitimacy is no longer based on appointment or recognition from higher authorities, but on popular votes. Governments at the higher levels find that it is increasingly difficult to deal with lower level officials. In this sense, the local election system promotes democratization by putting political pressure on government officials at higher levels.

However, at this stage, the apparent contradiction between members of the villagers' committees who are elected and their superiors who are appointed is not serious and may not necessarily end up being confrontational. It would appear that the two different systems are co-existing side by side and it is still too early to predict how the two systems will fare together in the future. For the moment, the authorities seemed to be encouraging the geographical expansion of the villagers' committee elections. According to an article in *People's Daily*, in 2003 alone, there were 929 counties across China covering Tianjin, Hebei, Shanxi, Inner Mongolia, Fujian, Jiangxi and Shaanxi that conducted elections to elect new villagers' committees. [25]

Concluding Remarks

We have discussed how political incrementalism was embedded in various aspects of institutional adjustment in the past two decades. Institutional building has occurred both within and without the regime. In order to maintain stability and order, the government has to implement within-system-adjustment to increase the efficiency of its governance. In order to accommodate the social forces arising from rapid economic development, it has to implement without-system-adjustment to change its relations with society.

Even though all these efforts in institutional building are not aimed at democratizing the country, the process of continuous institutional building has bred various democratic factors. Over the years, the leadership has quietly allowed grass roots democracy in the rural areas to grow and spread through direct election. With continuous institutional building, the Chinese political system tends to show its flexibility by being more accommodating towards social changes and democratic developments. The problem is that the Party still does not want growing social forces to influence and interrupt its plan of reform. The Party wants to use its own way to accommodate demands for political changes or democratization resulting from rapid economic changes, and cannot tolerate any spontaneous democratic movements forcing it to democratize the government. This is why the Party has used very brutal measures against political challenges from society.

Drastic socio-economic changes create great demands for political changes. This was what Chinese leaders learned from the 1989 pro-democracy movement. However, they also learned from the former Soviet Union and other East European countries that radical political reform and democratization would not only force the Communist Party out of power, but also bring chaos to the entire country. From whatever perspective, what they could do was to adopt an incremental approach to political reform, i.e., to accommodate social demands for political reform through institutional adjustment. The top leadership, however, is still not sure whether such incrementalism will be able to cope with the greatest political challenge, i.e. democratization. Incrementalism means that the leadership wants to retain the initiative to decide its own way of reforming the political system, but social demands for political reform are often far greater than the capacity of incrementalism could accommodate. Although political incrementalism has enabled the CCP to improve its governance while maintaining social stability, the rising demand for more vigorous political changes may pose the most severe challenge yet to the CCP's ability to effectively govern China in the future.

Notes

1   For example, Francis Fukuyama, "The End of History?", *The National Interest*, 16 (Summer 1989), pp. 3-18.

2   Tsuyoshi Hasegawa, "The Connection Between Political and Economic Reform in Communist Regimes," in Rozman (ed.) (1992:62).

3   Deng Xiaoping, "Guanyu zhengzhi tizhi gaige wenti" (Issues Related to Political System Reform, September-November, 1986), In Deng (1993:176).

4   Deng Xiaoping, "Reform System of the Party and State Leadership," in Deng (1984:302-25).

5   In Chinese literature in this regard, the most detailed discussion of power succession under Deng Xiaoping, see, Wu (1997). For a general discussion in English literature, see, Richard Baum, "The Road to Tiananmen: Chinese Politics in the 1980s," in MacFarquhar (ed.) (1997:340-71).

6   For a discussion of the role of ideology in China, see Schurmann (1968).

7   For a discussion of Deng's southern tour on China's development, see Wong and Zheng (eds) (2001).

8   Jiang Zemin, "Stresses to Strengthen Party Building and Steadfastly Lead the People to Facilitate the Development of Productive Force in Light of New Historical Conditions", *People's Daily*, May 18, 2000.

9   *Renmin Ribao*, "Quanmian jianshe xiaokangshehui de fendou mubiao" (The targets to achieve a comprehensive construction of a comfortable society), November 9, 2002. According to Dr Li Jinwen, one of the drafters of China's 10th Five Year Plan (2001-2005), this would mean achieving a GDP of around US$4 trillion by 2020 with a per capital income of US$3,100. See *The Sunday Times*, "Jiang maps out road to full modernization," November 10, 2002.

10 On the movement of technocracy, see Lee (1991); Cheng Li and Lynn White, "The Fifteenth Central Committee of the Chinese Communist Party: Full-Fledged Technocratic Leadership with Partial Control by Jiang Zemin," *Asian Survey*, vol. 38, no. 3 (March 1998), pp. 231-264).

11 Lee (1991); and Cheng Li and David Bachman, "Localism, Elitism, and Immobilism: Elite Formation and Social Change in Post-Mao China," *World Politics*, vol. 42, no. 1 (October 1989), pp. 64-94.

12 Li and White (1998); David Shambaugh, "The CCP's Fifteenth Congress: Technocrats in Command," *Issues and Studies*, vol. 34, no. 1 (January 1998), pp. 1-37.

13 For a discussion of this point, see Hass (1964).

14 For a discussion of this point, see Suleiman (1974:380).

15 Lee (1991:404).

16 The Central Committee of the CCP, "Guanyu jianli lao ganbu tuixiu zhidu de jueding" (The Decision to Establish the Retirement System for Aged Cadres), in The Office of Documentary Studies of the Central Committee of the CCP (ed.), *Shiyijie sanzhong quanhui yilai zhongyao wenxian xuanbian* (Selected Important Documents since the Third Plenum of the Eleventh Party Congress) (Beijing: Renmin chubanshe, 1987), pp. 411-421.

17 For a discussion, see, Wu Guoguang, *Zhulu shiwuda*.

18 For a discussion of this point, see, Zheng (1999b), chapter three.

19 Jenner (1992:1); Jack A. Goldstone, "The Coming Chinese Collapse," *Foreign Policy*, 99, 1995, p. 52; and David Bachman, "China in 1993: Dissolution, Frenzy, and/or Breakthrough?" *Asian Survey*, xxxiv (1), 1994, p. 30.

20 For assessments of the 1994 taxation reform, see Shaoguang Wang, "China's 1994 Fiscal Reform: An Initial Assessment," *Asian Survey*, xxxvii (9), 1997, pp. 801-17; and Hu Angang, "Fenshuizhi: pingjia yu jianyi" (The Taxation-Division System: Assessment and Recommendations), *Zhanlue yu guanli* (Strategy and Management), 18, 1996, pp. 1-9.

21 For discussions of the central banking system reform, see Bowles and White (1993) and Chen (1994).

22 Bain Ji, "31 Provincial Branches Replaced by Regional Ones," *The China Daily*, December 16, 1998.

23 Interviews in the Development Research Center, the State Council, May 6, 1998.

24 Cited in Jiang Wandi, "Grassroots Democracy Taking Root", *Beijing Review*, 39 (11), March 11-17, 1996, p. 11.

25 "Minzhengbu: zhongguo cunweihui huanjie xuanju gongzuo jiang juxu tuijin" (Ministry of Civil Affairs: China's villagers' committees election work will continue to push ahead), *Xinhua News*, May 5, 2004.

References

Bachman, David, "China in 1993: Dissolution, Frenzy, and/or Breakthrough?" *Asian Survey*, xxxiv (1), 1994.

Bowles, Paul and Gordon White, *The Political Economy of China's Financial Reforms: Finance in Late Development*, Boulder, CO.: Westview Press, 1993.

Chen Yuan, *Zhongguo jinrong tizhi gaige* (Reform in China's Financial System), Beijing: Zhongguo caizheng jingji chubanshe, 1994.

Deng Xiaoping, *Selected Works of Deng Xiaoping (1975-1982)*, Beijing: Foreign Languages Press, 1984.

Deng Xiaoping, *Deng Xiaoping wenxuan* (Selected Works of Deng Xiaoping), Vol. 3, Beijing: Renmin chubanshe, 1993.

Fukuyama, Francis, "The End of History?" *The National Interest*, 16, Summer, 1989.

Goldstone, Jack A., "The Coming Chinese Collapse," *Foreign Policy*, 99, 1995.

Hass, Ernst B., *Beyond the Nation-State: Functionalism and International Organization*, Stanford, CA: Stanford University Press, 1964.

Hu Angang, "Fenshuizhi: pingjia yu jianyi" (The Taxation-Division System: Assessment and Recommendations), *Zhanlue yu guanli* (Strategy and Management), 18, 1996.

Jenner, W. J. F., *The Tyranny of History: The Roots of China's Crisis*, London: The Penguin Press, 1992.

Lee Hong Yung, *From Revolutionary Cadres to Party Technocrats in Socialist China*, Berkeley, CA.: University of California Press, 1991.

Li Cheng and Lynn White, "The Fifteenth Central Committee of the Chinese Communist Party:

Full-Fledged Technocratic Leadership with Partial Control by Jiang Zemin," *Asian Survey*, Vol. 38, No. 3, March, 1998.

Li Cheng and David Bachman, "Localism, Elitism, and Immobilism: Elite Formation and Social Change in Post-Mao China," *World Politics*, Vol. 42, No. 1, October, 1989.

MacFarquhar, Roderick (ed.), *The Politics of China: The Eras of Mao and Deng*, second edition, New York: Cambridge University Press, 1997.

Rozman, Gilbert (ed.), *Dismantling Communism*, The Woodrow Wilson Center Press & The Johns Hopkins University Press, 1992.

Schurmann, Franz, *Ideology and Organization in Communist China*, Berkeley and Los Angeles: University of California Press, 1968.

Shambaugh, David, "The CCP's Fifteenth Congress: Technocrats in Command," *Issues and Studies*, Vol. 34, No. 1, January, 1998.

Shirk, Susan L., *The Political Logic of Economic Reform in China*, Berkeley, CA.: University of California Press, 1993.

Suleiman, Erza, *Politics, Power, and Bureaucracy in France: The Administrative Elite*, Princeton, NJ: Princeton University Press, 1974.

Wang Shaoguang, "China's 1994 Fiscal Reform: An Initial Assessment," *Asian Survey*, xxxvii (9), 1997.

Wong, John and Zheng Yongnian (eds), *The Nanxun Legacy and China's Development in the Post-Deng Era*, London & Singapore: Singapore University Press & World Scientific, 2001.

Wu Guoguang, *Zhao Ziyang yu zhengzhi gaige* (Political Reform under Zhao Ziyang), Hong Kong: The Pacific Century Institute, 1997.

Zheng Yongnian, *Zhu Rongji xinzheng: Zhongguo gaige de xin moshi* (Zhu Rongji's New Deal: A New Model for Reforming China), Singapore: World Scientific, 1999a.

Zheng Yongnian, *Discovering Chinese Nationalism in China*, Cambridge University Press, 1999b.

Chapter 7

De-Essentialising Chinese Enterprise: Transnationalism, Networks and Business Development

Edmund Terence Gomez

Chinese Culture, Business Networks and Transnationalism

A number of scholars have traced Chinese economic behaviour to cultural traditions.[1] In this tradition of scholarship, Chinese culture explains the dynamism of entrepreneurship among 'overseas' Chinese. Culture also characterizes the way Chinese businesses organize themselves. Redding,[2] for example, claims that enough commonalities exist among Chinese enterprises to allow him to posit the argument that cultural features explain their mode of business development. Chinese entrepreneurs expand not by enlarging an extant business but by creating new ones. Whitley,[3] though taking an institutional rather than a strictly cultural approach, characterizes the form of business organization among members of this ethnic community as the 'Chinese family business'.

A related body of literature argues that most East Asian business organizations tend to share a common characteristic of crucial reliance on business networks in coordinating production, distribution and consumption of products and services. This has prompted some scholars to proclaim 'network organization' to be a unique institutional feature of Asian – specifically Chinese – capitalism, a system that is distinctive from the western notion of bureaucratization and efficiency.[4] There are also many claims that what Chinese do is 'network capitalism' or '*guanxi* capitalism'.[5] This capitalism is said to provide Chinese firms in Southeast Asia with considerable competitive advantages.[6]

Along with the rise of studies tying culture with enterprise development, another body of literature dealing with Chinese business from a transnational perspective has served to create a linkage between identity and capitalism. Transnationalism, with its focus on migration and transnational business networks, is a vogue concept in much of the literature on ethnic minorities. According to this literature, ethnic Chinese of the diaspora share an essentially identical set of cultural traits, just as their businesses display an essentially uniform 'ethnic style' characterized by family firms and intra-ethnic business networks.

A transnational community has been defined as a social formation best exemplified by ethnic diasporas. It relates triadically to its globally dispersed self, the states it inhabits and its ancestral homeland.[7] Its medium is the network, dynamised by new technologies. Multiple identifications and a sense of cultural fluidity, represented as creolised or hybrid, mark its 'consciousness'. Economic transnationalism is chiefly the province of global corporations, but ethnic groups are also players in the world economy, by virtue of their remittances to and investments in the homelands. Governments, realizing the worth of this inward flow, play on the ethnic loyalty of 'nationals' abroad to gain access to their capital. Economic resources flow through diasporic networks as well as to the homeland. As technology speeds the globalization of politics, diasporas become politically more vocal, at both ends of the migration process.

Researchers claim that the networks that typify transnational communities work at the level of the diaspora as a whole as well as in its separate 'homelands' (ancestral and adopted), and that new technologies connect the triadic entity "with increasing speed and efficiency".[8] Studies assume that institutionalised ethnic networks permit diasporic co-ethnics to move capital across national boundaries.[9] Intra-ethnic business networks are based on a sense of group cohesion that facilitates the movement of funds across borders and the mutually beneficial pooling of resources in enterprise development.[10]

In the literature on transnationalism and the Chinese, Ong, in her attempt to "reorient the study of Chinese subjects" and with the development of her concept of 'flexible citizenship' has propagated strongly the view that "global capitalism in Asia is linked to new cultural representations of 'Chineseness' (rather than 'Japaneseness') in relation to transnational Asian capitalism."[11] Ong goes on to argue that 'overseas Chinese' and mainland China are becoming tied in production, trade, and finance 'circuits' leading to the rise of a form of 'fraternal network capitalism' and 'Chinese capitalism' which "has induced long-assimilated Thai and Indonesian subjects to reclaim their 'ethnic Chinese' status as they participate in regional business networks."[12] She fails to ask whether these long-assimilated Indonesians and Thais really are reclaiming their Chinese identity rather than, as business investors, acknowledging that ethnic identity is a tool that can be exploited to facilitate investment in China. Investment of this sort is, however, the result not of some atavistic impulse but of political exhortation by state authorities. Such discourse suggests that all ethnic Chinese in Southeast Asia, even those 'long-assimilated', celebrate as well as profit from the supposed rise of 'Chinese capitalism' in Asia.

This tripartite link between transnationalism, capital and identity has been most lucidly developed by Ong and Nonini's volume *Ungrounded Empires: Ungrounded Empires: The Cultural Politics of Modern Chinese Transnationalism*. Among Chinese migrants, Ong and Nonini argue during the transnational experience, migrants develop a 'third culture', one defined as a 'modern Chinese transnationalism' that "provides alternative visions in late capitalism to Western modernity and generates new and distinctive social arrangements, cultural discourses, practices, and subjectivities."[13] This third culture would include the deployment of economic strategies, such as the family firm and *guanxi* relations or networks to accumulate capital.[14]

Ong and Nonini point to the strength of the state in Asia and its capacity to control 'globalisation', and rightly maintain that much of the "new capitalism of the Asia-Pacific is state-driven and state-sponsored".[15] However, their argument that "modern Chinese transnationalism is expanding ever more rapidly across the Asia Pacific and indeed launching the capitalist development of China itself" is disappointing.[16] While Chinese–owned firms from East and Southeast Asia have invested in China, it is doubtful that they have driven the mainland's economic expansion over the past decade.

Some of Ong and Nonini's other contentions are likewise questionable. These include their assertion that "Chinese transnational capitalists act out flexible strategies of accumulation in networks that cut across political borders and are linked through second-tier global cities such as Shanghai, Guangzhou (Canton), Hong Kong, Taipei, Singapore, Bangkok and Kuala Lumpur. These overlapping business, social, and kinship networks stitch together dynamic, productive, financial, and marketing regions that are not contained by a single-nation or subject to its influence."[17] At another point, they suggest that "diasporic capitalist interests can subvert state disciplining by transferring economic capital out of their host countries to overseas locations, and thus act to transform national economies under the rubric of 'market forces'."[18]

On the one hand, they exaggerate the role played by Chinese-owned capital in driving the economic boom in East Asia; on the other hand, they minimise the capacity of the state to discipline Chinese capitalists and exaggerate the capitalists' ability to transfer their assets across borders. Their suggestion that Chinese capitalists in the region act as a cohesive unit by means of tightly-knit intra-ethnic 'networks' that enable them to emerge as a dynamo for economic growth in Asia is wrong in two respects. By creating a tripartite linkage of transnationalism, identity and capitalism, it tends both to essentialise patterns of enterprise development among Chinese and to homogenise ethnic communities of the diaspora.

In this type of theorising about this tripartite linkage in transnational settings, these theorists have served to 'essentialise capitalism' and intra-ethnic business networks. Redding and Hamilton,[19] though not writing within the perspective of transnational theory, have been the most vocal proponents of the growing transnational impact of Chinese businesses and networks. This homogenising of ethnic communities and culture has also been developed through arguments like the 'clash of civilization' by Huntington[20] and concepts like 'global tribes',[21] 'bamboo networks',[22] and 'Chinese commonwealth'.[23] Concepts like global tribes', 'bamboo networks' and transnationalism tend to perpetuate the impression that ethnic Chinese can think and act only as a group rather than as individuals.

In this article, I argue that the notion of a proliferation of powerful networks has little more basis in fact than the idea of a single world of Chinese capital. To support this contention, I provide a detailed analysis of investments in Britain by ethnic Chinese from East and Southeast Asia. Since a number of British Chinese in business were originally from East or Southeast Asia, this study will also determine whether – and how – enterprises owned by British Chinese deal with ethnic Chinese investors from East and Southeast Asia.

I define 'networks' here as tangible cooperative business ties between co-ethnics of the diaspora. A network with the economic clout of a 'global tribe' would need interlocking stock-ownership ties, a sharing of resources, and cooperation to the point of merger. An assessment will also be made of interlocking directorate links among Chinese-owned companies. The evidence from the manner of operations of ethnic Chinese capital from East and Southeast Asia in the UK will be used to advance an argument about the heterogeneity of Chinese capitalism.

Ethnic Chinese Investments in Britain

Table 1 provides a breakdown of the number of firms from East and Southeast Asia with investments in the UK; a large number of these companies are owned by ethnic Chinese. According to this list in Table 1,[24] a total of 275 companies from East and Southeast Asia have invested in the UK, of which approximately 41 percent are from Hong Kong, about 25 percent from Singapore and roughly 21 percent from Malaysia. Approximately 6 percent of these companies are from mainland China, while about 13 percent are from Taiwan. The companies from China are state-owned, as are some of the enterprises from Singapore and Malaysia. It is, however, worth noting that state-owned Singaporean companies have been used by the government to encourage intra-Chinese business cooperation. Table 2 provides a sample of companies from these countries, identified as being owned by ethnic Chinese, with investments in Britain.

Table 1: Companies from East Asia which own firms in Britain

Country	Number of firms
Hong Kong	114
Singapore	68*
Malaysia	59*
China	17
Taiwan	10
Thailand	5*
Philippines	2*

* Not all companies are owned by ethnic Chinese

Table 2: Ethnic Chinese-owned companies from East Asia investing in Britain

China

Trading (Import-Export)

Company (Incorporation)	Activity	Location	Paid-up Capital	Turnover	Pre-Tax Profit	No. of Employees	Ultimate Holding Company
Yuan Mei International (UK) Ltd (29/7/93)	Industrial raw material trader	Middlesex	2	5,725,143	3,278	n.a	China Tunshu Guangdong Tea Import & Export Corp
Hunan (UK) (1/7/88)	Importers & exporters	Surrey	1,000	3,020,204	189,907	2	Hunan Trading Co Ltd
Sinochem (UK) Ltd (19/5/86)	Petroleum products trader	London	510,000	203,755,000	1,246,00	9	Xiao Yuan Shi Ji Mao Jiao
Tylong International Ltd (31/8/93)	Chemical petroleum trader	London	74,000	55,634,000	-75,000	2	China National Chemicals Import & Export (Sinochem)
Top Glory (London) Ltd (17/11/86)	Cereals, oils and foodstuff trader	London	800,000	37,164,000	-39,400	9	China National Cereals, Oils & Foodstuffs
Kimet International Ltd (31/12/85)	Import & distribution of metal products	Warwick	100,000	2,584,170	-1,036,963	23	China National Metals & Mines Import & Export Corp
Douglun Ltd (9/2/89)	Pharmaceutical raw materials trader	London	100	2,172,717	16,979	n.a	Northeast Pharm Corp
China Waren Ltd (6/1/88)	Import & sale of Chinese art work	Wimbeldon	30,000	629,424	103,389	4	China National Arts & Crafts Import & Export Corp

Company (Incorporation)	Activity	Location	Paid-up Capital	Turnover	Pre-Tax Profit	No. of Employees	Ultimate Holding Company
Professional Services							
The Scottish Lion Insurance Co Ltd (22/11/47)	Marine, aviation, transit insurance	Edinburgh	47,000,000	n.a	-9,881,000	21	China Merchants Holdings Co Ltd
Houlder Insurance Services Ltd (18/12/13)	Insurance & reinsurance	London	2,600,000	2,242,000	89,000	30	China Merchants Holdings Co Ltd
CIC Holdings Ltd (22/2/93)	General insurance & reinsurance	London	17,208,000	n.a	1,059,000	40	People's Insurance Company of China
General Services							
Cosco (UK) Ltd (2/2/88)	Shipping agent	Essex	200,000	16,341,00	-696,000	306	China Ocean Shipping Co
Crystal Logistics Ltd (6/12/91)	Freight agency	Essex	60,000	11,546,000	-449,000	23	China Ocean Shipping Co

Company (Incorporation)	Activity	Location	Paid-up Capital	Turnover	Pre-Tax Profit	No. of Employees	Ultimate Holding Company
Taiwan							
Computer							
Protac International Ltd (1/6/94)	Distribution of computer products	London	100,000	24,755,000	237,000	30	EXCEL Corp
Longshine Technology Ltd (26/4/90)	Distributor of computer products, software consultancy	London	200,000	1,176,906	3,002	4	Longshine Electronics Corp
CTX Europe Ltd (13/1/94)	Sale of VDU monitors	Herts.	3,678,000	84,148,000	-553,000	75	Chuntex Electronic Corp.
Elitegroup Computer Systems (UK) Ltd (19/8/89)	Marketing of computer products	London	100,000	7,896,024	-23,550	18	Elitegroup Computer Systems
Wyse Technology (UK) Ltd (9/9/85)	Marketing computers	Twyford	2	2,155,172	24,962	22	Channel Overseas Corp Ltd
Mitac Europe Ltd (1/11/88)	Supply & maintenance of electronic & data processing equipment	Telford	3,000,000	131,211,000	-230,000	314	Mitac International Corp

Company (Incorporation)	Activity	Location	Paid-up Capital	Turnover	Pre-Tax Profit	No. of Employees	Ultimate Holding Company
Manufacturing							
Europa Magnetics Corp Ltd (4/6/93)	Manufacture of magnetic floppy discs	Cramlington	18,750,000	22,293,000	1,349,000	323	CMC Corporation
Tatung (UK) Ltd (28/7/80)	Manufacturer of televisions, computers & computer components	Telford	22,633,000	102,968,000	-2,466,000	550	Tatung Co
Trading (Import-Export)							
China General (Europe) Ltd (2/8/71)	Import agents	Manchester	1,000	2,833,731	242,515	5	China General Plastics Corp
Pro-Kennex (UK) Ltd (31/1/83)	Distributor of sports equipment	Nottingham	500,000	2,688,714	-236,452	13	Kunnan Enterprises Ltd

Company (Incorporation)	Activity	Location	Paid-up Capital	Turnover	Pre-Tax Profit	No. of Employees	Ultimate Holding Company
Malaysia							
Wholesaling and Retailing							
Ramus Tile Co. Ltd (18/7/24)	Wholesaler of British & imported ceramic wall	Cheshire	24,000	20,808,000	-1,426,000	121	Hong Leong Co (Malaysia) Bhd
Crabtree & Evelyn Holdings Ltd (29/2/96)	Distribution & retailing of toiletries & cosmetics	London	50,000	72,490,000	-1,892,000	1,879	Kuala Lumpur Kepong Bhd
Intrapac (UK) Ltd (31/3/95)	Sale of parts & equipment	Fife	1,750,000	4,210,162	120,260	80	Intra-Muda Holdings Sdn Bhd
Laura Ashley Holdings plc	Garment retailing	London	11,900,000	344,900,000	-49,300,000	3,657	Malayan United Industries Bhd
William Jacks plc (26/7/26)	Sale of cars	Ascot	4,980,000	109,292,000	1,206,000	367	Johan Holdings Bhd

Company (Incorporation)	Activity	Location	Paid-up Capital	Turnover	Pre-Tax Profit	No. of Employees	Ultimate Holding Company
Services							
Millennium Group Ltd	Investment Holding						George Town Holdings Bhd
Third Millennium Studios Ltd (16/9/94)	Business Consultancy	London	100	1,279,047	45,724	2	George Town Holdings Bhd
Pengkalen (UK) Ltd (25/9/59)	Investment holding company	London	7,905,000	37,326,000	-10,166,000	145	Pengkalen Holdings Bhd
Mclean & Gibson (International) Ltd (15/1/81)	Engineering services	Fife	1,002,500	240,000	62,421	64	Intra-Muda Holdings Sdn Bhd
Banking & Finance							
Benchmark Group plc (28/8/69)	Holding company for companies involved in banking, finance, and property development	London	30,140,000	8,483,000	4,218,000	n.a	Hong Leong Co. (Malaysia) Bhd

Company (Incorporation)	Activity	Location	Paid-up Capital	Turnover	Pre-Tax Profit	No. of Employees	Ultimate Holding Company
Manufacturing							
Yule Catto & Co plc (16/8/08)	Manufacture of rubber products		13,624,000	367,170,000	38,050,000	3,384	Kuala-Lumpur Kepong (KLK) Bhd
Beel Industrial Boilers Ltd (11/1/88)	Manufacture and marketing of industrial boilers	Lincoln	1,219,000	7,431,000	-74,000	154	Mechmar Corp (Malaysia) Bhd
AAF Ltd (31/3/66)	Manufacture & marketing of mechanical products	Cramlington	125,000	44,871,000	2,786,000	392	Hong Leong Co (Malaysia) Bhd (& AAF Mcquay Int. Inc [USA})
Singapore							
Services							
Millennium & Copthorne Hotels plc	Ownership & management of hotels	London	43,500,000	202,600,000	50,200,000	3,464	Hong Leong Investment Holdings plc
STA Travel Ltd	Travel agents	London	305,000	114,713,000	274,000	353	STA Travel (Holdings) Pte Ltd

Company (Incorporation)	Activity	Location	Paid-up Capital	Turnover	Pre-Tax Profit	No. of Employees	Ultimate Holding Company
Property							
Validhill Ltd	Real estate agent	London	10,000	474,569	91,531	4	Parkway Holdings Ltd
Nuptine Properties Ltd (26/8/87)	Property agent	London					Parkway Holdings Ltd
Hazeldean Ltd	Property investment						Times Publishing Ltd
Wholesaling and retailing							
N.C.H. Edible Oils (UK) Ltd	Sale of edible oils & tin products	Birmingham	600,000	1,892,050	-219,678	3	Ngo Chew Hong (Holdings) Pte Ltd
Wearnes Computer Systems Europe Ld (30/3/90)	Sale of personal computers	London	100,000	2,678,000	33,000	7	Wearnes Technology Pte Ltd
IPC Corporation (UK) Ltd (4/5/84)	Importer & distributor of EPOS network system		1,182,738	11,081,000	2,509,000	60	IPC Corporation Ltd

Company (Incorporation)	Activity	Location	Paid-up Capital	Turnover	Pre-Tax Profit	No. of Employees	Ultimate Holding Company
Manufacturing							
Wearnes Hollingsworth Ltd (14/9/61)	Manufacture of electronic components	Castleton	2,800,586	5,383,898	326,788	124	Wearnes Technology Pte Ltd
TPL Printers (UK) Ltd (3/11/76)	Manufacture & printing of binders	Hartlebury	5,415,000	15,618,000	299,000	181	Times Publishing Ltd
Igel International Ltd (12/1/79)	Manufacturer and sale of contact lenses			1,776,426	202,775	49	Alliance Technology & Development Ltd
Hong Kong							
Services							
Sing Tao (UK) Ltd (1/2/88)	Publication of Chinese daily newspaper	London	100	2,391,949	-83,865	37	Sing Tao Ltd
Port of Felixstowe Ltd (8/3/91)	Operation of Port of Felixstowe	Felixstowe	100,000	128,391,000	37,163	1,924	Hutchison Whampoa Ltd
Orange plc (4/94)	Telecommunications operator	London					Hutchison Whampoa Ltd
Thamesport (London) Ltd (11/11/87)	Operator of international container	London	n.a	14,133,000	1,097,000	225	Hutchison Whampoa Ltd

Company (Incorporation)	Activity	Location	Paid-up Capital	Turnover	Pre-Tax Profit	No. of Employees	Ultimate Holding Company
Tumble Tots (UK) Ltd (22/3/83)	Operation of active physical programs for children	Halesowen	1,800,000	1,087,000	128,000	15	Jack Chia Holdings (Hong Kong) Ltd
MTS (Holdings) Ltd R.S. Stokvis & Sons Ltd (27/1/60)	Construction specialists	Surrey	250,000	11,108,000	696,000	77	First Pacific Co. Ltd
Hutchison Whampoa (Europe) Ltd (17/6/85)	Consultancy & information services	London	1,000	n.a	115,645	15	Hutchison Whampoa Ltd
AHK Air Hong Kong (UK) Ltd (6/2/91)	Air freight services	Middlesex	100	8,202,255	-127,393	10	AHK Hong Kong Ltd
Tileman Engineering Ltd (24/4/89)	Civil engineering	London	1,000,000	22,061,000	402,000	11	Hopewell Holdings Ltd
Hecny Freight Ltd (21/3/51)	Freight forwarding agents	London	785,164	1,002,639	-170,119	7	Hecny Transportation Ltd
Wholesaling & Retailing							
Trendairo Ltd (28/1/88)	Import & distribution of garments	Manchester	100	7,268,124	13,883	86	Yangtzekiang Garment Manufacturing Co Ltd
GP Batteries (UK) Ltd (28/4/93)	Distribution of batteries	Somerset	40,000	1,987,216,000	48,968,000	6	GP Battery Technology (Hong Kong) Ltd

Company (Incorporation)	Activity	Location	Paid-up Capital	Turnover	Pre-Tax Profit	No. of Employees	Ultimate Holding Company
Fang Brothers (UK) Ltd (28/4/92)	Textile wholesalers	London	2	n.a	87,477	10	SC Fang & Sons (Holdings) Ltd, Kenneth Fang
QDI Computer (UK) Ltd (17/3/92)	Sale of computer components	Slough	50,000	13,127,000	-333,000	14	Newford International Ltd
Unmix (UK) Ltd (6/4/87)	Textile merchanting	London	200,000	26,270,000	103,000	76	Unmix Ltd
Stokvis Tapes (UK) Ltd (24/10/73)	Distribution of adhesive tapes	Herts	100,000	2,875,733	186,165	17	First Pacific Co Ltd
*Newey & Eyre Group Ltd (8/5/47)	Distribution of electrical products	Birmingham	38,280,000	437,518,000	9,564,000	2,797	First Pacific Co Ltd
Halina Marketing (UK) Ltd (4/6/90)	Distributing photographic equipment	Herts	300,000	7,580,688	-46,087	27	W.Haking Enterprises Ltd
Temenos Systems (UK) Ltd (19/12/85)	Development & marketing of Globus, an integrated banking system	London	2,198,844	5,741,275	980,852	47	CTW Ltd
Stelux Watch (UK) Ltd (16/6/44)	Import, assembly & distribution of watches	Lichfield	3,042,000	13,519,000	3,264,000	51	Stelux Holdings Ltd
Harvey Nichols & Co Ltd (1/12/83)	Retailing of high quality clothes, accessories, household items	London	11,000,000	110,006,000	12,018,000	726	Dickson Concept (Int.) Ltd

Company (Incorporation)	Activity	Location	Paid-up Capital	Turnover	Pre-Tax Profit	No. of Employees	Ultimate Holding Company
Property and Hotels							
Grandcrest Projects Ltd (4/3/94)	Property development	London	2	5,372,900	815,475	n.a	Sincere Company Ltd
Combe Grove Manor Hotel & Country Club Ltd (13/1/86)	Developing & running a country club & sports complex	Bath	4,350,000	2,226,400	635,012	95	Jack Chia Holdings (Hong Kong) Ltd
Hotel Property Investors (UK) Ltd (9/10/80)	Holding company, hotels & restaurants	Middlesex	18,730,000	31,050,000	4,418,000	699	New World Developments Co Ltd
Manufacturing							
Herrburger Brooks plc (30/4/20)	Manufacture of piano keyboards		1,885,740	5,372,487	-446,830	225	Harmony Piano Co Ltd
Rogers International (UK) Ltd	Manufacture & distribution of electric components	London	500,000	2,765,224	-916,534	42	Wo Kee Hong (Holdings) Ltd

Company (Incorporation)	Activity	Location	Paid-up Capital	Turnover	Pre-Tax Profit	No. of Employees	Ultimate Holding Company
Lion Mark Holdings Ltd (8/9/83)	Holding company for group engaged in food manufacturing, processing & distribution	Cheshire	1,571,000	43,881,000	687,000	405	Chinney Holdings Ltd
Blue Bird Confectionery Ltd (12/12/79)	Manufacture & distribution of sugar baded confectionery	Halesowen	5,000,000	29,386,000	620,000	391	Jack Chia Holdings (Hong Kong) Ltd
Financial Services							
Swire Pacific I B Ltd (31/10/90)	Investment holding company	London	n.a	18,382,000	-1,582,000	356	Swire Pacific Ltd
Sun Hung Kai Securities (UK) Ltd (30/11/73)	Administrative & other financial intermediation, business services	London	605,000	1,310,464	107,236	11	Sun Hung Kai Securities Ltd

Note: The list of Singapore companies does not include those that are state-owned.

*Newey & Eyre Group Ltd is wholly owned by Hagemeyer (UK) Holdings Ltd, which was specifically established to hold the equity of the Newey & Eyre Group.

The list in Table 2 indicates the involvement of a number of major Chinese-owned firms from East and Southeast Asia in the British economy. Among the most prominent names include Hong Kong's Li Ka-shing, Dickson Poon and the Fang and Jack Chia families, Taiwan's Tatung Group, Indonesia's Oei Hong Leong and Liem Sioe Leong, Singapore's Hong Leong Group owned by the Kwek family and Ong Beng Seng, and a number of major state-owned enterprises from China, including China National Chemicals & Export Corp (Sinochem). A large number of Chinese from Malaysia invest in the UK, including Quek Leng Chan (Hong Leong Group), Vincent Tan Chee Yioun (Berjaya Group), Khoo Kay Peng (MUI Group) and the family of the late Lee Loy Seng (KL-Kepong Group). To review the extent to which there is intra-ethnic business cooperation, or networks, among Chinese enterprises from Asia, we review the operations and ownership patterns of most of the companies from Asia listed in Table 2.

China

The major investors in the UK from China are large national foreign trade corporations controlled by the government in the mainland. The most prominent firms with interests in the UK include China National Cereals, Oils & Foodstuffs Corp, China National Arts & Crafts Import & Export Corp, China National Chemicals & Export Corp and China National Metals & Mines Import & Export Corp.[25] All the companies established in the UK by enterprises from China were incorporated after 1985.

Among the largest Chinese trading companies, in terms of volume of turnover, are those involved in petroleum trade; none of these companies, however, employs a large number of employees. For example, China National Chemicals & Export Corp, also known as Sinochem, owns the petroleum trader, Sinochem (UK) Ltd, which registered a significantly large turnover of £203.755 million, but has only nine employees. Sinochem also owns Tylong International Ltd, another chemical petroleum trader, which has a turnover of £55.634 million, but has only two employees. Sinochem is the state-owned company responsible for handling products produced by the mainland government's Ministry of Chemical Industry.[26]

The only other trading company from China which has registered a high turnover is Top Glory (London) Ltd, a cereals, oils and foodstuff trader owned by another Chinese state-owned trading company, China National Cereals, Oils & Foodstuffs Corp. Top Glory has a reputation of consistently posting the highest turnover among the trading companies, but has only nine employees. The only Chinese company with more than ten employees is Kimet International Ltd, a metal products importer and distributor which has 23 employees; this company is owned by the state enterprise, China National Metals & Mines Import & Export Corp. All the companies involved in international trade, with the exception of Kimet International, are based in the vicinity of London which has the largest concentration of ethnic Chinese in the UK as well as firms owned by this community.

Of the two companies involved in shipping and freight services, Cosco (UK) Ltd and Crystal Logistics Ltd, both operate out of Essex and are owned by China Shipping Co, another state enterprise. Cosco (UK), incorporated in February 1988, has 306 employees, while Crystal Logistics, incorporated in December 1991, has only 23 employees.

Firms from the mainland have also invested in the insurance sector. The China Merchants Holdings Co Ltd acquired a large interest in two insurance companies, The Scottish Lion Insurance Co Ltd, a group involved primarily in marine and aviation insurance incorporated in 1947, and Houlder Insurance Services Ltd, a general insurance and reinsurance company incorporated in December 1913. CIC Holdings Ltd, also a general insurance and reinsurance company incorporated in 1993, was established by the People's Insurance Company of China.

None of the companies from China investing in the UK has ventured into manufacturing, remaining primarily in the services and trading sectors. Despite the involvement of mainland firms in trading, shipping and insurance services, there is no evidence of joint activities with companies owned by ethnic Chinese from Asia. Company records of all these corporations reveal that even firms involved in food-related products have not established major business linkages with British Chinese companies.

Taiwan

Of the 10 companies from Taiwan in this sample, all but two are involved in the computer industry. Six of the eight companies in the computer industry are involved in the distribution and maintenance of computer products, while the remaining two have established enterprises to manufacture computer-related products. Two of these 10 companies, China General (Europe) Ltd and Pro-Kennex (UK) Ltd, are involved in international trading, of plastic products and sports equipment respectively. All but one of these 10 companies was established after 1980; seven of these nine companies were incorporated after the mid-1980s, a trend similar to the companies from mainland China investing in the UK. However, unlike some enterprises from China, none of the Taiwanese firms has acquired an interest in a major British company. Nor is there any evidence that Taiwanese firms are involved in finance, insurance, banking or in the property sector.

One of Taiwan's leading enterprises with investments in the UK is the Tatung Group. This conglomerate is a home electric appliances manufacturer that has diversified into electronics, communications, construction, building materials and publishing. The Group's UK subsidiary, Tatung (UK) Ltd, incorporated in 1980, is involved in the manufacture of electrical products, including televisions and computers, and also producers computer components. Employing about 550 personnel, Tatung (UK) is a major foreign enterprise, capitalized at about £22.633 million and registering a turnover of £102.968 million.

Another major Taiwanese company involved in the electronics sector with more than 300 staff, a capital investment of £3.678 million, and a turnover of more than £100 million is Mitac Europe Ltd, controlled by the Mitac International Corporation. Taiwan's CMC Corp has a floppy disc-manufacturing subsidiary, Europa Magnetics Corp Ltd, which has a paid-up capital of £18.750 million and employs 323 people. Another large company, in terms of turnover and number of employees, is CTX Europe Ltd, controlled by Chuntex Electronic Corporation; this company has a paid-up capital of £3 million and employs about 75 people.

There are other major companies from Taiwan, which are not in this sample, which have invested, or are planning to invest, in the manufacturing sector in the UK. The Acer Group, which emerged as the seventh-largest maker of personal computers in the world in 1997, had, by early 1998, begun construction of a factory in Cardiff and was expected to invest £200 million in this new venture to produce computer monitors.[27] By 1998, 80 percent of Taiwanese investments in Europe were in the UK; by this year, a total of £330 million had been invested in Britain by Taiwanese firms, and 17 companies were involved in manufacturing.[28]

Unlike the companies from China which are situated primarily in the vicinity of the London area, Taiwanese–owned companies are situated throughout the UK, with a number located in Telford, a small town at the border of Wales and England. In spite of the proximity of Taiwanese enterprises with each other in the UK, company records do not indicate any evidence of significant inter-company dealings. Nor is there any evidence that any of these Taiwanese companies work closely with other companies owned by ethnic Chinese from Asia or in the UK. There is, however, some evidence that Taiwanese enterprises employ the services of professionals, like accountants, lawyers and auditors, who are ethnic Chinese and based in the UK.

Hong Kong

Economic sectors in the UK in which Hong Kong firms have investments are diverse and include manufacturing, financial services, wholesaling and retailing, services, property and hotels. Hong Kong's Li Ka-shing, through his main holding company, Hutchison Whampoa Ltd, probably has the largest amount of investments in the UK among the ethnic Chinese investors from East Asia. Indonesia's Liem Sioe Leong, reputedly the second richest man in Asia after the Sultan of Brunei, has investments in the UK through his main publicly-listed holding company in Hong Kong, First Pacific Co Ltd.

Li's two most important enterprises in the UK are Port of Felixstowe Ltd and Orange plc. Port of Felixstowe, a company incorporated in March 1991, manages the Felixstowe dockyard, the largest container port in Britain. This company had a massive turnover of £128.391 million, with a total of 1,924 employees in 1998. Hutchison Whampoa also operates another international container company, Thamesport (London) Ltd, a company incorporated in 1987, and which, according to company reports filed in 1997, registered a turnover of £14.133 million; this company has 225 employees.

Hutchison Whampoa has a 50 percent stake in Orange plc, a company incorporated on 5 October 1995 and involved in the mobile telephone industry. This was a second attempt by Li to move into the UK telecommunications sector after an earlier attempt to promote Hutchison Whampoa's Rabbit cordless telephones failed to make an impact, eventually closing down in 1993.[29] Orange, in which Hutchison Whampoa invested £752 million, is a joint-venture with British Aerospace. Although Orange ran up huge losses in its first three years of operation, by 1996 it had managed to attract such a large number of subscribers to its network that it had emerged, after Cellnet and Vodafone, as Britain's third largest cellular telephone company.[30] The company is expected to secure at least 25 percent of Britain's cellular telephone market by the year 2000.[31] Orange, which has 18 subsidiaries involved in a range of related activities, was listed on the London Stock Exchange in March 1996. Hutchison Whampoa also owns a consultancy and information company, Hutchison Whampoa (Europe) Ltd, which is based in London.[32]

Liem Sioe Leong's First Pacific[33] has control over a number of major companies in the UK including R.S. Stokvis & Sons Ltd, a construction specialists and Stokvis Tapes (UK) Ltd, a distributor of adhesive tapes. First

Pacific has control over Hagemeyer, the electrical products manufacturer from Holland, which has begun to make an impact in this sector in the UK.

Another major Hong Kong company with investments in the UK is Jack Chia Holdings (Hong Kong) Ltd. This holding company has an interest in three companies: Tumble Tots (UK) Ltd, a company incorporated in 1983 and which runs active physical programs for children; Combe Grove Manor Hotel & Country Club Ltd, incorporated in 1986 and manages a country club and sports complex; and Blue Bird Confectionery Ltd, a company incorporated in 1979 and is involved in the manufacture and distribution of sugar-based confectionery. Blue Bird Confectionery, the largest of these three companies, has a paid-up capital of £5 million and employs 391 workers. Jack Chia (Holdings) Group also has an interest in public-listed Boustead plc.

Jack Chia Holdings (Hong Kong), an investment holding company, is a well-diversified group, involved in a varied number of activities, with investments, apart from the UK, in France, Australia, Taiwan, Malaysia, Singapore, Thailand, Indonesia and the Philippines. The companies in the Jack Chia Holdings Group are involved in the manufacture of pharmaceuticals, confectionery and trades machine tools; the import, wholesale, and retail of books, magazines, and stationery; the publishing of books and magazines; and investments in property and hotels.

A number of other companies from Hong Kong have huge investments the UK's manufacturing sector. Lion Mark Holdings Ltd, incorporated in 1983, based in Cheshire and owned by Chinney Holdings Ltd, is a holding company for firms engaged in food manufacturing, processing and distribution. Lion Mark, capitalized at £1.571 million, has 405 employees. Herrburger Brooks plc, a piano keyboard manufacturing company incorporated in 1920, is owned by the Harmony Piano Co Ltd and has 225 employees. Rogers International (UK) Ltd, owned by Wo Kee Hong (Holdings) Ltd, manufactures and distributes electric components.

Hong Kong companies are also involved in wholesaling, retailing and distribution, involving a diverse range of products. Among them is Fang Brothers (UK) Ltd, owned by S.C. Fang & Sons (Holdings), linked to one of the two famous Fang brothers – the other was S.H. Fang. The Fang brothers were refugees from Shanghai who had managed to develop a global textile business with interests in North America, Canada, Panama and a number of Southeast Asian countries. Another prominent firm is Stelux Watch (UK) Ltd, a company involved in the import, assembly and distribution of watches. Stelux Watch is owned by Stelux Holdings, which is, in turn, owned by Mongkol Kanjanapas – he is also known as Wong Chue Meng – who has a number of investments in Hong Kong.[34] Unlike the companies from Taiwan, only one company in this sample of companies from Hong Kong is involved in the sale of computer components, QDI Computer (UK) Ltd. Incorporated in 1992, QDI Computer has a paid-up capital of £50,000 and has only 14 employees.

The most prominent British company controlled by an ethnic Chinese from Hong Kong is probably Harvey Nichols & Co Ltd, an upmarket retailer of clothes, accessories and household items. This prominent retailing outlet is wholly-owned by publicly-listed Harvey Nichols Group plc, of which Dickson Concepts Ltd owns a controlling 50.1 percent stake. Dickson Concepts, one of the largest dealers of luxury goods in Hong Kong, is owned by Dickson Poon. The Harvey Nichols Group also wholly-owns Harvey Nichols Restaurants Ltd, which operates London's Oxo Tower restaurants.[35] Since its takeover by Dickson Concepts, Harvey Nichols has begun expanding its operations outside London, opening a branch in Leeds, with plans to open outlets in Manchester or Newcastle and in either Edinburgh or Glasgow.[36] The Harvey Nichols Group's turnover has also increased appreciably since its takeover by Dickson, increasing almost three-fold between 1994 and 1998, from £50.607 million to £128.540 million,[37] while the number of employees in the Group has increased from 768 to 1,307.

Hotel Property Investors (UK) Ltd, a holding company of firms in the hotels and restaurant industries with a paid-up capital of £18.730 million, is owned by New World Developments Co Ltd, a company controlled by Cheng Yu-teng, one of Hong Kong's largest property owners. Hotel Property

Investors (UK) has around 700 employees. Cheng also owns an interest in major hotels in the United States, China and a few Southeast Asian countries. Sing Tao (UK) Ltd is well-known in the UK among ethnic Chinese as it is the publisher of a Chinese daily newspaper; with a paid-up capital of £100, the company has 37 employees. Tileman Engineering Ltd, a company incorporated in 1988 and with a paid–up capital of £1 million and 11 employees, is controlled by Hopewell Holdings Ltd, owned by the prominent Hong Kong businessman, Gordon Wu, who is heavily involved in infrastructure engineering and power supply in Asia. Another investor from Hong Kong is David Li Fook-wo who has control of the Bank of East Asia, which announced in January 1998 its intention to buy the Asian equities and corporate finance operations of National Westminster Bank.[38]

Singapore

The 11 companies in the sample in Table 2 owned by firms from Singapore are involved in a wide range of activities, including hotels, manufacturing, property and trading. Singaporean companies have a conspicuous presence in the British hotels sector. From the mid-1990s, the hotels sector began registering an exceptional rise in turnover, attracting takeover bids by companies from East Asia. In 1997, *The Guardian* reported the results of a survey of the hotels sector as such: "hotels are enjoying an average 3 percent rise in occupancy rates to nearly 73 percent, and have managed to increase room prices by an average 9.6 percent."[39]

The largest British enterprise owned by a Singaporean firm is Millennium & Capthorne Hotels plc, a major hotel chain, with nearly 3,500 employees, and a paid-up capital of £43.5 million. The Millennium & Capthorne Group is the largest company, in terms of turnover and number of employees, owned by an ethnic Chinese from Singapore in this sample. The Millennium & Capthorne Group is controlled by the Hong Leong Investment

Holdings Group, owned by the members of the Kwek family who are developing their own corporate base independently of the Malaysian-based Hong Leong Group headed by their cousin, Quek Leng Chan. The Singapore-based Hong Leong Investment Holdings Group, through CDL Hotels International, has a 55 percent stake in Millennium & Capthorne Hotels, whose chairman is Kwek Leng Beng; the CDL Group also reportedly owns the Gloucester Hotel, the Chelsea, and the Bailey.[40] The Millennium & Capthorne Hotels Group also has 27 subsidiaries, most of which operate hotels throughout the UK; by 1998, this Group also owned or managed 21 hotels in Europe.[41] Other Singaporean hoteliers – which are not in this sample base – own a number of other hotels in London. For example, the Raffles Group, which runs a luxury hotel in Singapore, acquired the prestigious Brown's Hotel in London from the Granada Group in June 1997.[42] Between 1992 and 1995, it was estimated that the value of Singaporean investments in London hotels was about £300 million.[43] The leading Singaporean investor in the British hotels sector is probably Ong Beng Seng who, through his Singapore-based publicly-listed Hotels Properties Ltd, owns The Inn on the Park, the Metropolitan Hotel, The Halkin, and the Four Seasons Hotel (all based in London) as well as a 30 percent interest in the Canary Riverside Hotel. Ong, with his wife Christina Ong, also acquired a 11 percent stake in Virgin Cinemas, controlled by Richard Branson, and owns the promotion company Lushington Entertainments Ltd.[44] Apart from this, Christina Ong owns the UK franchise for Armani, Prada, Guess and Donna Karan brand products.[45] In 1997, Christina Ong, then reputedly the ninth richest woman in the UK, acquired shop lots in London's Bond Street, Sloane Street and Brompton Street, as well as in Manchester and Glasgow, which served as outlets for her various range of designer products.[46] Ong and Christina also have an interest in the Hard Rock and Planet Hollywood franchises in Asia and own the Haagen-Daz franchise for Southeast Asia.[47]

Investments by Singaporeans in the British property market, particularly in the London area, have been increasing since the early 1990s. This has been attributed to "good capital gains, high rental yields, no restrictions on foreign buyers, a favourable tax regime, and an open and established residential property market".[48] Singapore-based companies, like Scotts Holdings Ltd, run several serviced apartments in the City, while the Noel Group owns 12 apartments at Lancaster Gate, Ho Bee Development Ltd has acquired flats in Euston and near the Strand, while Liang Court Ltd has development projects in Kensington and Hampsted.[49] Oei Hong Leong, the Indonesian tycoon whose family controls the Sinar Mas Group, the second largest business empire in Indonesia, and who operates out of Singapore and Hong Kong through his publicly-listed investment holding company, China Strategic Holdings Ltd, acquired in 1995 a controlling stake in publicly-listed Bolton Group.[50] Another shareholder of China Strategic Holdings, with almost 10 percent of the company's equity, is Li Ka-shing's Hutchison Whampoa Ltd.[51] In 1996, it was also reported that Albert Reynolds, the former Irish Prime Minister, had joined the board of directors of China Strategic Holdings;[52] Reynolds had, however, been involved in business before venturing into politics.

Another leading company controlled by Singaporean Chinese is STA Travel Ltd, one of the UK's leading travel agencies, which employs around 350 people. One Singaporean company controlled by ethnic Chinese with a large number of investments in the UK is the Oversea-Chinese Banking Corporation (OCBC) Group. OCBC's investments in the UK are held through Times Publishing Ltd and Wearnes Technology Pte Ltd. Times Publishing has an interest in TPL Printers (UK) Ltd, a manufacturer and printer of binders, which employs around 180 people, while Wearnes Technology owns Wearnes Hollingsworth Ltd, a company with 124 employees and involved in the manufacture of electronic components. Wearnes Technology also has an interest in Wearnes Computer Systems Europe Ltd, a distributor of personal computers.

Singaporean interests in the UK have been secured primarily through acquisitions. There is, however, evidence of Singaporean Chinese investing in manufacturing by establishing new enterprises or subsidiaries; TPL Printers (UK) Ltd, for example is a binder's manufacturer.

Malaysia

Table 2 indicates that the companies from Malaysia owned by ethnic Chinese are involved in a range of activities, including retailing, finance, manufacturing and services. A major investment in the UK by Malayan United Industries (MUI), owned by Khoo Kay Peng, is its acquisition of a 40 percent interest in Laura Ashley Holdings plc, a major retailing outlet. Laura Ashley, which had an issued capital of £11.900 million and employed almost 4,700 people in 1994, is also involved in the designing and manufacturing of garments, accessories, and home furnishings. The MUI Group's acquisition into Laura Ashley, making it the company's largest single shareholder, was seen as a "bail-out" by the Malaysian firm.[53] By the early 1990s, Laura Ashley, which had been founded by Laura and Bernard Ashley,[54] was still the ninth largest garment retailer group in the UK, with 178 branches.[55] Laura Ashley also had outlets in 34 countries including the US, Australia, Canada, and major Asian cities.[56] In 1998, although Laura Ashley registered a turnover of £344.900 million, the company also registered a loss of £49.300 million. In 1999, as Laura Ashley continued to register poor sales, Pat Robertson, a reportedly close associate of Khoo, and the former US Republican presidential candidate in 1988, was appointed to the company's board of directors. Robertson then had an interest in the garment retailing sector in the UK as well as a 2 percent stake in Laura Ashley.[57]

The well-diversified Hong Leong Group, controlled by Quek Leng Chan, is the Malaysian company that probably has the most diverse range of interests in the UK. In 1993, the Hong Leong Group acquired a 57.5 percent stake in Ramus Holdings plc which owns the Ramus Tile Co Ltd, a long-established wholesaler of ceramic material and self-assembly kitchen furniture. In 1995, the Hong Leong Group's wholly-owned American company, McQuay International Inc, acquired AAF Ltd, a company involved in the manufacture and marketing of air-condition, refrigeration, and freezer systems and products. McQuay International Inc, through AAF-McQuay (UK) Ltd, owns AAF Ltd which, in turn, has a number of subsidiaries involved in related business, including the sale of air filtration products.

AAF, incorporated in 1966, has 392 employees, and company accounts for the year 1997 indicate that it had a turnover of £44.871 million. The Hong Leong Group also acquired Benchmark Bank plc, renaming it Dao Heng Bank (London) plc; this was an attempt by the Hong Leong Group to develop its banking and finance operations abroad. Dao Heng Bank (London) was to be part of the Hong Leong Group's attempt to build up its Hong Kong-based Dao Heng Bank Group, which had been enlarged rapidly through a series of acquisitions and mergers since the mid-1980s, enabling the Hong Leong Group to create the fifth largest bank network in the territory.[58]

The Kuala Lumpur Kepong (KLK) Group, involved primarily in plantations and property development and owned by the Lee family, acquired in 1996 a controlling stake in the major toiletries and cosmetics company, Crabtree & Evelyn Ltd. Established in 1972 by two Englishmen, George Crabtree and John Evelyn, Crabtree & Evelyn has its headquarters in the US, but has outlets throughout Asia, as well as in Australia and New Zealand.[59] The Crabtree & Evelyn Group employs about 1,900 people. The KLK Group also has a 29 percent stake in Yule Catto & Co plc, a publicly-listed manufacturer of rubber threads and latex examination gloves. Yule Catto & Co, incorporated in 1908, employs about 3,400 people. While Yule Catto & Co is involved in an industry that is related to the KLK Group's mainstay activity in Malaysia, i.e. rubber production, the latter's acquisition of Crabtree & Evelyn indicates a new trend, since the mid-1990s, by the KLK Group, to diversify its activities.[60]

The Johan Holdings Group, controlled by Tan Kay Hock and involved primarily in the trading of engineering products and the manufacture of brass products, has a 59 percent stake in William Jacks plc, also a company quoted on the London Stock Exchange. William Jacks, incorporated in 1926, is an investment holding company, its subsidiaries involved primarily in the sale of motor vehicles. William Jacks has almost 400 employees.

A number of other Malaysian Chinese-owned enterprises have investments in the UK. The Pengkalen Holdings Group, controlled by the Tan family, has a UK-based subsidiary, Pengkalen (UK) Ltd, an investment holding company which employs 145 people. Pengkalen (UK) has a long list of subsidiaries some of which, like Central Cocoa Pte Ltd, Meltis Holdings Ltd and Network Foods Australia Ltd, are involved in the manufacture and trading of cocoa products. George Town Holdings Bhd, the retailing company in which T.T. Phua has a joint controlling interest, has a stake in the British company, Millennium Group Ltd, which owns Third Millennium Studios Ltd and Super Millennium (UK) Ltd. Mega First, another company owned by a Malaysian Chinese, bought Bloxwich Engineering Ltd in 1995, a British company which produces door closure systems.[61]

Intra–Ethnic Networking?

Although there has been much overlap in areas of investment in the UK by leading Chinese capitalists from Asia, there is evidence of only one interlocking stock ownership tie among these businessmen. This involves Oei Hong Leong, the Indonesian tycoon who, through his holding company, China Strategic Holdings Ltd, has a controlling stake in public-listed Bolton Group. Li Ka-shing's Hutchison Whampoa owns about 10 percent of Bolton's equity, but it does not appear the he plays an active part in the management of this Group. There is no evidence of any interlocking directorships among any of the ethnic Chinese capitalists from Asia investing in the UK.

Although Li is reputed to have established intra-ethnic business linkages through investments outside Hong Kong, and although he has considerable interests in the UK, there is no evidence of any business cooperation between him and other leading Chinese entrepreneurs. Li has shown a preference to work with non-Chinese companies or businessmen, evident in his choice of partner for his venture into telecommunications, i.e. British Aerospace. The former Irish Prime Minister, Albert Reynolds, is a director of China Strategic Holdings, in which Li also has an interest. Similarly, Singapore's Ong family has interlocking ownership ties in a company owned by Richard Branson. Malaysian Chinese have cooperated with non-Chinese businessmen and enterprises, for example Khoo Kay Peng's involvement of Pat Robertson in Laura Ashley. There is no indication that Malaysian Chinese businessmen have sought out or worked with British Chinese with investments in similar areas of business.

The sample indicates that enterprises owned by some of Hong Kong's wealthiest businessmen, including Li Ka-shing, Cheng Yu-teng, Gordon Wu and Dickson Poon, have a larger volume of investments in the UK than ethnic Chinese from the rest of Asia. Interestingly, in spite of the numerous investments by leading Hong Kong capitalists in Britain, there is no evidence of any interlocking business ties between any of these businessmen to promote their interests in a foreign environment.

This sample of ethnic Chinese companies from Asia also indicates that even though investments by ethnic Chinese from this region in Britain have been growing, there is no indication of endeavours by them to establish intra-ethnic business ties with British Chinese in business. There is, for example, no evidence that the Chinese from different regions have forged joint-ventures, nor is there any evidence that British Chinese have benefited in the form of sub-contracts or serve as suppliers to Chinese investors from Asia.

Chinese enterprises in Hong Kong have a reputation in the garment industry, which has also been established abroad, for example in the US. In Britain, although there are three Hong Kong companies involved in textile distribution, including the famous Fang Brothers (UK), there is little evidence that they have established ties with British Chinese businessmen who were originally from Hong Kong; nor is there any evidence that there is significant global textile trade with other Chinese businessmen, even though Fang Brothers has established subsidiaries worldwide. All three of these Hong Kong companies have remained relatively small enterprises and do not appear to have been able, based on their turnovers, to make much of an impact in the UK textile sector. British Chinese have long been a prominent presence in the food catering, wholesaling and retailing sector, and since the early 1980s have begun to make in-roads into the high tech computer sector.[62] Many of these British Chinese in these sectors were originally from Hong Kong, Taiwan and Southeast Asia. Investors from these countries have begun to make a presence in the computer sector (especially those from Taiwan), while others have been involved in food trading (for example from China) and retailing; yet, there is no evidence of any intra-ethnic business cooperation among these businessmen in the UK.

From the pattern of investments by ethnic Chinese from Asia, it is obvious that the inflow of capital by these capitalists into the UK began to increase appreciably after the late 1980s. Chinese businessmen from different countries in the Asian region also seem to have a different pattern of investment. While Taiwanese companies have ventured primarily into manufacturing and distribution of computer products, the enterprises from China are involved principally in international trade. Key areas of investment by companies from Singapore are in hotels and the property sectors, though a group of companies have also invested in manufacturing but on a much smaller scale than the companies from Taiwan. Businessmen from Hong Kong and Singapore have acquired publicly-quoted companies, which would probably enable them to use the London Stock Exchange to raise capital for corporate expansion. There is, however, no evidence of any Chinese from Taiwan or China who have acquired an interest in a quoted company; nor have they listed any of their firms which have invested in the UK on the local stock exchange. In their home countries, the Chinese from Hong Kong and Singapore have shown a greater proclivity to use the stock exchange as a source of funding, an option that is not as frequently used by Chinese businessmen from Taiwan.

Malaysian-owned firms, including the Benchmark Group, Ramus Tile, AAF, William Jacks, and Laura Ashley, all long-established British enterprises, were acquired through a spate of acquisitions between the late 1980s to the mid-1990s. Malaysian Chinese investors in the UK have not invested in new subsidiaries involved in manufacturing, though they have acquired an interest in companies in this sector. In other words, there is no evidence that any Malaysian company has established a new enterprise in Britain, particularly in the manufacturing sector as evident among Taiwanese companies. The trend emerging from this study of Malaysian companies in the UK indicates a proclivity for acquiring well-established, usually public-listed British companies involved in the retailing, finance, manufacturing and services.

Although the sample in Table 2 indicates a growing presence by ethnic Chinese capitalists from Asia in the UK economy, there is little evidence to support the argument that when ethnic Chinese groups cross-borders for investment purposes, common ethnic identity has served as an important mechanism for promoting joint business cooperation. Even capitalists from the same country have shown no proclivity for conducting joint business ventures in a foreign environment. There is little evidence from this study of investments in the UK by ethnic Chinese from East Asia to suggest that the creation of co-ethnic business networks that will enable ethnic Chinese capital to emerge as Asia's business dynamo and as a major force in terms of its asset base. There is also no evidence that any big ethnic Chinese companies have instituted interlocking stock ownership and directorate links of any significance with other Chinese–owned companies, when they cross borders.

Conclusion

The basis on which the concept of transnationalism rests is the belief that there exists a pan-ethnic unity among ethnic Chinese in different countries which facilitates the development of Chinese enterprise in a global perspective. Transnational networks, said to explain the phenomenal strength of Chinese capitalism, are often attributed to the emergence of new means of communication. However, this study of Asian Chinese investments in the UK provides no evidence to support the argument that co-ethnics of the diaspora work together to promote their investments. Nor is there any evidence of intra-ethnic business cooperation among ethnic Chinese from Taiwan and Hong Kong, territories dominated by the Chinese.

This would suggest that the issue of common ethnic identity is of little importance in transnational business transactions undertaken by ethnic Chinese from Asia. Ethnicity is a political construct that has been used to justify state policies and endeavours (in a national perspective) and to promote or enhance economic pursuits (in an international perspective). At both levels, however, there is little evidence that common ethnicity promotes economic pursuits as well as helps unify a community. This study suggests that though individual businessmen could tap into or use these political constructs when it suits their business interests since some state leaders promote this idea of greater cross-border intra-ethnic business cooperation, there is little indication that their ethnic identity has served as an important tool to facilitate business deals. Among Malaysian Chinese businessmen, the fact that there is little business cooperation in the UK is not surprising given that even within Malaysia, where these businessmen face much discrimination from the state, they have found little benefit from promoting close intra-ethnic business collaboration.[63] There is also no evidence that in Malaysia the promotion of a common ethnic identity is of any importance to leading Chinese businessmen in the development of their enterprise.

This suggests that the concept of transnationalism not only provides little insight into the diversity in the forms of corporate development of Chinese business groups when they cross-borders, it presents a false idea, that ethnicity, based on common cultural formulations, functions as an important unifying factor. The extent of intra-ethnic cooperation among Chinese entrepreneurs is not as significant as the concept suggests and the potential influence of Chinese capital coalescing and emerging as a major force in the global economy due to the networks consolidated by their common ethnicity is untrue. These research findings also bring into question the notion of a distinct type of "Chinese capitalism". It indicates that there is a need to 'de-essential capital', that is to challenge the idea that all Chinese businesses subscribe to some common method of enterprise development or that they possess characteristics original only to them that facilitate the growth of their firms.

Notes

1 Redding, 1990; Bond and Hofstede, 1990; Rozman, 1991.
2 Redding, 1988.
3 Whitley, 1992.
4 Biggart and Hamilton, 1997:51; Whitley, 1992.
5 See, for example, Hamilton, 1996.
6 Yeung and Olds, 2000.
7 See, for example, Portes, Guarnizo and Landolt, 1999.
8 Vertovec, 1999.
9 Kao, 1993; Ong and Nonini, 1997; Ong, 1999.
10 Redding, 1990; Lever-Tracy, Ip and Tracy, 1996; Yeung and Olds, 2000.
11 Ong, 1999:7.
12 Ong, 1999:7.
13 Ong and Nonini, 1997:11.
14 Ong and Nonini, 1997:21.
15 Ong and Nonini, 1997:323-332.
16 Ong and Nonini, 1997:323.
17 Ong and Nonini, 1997:323.
18 Ong and Nonini 1997:325.
19 Redding, 1990; Hamilton, 1996.
20 Huntington, 1996.
21 Kotkin, 1993.
22 Weidebaum and Hughes, 1996.
23 Kao, 1993.
24 The number of companies from East and Southeast Asia investing in the UK, listed in Table 1, was adopted from the Financial Analysis Made Easy (FAME) CD-ROM programme. Based on my own research, the number of companies from Taiwan and Hong Kong investing in the UK is considerably greater than that listed in Table 1.
25 See Chen, 1995:252-53.
26 Chen, 1995:252-53.
27 *Asia, Inc.* June 1997; *The Sunday Times* 15/3/98.
28 *The Sunday Times* 15/3/98.
29 See *Far Eastern Economic Review* 15/8/96.
30 Between 1995 and 1997, Orange's turnover increased almost 13-fold, from £72 million to £913.7 million, while its employees more than doubled, from 2,409 to 4,939. By early 1999, although Orange had yet to register a profit, the value of the company had quadrupled, with an estimated worth of £11 billion (*The Times* 22/1/99).

31 Chan, 1996: 215; *Asia, Inc.* December 1996.

32 *Far Eastern Economic Review* 15/8/96; *Newsweek* 10/11/97.

33 First Pacific, controlled by Liem's son, Anthony, has substantial business interests in the Philippines, and is run by a professional management team.

34 Hiscock, 1997:271.

35 *The Times* 23/6/98.

36 See *The Times* 23/6/98.

37 During the same period, there has also been a more than ten-fold increase in pre-tax profits, from £1.345 million to £14.067 million.

38 *Financial Times* 27/1/98.

39 *The Guardian* 9/6/97.

40 See *Financial Times* 9/6/95.

41 *Financial Times* 3/3/98.

42 *The Guardian* 9/6/97.

43 See *Financial Times* 9/6/95.

44 *Malaysian Business* 1/8/96; *The Observer* 23/2/97.

45 *The Times* 2/6/98.

46 See *The Observer* 23/2/97.

47 *The Observer* 23/2/97.

48 *Financial Times* 7/6/97.

49 *Financial Times* 7/6/97.

50 *Financial Times* 23/3/95.

51 Hiscock 1997: 57-58.

52 See *Financial Times* 6/2/96.

53 *The Times* 18/4/98.

54 The Laura Ashley takeover was implemented when MUI injected £43 million into the company, leading to an increase in the company's paid-up capital. Following the MUI takeover, Bernard Ashley's stake in Laura Ashley was reduced from 35 percent to 21 percent. Another shareholder then of Laura Ashley was the Japanese retailer, Jusco, whose stake in the company was reduced from 15 percent to 9 percent (*The Times* 18/4/98). Bernard Ashley subsequently lost management control of the company (see *The Times* 22/1/99).

55 Thomas, 1998: 69.

56 *The Star* [Malaysia] 17/4/98.

57 See *The Times* 22/1/99.

58 The Hong Leong subsequently divested its interests in the Sao Heng Bank Group, but retained its interests in the financial sector in Malaysia through the Hong Leong Bank and Hong Leong Finance.

59 *The Star* [Malaysia] 6/7/98.

60 See Gomez 1999.

61 *Financial Times* 9/6/95.

62 Gomez 1998.
63 For an analysis of the development of the MUI, Hong Leong and KLK groups in Malaysia, see Gomez (1999). Of these three groups, only Khoo Kay Peng's MUI group has attempted to forge a merger with other Chinese business groups. The proposed merger failed to materialise and led to a bitter public corporate dispute between the businessmen involved.

References

Benton, G. and E.T. Gomez, *Chinatown and Transnationalism: Ethnic Chinese in Europe and Southeast Asia*, Canberra: Centre for the Study of the Chinese Southern Diaspora, Australian National University, 2001.

Biggart, Nicole W. and Gary G. Hamilton, "On the Limits of a Firm-Based Theory to Explain Business Networks", in Marco Orrù, Nicole Woolsey Biggart, and Gary G. Hamilton (eds), *The Economic Organization of East Asian Capitalism*, Thousand Oaks, CA: Sage Publications, 1997.

Bond, M.H. and G. Hofstede, "The Cash Value of Confucian Values", in S.R. Clegg and S.G. Redding (eds), *Capitalism in Contrasting Cultures*. New York: de Gruyter, 1990.

Chan Yiu Man and C. Chan, "The Chinese in Britain", *New Community* 23 (1), 1997.

Chen Min, *Asian Management Systems: Chinese, Japanese and Korean Styles of Business*, London: Routledge, 1995

Fukuyama, F., *Trust: The Social Virtues and the Creation of Prosperity*, New York: Random House, 1995.

Gomez, Edmund Terence, *Chinese Business in Britain*. Unpublished manuscript, 1998.

Gomez, Edmund Terence, *Chinese Business in Malaysia: Accumulation, Ascendance, Accommodation*. Honolulu: University of Hawaii Press, 1999.

Gomez, Edmund Terence and Hsin-Huang Michael Hsiao (eds), *Chinese Business in Southeast Asia: Contesting Cultural Explanations, Understanding Entrepreneurship*. Richmond: Curzon, 2001.

Gomez, Edmund Terence and Hsin-Huang Michael Hsiao (eds), *Chinese Enterprise, Transnationalism, and Identity*, London: RoutledgeCurzon, 2004.

Guarnizo, L.E. and M.P. Smith, "The Locations of Transnationalism", in *Transnationalism from Below*, M.P. Smith and L.E. Guarnizo (eds), New Brunswick, NJ: Transaction Publishers, 1998.

Hamilton, G., *Asian Business Networks*, Berlin: W. de Gruyter, 1996.

Hamilton, G. and Nicole W. Biggart, "Market, Culture, and Authority: A Comparative Analysis of Management and Organization in the Far East", *American Journal of Sociology* 94, 1988.

Hiscock, G., *Asia's Wealth Club*, London: Nicholas Breasley Publishing, 1997.

Huntington, S. P., *The Clash of Civilizations and the Remaking of World Order*, New York:

Simon & Schuster, 1996.

Kao, J., "The Worldwide Web of Chinese Business", *Harvard Business Review*, March–April, 1993.

Kotkin, J., *Tribes: How Race, Religion, and Identity Determine Success in the New Global Economy*, New York: Random House, 1993.

Lever-Tracy, C., D. Ip, and N. Tracy, *The Chinese Diaspora and Mainland China: An Emerging Economic Synergy*, London: Macmillan, 1996.

Liu Hong, "Old linkages, New networks: The Globalization of Overseas Chinese Voluntary Associations and its Implications", *China Quarterly* 155, September, 1998.

Ong, A. and D.M. Nonini (eds), *Ungrounded Empires: The Cultural Politics of Modern Chinese Transnationalism*, London: Routledge, 1994.

Ong, A.., *Flexible Citizenship: The Cultural Logics of Transnationality*. Durham: Duke University Press, 1999.

Portes, A., L.E. Guarnizo, and P. Landolt, "Introduction: Pitfalls and Promise of an Emergent Field", *Ethnic and Racial Studies*, special issue (*Transnational Communities*), 22 (2), March, 1999.

Redding, S. Gordon, *The Spirit of Chinese Capitalism*, Berlin: de Gruyter, 1990.

Redding, S. Gordon, "The Role of the Entrepreneur in the New Asian Capitalism", In P.L. Berger and H.H.M. Hsiao (eds), *In Search of An East Asian Development Model*, New Brunswick, NJ: Transaction Books, 1988.

Rozman, G., *The East Asian Region: Confucian Heritage and its Modern Adaptation*, Princeton: Princeton University Press, 1991.

Smith, Michael Peter and Luis Eduardo Guarnizo (eds), *Transnationalism From Below*, New Brunswick (NJ): Transaction Publishers, 1999.

Smith, Michael Peter, *Transnational Urbanism: Locating Globalization,* Oxford: Blackwell, 2001.

Thomas, M., "The UK Market Environment", in Stephen Fox (ed.), *The European Business Environment: UK*, London: International Thomson Business Press, 1998.

Tu Wei-ming (ed.), *The Living Tree: The Meaning of Being Chinese Today*. Stanford: Stanford University Press, 1994.

Vertovec, S., "Conceiving and Researching Transnationalism", *Ethnic and Racial Studies*, special issue 22 (2) (March), *Transnational Communities*, 1999.

Vertovec, S. and R. Cohen (eds), *Migration, Diasporas and Transnationalism*. Cheltenham: Elgar, 1999.

Weidenbaum, M. and S. Hughes, *The Bamboo Network*, New York: The Free Press, 1996.

Whitley, R.D., *Business Systems in East Asia: Firms, Markets, and Societies*. London: Sage Publications, 1992..

Yeung, H.W.C. and K. Olds (eds), *Globalization of Chinese Business Firms*, Basingstoke: Macmillan, 2000.

Newspapers and Magazines

Far Eastern Economic Review
Financial Times
The Guardian (UK)
Malaysian Business
Newsweek
The Observer (UK)
The Star (Malaysia)
The Sunday Times (UK)
The Times (UK)

III

China and Southeast Asia: Regional Perspectives

Chapter 8

China's Peaceful Rise in Interaction with ASEAN

Wang Hailiang

China's Peaceful Rise

China's peaceful rise is an interesting topic for many people over the world because China is the most populous country and one of the permanent members of the security council of UN. China's peaceful rise as a conception contains very rich connotation and significance either in theoretic perspective or in practical perspective. The background of China's peaceful rise, in my opinion, is economic globalization in the international area and reform and opening in the domestic area. To study the issue one has to observe economic, political, social, cultural, and security aspects. For this presentation, it is better to concentrate attention on the political and security relations between China and ASEAN. In other words, I should focus on the impact of China's peaceful rise on her political and security relations with ASEAN.

Principally, the most important thing for one to observe China's relations with the outside world today is the fundamental concepts of "new view of security" and "common interests". The very core of new view of security at least contains that China's security is not isolated and absolute but mutual and common with the neighboring countries and the international community; China pursues broader and sustainable security covering both traditional national security and non-traditional human security; China options to cooperate with other nations to establish the new mechanism of international security against non-traditional threats. (Zhang and Huang *et al.*, 2004:3) A very persuasive example is the Shanghai Cooperation Organization. Common interests are where China can meet with and cooperate with other nations to make efforts for the welfares of all concerned. The six-party talks in Beijing are a good case.

The concern over China's rise is typical, for the rise of a big nation inevitably influences its environment if not changing the structure and order of the world it is in. Popular and natural as it is, the concern does not equal reasonable fear for threat. "China's rising draws people's attention to the possible challenges brought to the region by a prosperous and powerful China. In the past, China influenced the development of its neighbors." (Wang, 2004) Yes, many can not forget the historic periods when China was powerful, yet this time China's rise is in a completely new historic setting in which China must observe international rules to keep pace with the development in a globalizing world and must behave well to convince the international community on sensitive international issues. Of course, China must be very careful in dealing with issues concerning its neighbors. Otherwise, China's competitor, not to say its rival, will take chances to demonize China as a threat or at least as an uncertainty in the region so as to form a hostile alliance against it in its vicinity. China will not be so unwise as to offer its competitor or rival an excuse to block its way of rise or even to contain it as a rising power. In effect, China has no intention, nor will to threat its neighbors, not mention threatening the existing powers. I fully agree with the opinion that "it is a kind of misunderstanding to say China will get over and threaten other powers." *(ibid.)* In my opinion, China needs good relations with other powers as much as she needs a peaceful environment for socioeconomic development. One cannot imagine China with a heavy burden to reduce poverty in her hinterland challenges the developed powers. To develop the economy and enrich the people, China needs peace and goodwill from other nations. China is endeavoring to build a new international order of justice and fairness that will not be dominated by one nation, yet it is wise for China not to choose confrontation against the dominant power. What China has done in the international arena, either globally or regionally, in recent years proves the peaceful nature of China's rise.

A Responsible Power in an Insecure World

Contradictions prevail in our world, that is to say, internationally economic progress has been accompanied by political conflicts, territorial disputes, international wars, terrorism, etc., teaching men about a bit of philosophy with which to ponder over the world and human society. In reality, we have not won real peace by getting rid of the Cold War, and our socioeconomic development is vulnerable in such an insecure environment. As it is seen, the post Cold War world is still inflicted with regional conflicts and sporadic wars, with the disturbing tortuous Middle East peace process weaving up and down, the unstable situation in Iraq occupied by the Allied troops, the ambushing terrorist forces ready to attack, the potential crisis across the Taiwan Straits, and the Korean nuclear threat. This general pattern of global insecurity naturally affects China, ASEAN as well as the Asia-Pacific from various directions. So, "how insecure is Pacific Asia?" is a very practical question.[1]

In Pacific Asia, danger is still hanging on in the Korean peninsula, the very core of the Northeast Asian security structure, though the process of the Six-party Talk brings hope of peace and stability to the region. The situation there, however, is too complicated to be improved in a short time. The key issue is to reach compromise instead of one side forcing the other to surrender. So long as the US is not going to change its way of behavior and reduce the high pressure, the DPRK will surely maintain its powerful military potential as well as stern posture. One has many reasons to regard the peninsula as a flashpoint in pacific Asia. The efforts China took to facilitate the three rounds of Six-party negotiation in Beijing show that China is a responsible regional power that really wants to keep regional stability for the benefits of all sides concerned and the region as a whole.

In the lower part of Northeast Asia, Taiwan remains problematic in terms of both political relations with China mainland and security relations with USA and Japan. As the Chinese government means what it has declared about her strong will and determination against Taiwan seeking independence, any indiscreet move of Taiwan authorities toward independence will incur perilous military actions across the straits. In a way, the true danger lies in US policy as well as intention on the Taiwan issue. It is quite clear that all sides concerned know that any trial to change the status quo is dangerous to the peace and stability in the region. In the statement by Chinese government on May 17, 2004, however, the authorities reiterate that it will not give up efforts to solve the Taiwan issue peacefully though it will not promise to abandon military means as the last option. China's spirit of responsibility is seen clearly again. In this case, the best choice for the countries in East Asia is to maintain their policy on the issue, drawing a clear line between their political ground and their economic interests, that is, between their One China policy and their non-official relations with Taiwan. If China's neighbors take care not to send mistaking signals to Taiwan, they contribute not only to the solution of the Taiwan issue but also to the stability and security of the region.

Southeast Asia, free from economic and political crises, looks more stable. One has enough reasons to say that "with the current tension and uncertainty in cross-Straits relations and on the Korean Peninsula, China's relations with Southeast Asia have become a major factoring consolidating regional stability." (Teo, 2004) China and ASEAN have come to an agreement as to build a neighborly partnership of mutual confidence, which denotes to the principle of peaceful solution to disputes between them, and have reached consensus on concrete means to maintain the status quo on the territorial problems among the claimants. Out of various reasons, China is regarded by some to as a potential threat to the Southeast Asian countries who have drawn a variety of bilateral defense treaties. Moreover, most ASEAN countries are racing for arms imports despite their initiatives in the process of ARF. However, just as Premier Wen Jiabao described in early March this year, China is a friendly elephant that poses no threat to ASEAN. In fact, China has successfully cultivated its partnership with ASEAN in political, security, economic, and cultural areas, laying a solid standing within ASEAN through soft influence. As a result, "ASEAN countries today embrace unequivocally and acknowledge publicly the one-China policy, and actively engage Beijing in regional co-operation." *(ibid.)* After all, China's rise in economic, political and soft power, ASEAN's softened threat perception of China and the rise of ethnic Chinese power in Southeast Asia presage optimistic future development and growth in China-ASEAN relations.

Cooperate for Common Interests

Looking at the issue from the fore-mentioned conditions in the region, I must say that China shares interests with her neighbors and common security should be one of the most important and substantial part of the common interests. "...China's relationship to her neighboring countries is an important symbol." (Wang, 2004) Among China's neighbors, ASEAN is the only regional grouping with geo-strategic advantage and influence. After some ten years of communications and interactions, China's relationship to ASEAN is getting better and better and closer and closer. ASEAN countries have witnessed a perceptual change regarding China, from a "China threat" to a rising benign China, with ample opportunities for ASEAN. Three decisive factors ushered in the perceptual change. First, China's policy of political stabilization and strategic engagement with ASEAN has reassured ASEAN leaders. Second, China provides economic opportunities for ASEAN through trade surpluses accorded to ASEAN countries in general and the financial support given ASEAN during the Asian Financial Crisis in 1997-98 in particular. Third, Beijing's new and active diplomacy, which presents a responsible regional player and stabilizer, has "considerably reduced the former perception of this country as a military or political threat." (Teo, *op.cit.*) This general pattern of China-ASEAN political and security relations eases people's worry about unsafe scenarios in the region.

Although with radical changes in the power pattern of the Pacific-Asia, for instance, the economic and military rise of several Asian states, and the Russian military phase-out from the Asia Pacific, "for the first time, in almost a century and a half, the future of the international order in the Western Pacific is largely in Asian hands,"[2] one still sees the prevalent influence of U.S. in the region. Then, the questions to be answered by ASEAN as well as other regional partners are what kind of order to build and how to build it without bringing harm to any side. Judging by ASEAN's efforts to establish such international cooperative mechanisms and processes as APEC, ARF, and ASEM, it is seen that ASEAN intends to build up a highly cooperative international order in the region. China, as ASEAN's neighbor, continuously took part in the regional construction of cooperation hand in hand with ASEAN. China took part in the Southeast Asian Non-nuclear Zone and Southeast Asian Treaty of Amity and Cooperation while continuously promoting the 10+1 process and the China-ASEAN free trade agreement. These developments in China-ASEAN relationship has laid a solid foundation for the cooperation between the two sides in establishing a fair regional order, which should, first of all, be of equity and equality in character, without any country dominating the others. For such an equal and cooperative order, a power structure of multi-polarity seems acceptable to most concerning states. Of this power pattern of multi-polarity, ASEAN can be one of the poles as US, Japan, China, and Russia are. Yet, the reality is that ASEAN is not interested in the status of a pole, but oftentimes supportive to US playing the leading role, especially in the area of security, in other words, being the single pole. There are some objective reasons for this choice since ASEAN always regards itself as small and weak depending on the American military umbrella. In fact, ASEAN should and can enhance its status and play its proper role by supporting a multi-polarized power pattern. It is doubtless that with the great political, economic, and military changes in the region, a one-pole power structure is fragile and ineffective for maintaining peace and stability. Recognizing the necessity of multi-polarity for power structure dose not necessarily discard the special, important, and positive role the US plays in Pacific Asia. In a strategic sense, however, it is too sensitive for the US military to return to the Philippines and settle in the Malacca Strait even though such a presence sounds reasonable in a way. The recent discussion by both regional and international media on the scenario of US military presence in the Malacca Strait tells people that such a move can bring troubles to the strait and cause instability in the region. Therefore, with a multi-polarized power pattern emerging, the fore-mentioned cooperative mechanisms and processes will work better than now, the interests of all parties involved will be more ensured, and the stability as well as prosperity of the region better maintained.

ASEAN's Status in China's Perspective

The changes of global political pattern after the ending of the Cold War have added to the lifting of ASEAN's status in the international arena. The status of ASEAN can be analyzed on two levels, strategic one and operational one. Strategically, there are two dimensions, i.e. global dimension and regional dimension. Viewed in the global dimension, ASEAN holds the key position of strategy because of Southeast Asia's geographical location. With the weakening of Russia's potential power and NATO expansion, the European Union found US the emerging contender in the East. In Pacific Asia, unwilling to sit and watch US and Japan take the lion's share of the market, EU hurries to the region competing with US and Japan. Through the pass of Southeast Asia, West Europe directly marches into East Asia with the target on China market. In this process, ASEAN opens more to Europe, plays more functions between Europe and East Asia, and keeps balance between

EU and US. This strategic relationship is signified by ASEM cosponsored by ASEAN and EU with an intention to balance APEC. Here, one easily appreciates ASEAN's pivotal position among these global powers or world poles if you would like to call them so. A rising force as it is, ASEAN needs to maintain strategic balance among the powers who all stress ASEAN's strategic status. For instance, ASEAN is on good term with US and Europe, in good relation with Japan and China, and also in touch with India and Russia. With these powers embraced into one diplomatic network, ASEAN could well be the very pivot of global strategic structure. Militarily, because of the strategic value of Southeast Asia, ASEAN itself is on the whole safe and secured, for the powers do not like it to be in a fragile or even perilous state, nor allow it to be controlled by one power. This determines ASEAN's security relations with the powers that make the centrality of ASEAN possible.

The importance of ASEAN in world dimension also lies in the reality that the straits in Southeast Asia are the throats of the world lifeline for economic powers. It is this perception that motivates US in forming a network of military alliance, UK in strengthening the Five Power Treaty, China in carefully handling the issue of South China Sea, and Russia in keeping its influence by selling arms to some five ASEAN states. In this regard, ASEAN is rich in strategic resources and qualified for the status of a powerful grouping, especially in political area. With the speeding of economic globalization, ASEAN will be more and more evaluated and respected by the powers and other forces.

In the Asia Pacific dimension, ASEAN is more outstanding in strategic as well as political status. Strategically, Southeast Asia is the must way for the American military forces to enter the Indian Ocean and the Persian Gulf and also one of the American fingers to control the Pacific Asia (the other fingers being Japan, South Korea, Taiwan and Australia). No matter how contradictory in culture and values they are to each other, ASEAN and US are strategic partners. On US side, military alliances with various individual ASEAN states both serve its security aims and help with its strategic partnership with the regional grouping. On ASEAN side, with this American military commitment, it is better positioned to cope with other Asia Pacific powers. For Japan, an economic power heavily depending on the worldwide market Arabian oil resources, ASEAN means the key pass on Japan's sea-lanes. Japan has reasons to assist ASEAN economically and care about the security of the region. ASEAN needs Japan for economic support and even for a kind of balance concerning a rising China. However, ASEAN is not to offer assistance to Japan in rearming itself. Evidently, even when ASEAN takes a position of limited support to Japan's military ambition, Japan will not easily succeed. In this respect, ASEAN has the same interests with China and US, both of whom are checked by the former in the general power structure of the region. So, with such a favorable bargaining position and operational resources, ASEAN holds the status equal to those of the powers of the region. In another word, enhanced by its special advantages, ASEAN can be one of the four active parts of the Pacific Asian political game or one of the five if Russia is included.

Roles ASEAN and China Play

The past 36 years have proved that ASEAN's successes are not confined to the sub-region of Southeast Asia itself. With the "ASEAN Spirit" and the "ASEAN Way", the regional grouping has not only paved the way for peaceful development in Southeast Asia but has also provided the Asia-Pacific with the mechanisms and conditions for achieving stability and prosperity. And it has contributed in deed as well as ideas to Asia-Pacific security by playing the leading role in the ARF. ASEAN is a modern regional community of nation-states seeking to integrate into the global village; hence its value is much higher than simple and pure regionalism. It is this aspect of ASEAN that is a model for countries that have recently started opening up to the outside world. China is one of these countries, and it has shown respect to this model by some positive actions in the multi-lateral co-operations initiated by ASEAN.[3]

Besides its fore-mentioned role as a model, ASEAN is an important factor in Asia-Pacific balance of power. The Asia-Pacific major powers — China, US and Japan — are in an unstable triangular relationship that can show a certain degree of imbalance of power. ASEAN, in its special position and with its bargaining clout and soft power, plays the role of keeping the needed balance so that the grand triangle will be stable. In this regard, how ASEAN uses its weight matters. Evidently, should this weight be placed improperly, the Asia-Pacific balance of power would be slanted or even overturned, menacing the stability and security of the region. Aware of its subtle relationships with the major powers, ASEAN is now playing the game well in the regional strategic structure to the effect of providing equilibrium.[4]

ASEAN's role to keep the Asia-Pacific balance is not absolutely contradictory with ASEAN's support to the American military presence in East Asia. Though an international order is now taking shape in the region with a lot of changes that require readjustment of policy and ASEAN is well in the center of diplomatic arena, the US assumes clearly the superior status closely related to the regional stability. China as well as ASEAN recognizes the positive role of the American military presence in East Asia. In China's view, however, the US-Japan security treaty should not be the stepping-stone for Japan to be rearmed into a military power, something rejected even by the Japanese people. The treaty should also not be directed against China. It is only natural for China to warn against specifying the Taiwan Straits in the geographical scope of the US-Japan defense alliance, for such a move is sure to cause tension and insecurity. It is significant that ASEAN diplomats have shown their concern on the matter. This indicates that if China is endangered by the US and Japan, its immediate neighbors like the ASEAN nations will not be as secure as they are now. As the security pattern and situation are quite dynamic and complex, "the obvious conclusion is that the political roles of ASEAN members in the Pacific require adjustment, and considerable agility will be required if ASEAN's own position in the Pacific international system is to be maintained or enhanced.[5] A misunderstood and isolated China is not needed in this era of cooperation and comprehensive security. Strategically speaking, if ASEAN considers the current level of US military presence plus Japan's economic assistance sufficient to keep stability and balance of power and holds its own weight in reserve instead of placing it on the US-Japan side, then China will have more confidence in ASEAN.

As for the Spratlys and the South China Sea, the prospects are not necessarily as pessimistic as predicted by some analysts, though it will take time and effort. All parties concerned have interests in a peaceful solution. However, the claimant states have to realize that security is the first priority for all of them even though sovereignty, territory and economic gains are very important to each of them. So long as they care for mutual security, respect the interests of their partners and keep talking, there will be progress. After confidence is built up among the claimants, multilateral discussions will not be as difficult as they are now. There are good grounds to believe that ASEAN and China will develop more confidence in each other. Firstly, ASEAN and China have security dialogues, which prepare the conditions for long-term security consensus and relations. Secondly, ASEAN and China have agreed upon establishing neighborly partnership of mutual confidence. Thirdly, China needs a peaceful environment for its economic development that will take a long time to reach the desired level. Fourthly, China is stepping up reform and opening up to the outside world, learning more and more international concepts and norms for a more skilled diplomacy. As China integrates with the global community, it will abide by more and more international rules, resorting to legal and peaceful means for solutions to disputes with other countries as long as it is not contained or bullied. Fifthly, culturally speaking, China shares values with the Southeast Asian nations, which means they can stand on the same ground against western pressures concerning, for instance, human rights. Last but not least, geo-economically and geo-politically, China and ASEAN need each other for solving common problems affecting regional security such as the environment, transnational crimes, illegal immigration, piracy, cross-border terrorism and so on.

Conclusion

In conclusion, so long as ASEAN properly estimates and utilizes its unique status and the relative roles in the new international order of the Asia-Pacific and carefully as well as rightly deals with its relations with China, US, Japan, and other forces, keeping the Asia-Pacific balance of power as acceptable to all parties concerned, the Southeast Asia will enjoy peace, stability, and prosperity, so will, perhaps, the region of Pacific Asia as a whole. On China's part, it is obviously essential for her to maintain good relations with ASEAN for mutual benefits and regional welfare by being more responsible and cooperative with more efforts of coordinating interests and actions with ASEAN in the interaction between the parties.

Notes

1 Gerald Segal: *How Insecure Is Pacific Asia? International Affairs* 73,2 (1997) 235-249.
2 David Wurfel and Bruce Burton edited: *Southeast Asia in the New World Order: The Political Economy of a Dynamic Region,* Macmillan, 1996, p.9.
3 Wang Hailiang: *The Role of Asean from China's Perspective,* in *Trends,* No.85, Sept. 27-28, 1997, *The Business Times,* weekend edition, Singapore
4 Lee Kuan Yew's speech: *Why the China-US-Japan balance of power is so vital, The Straits Times,* Sept. 13, 1997.
5 Donald Crone: *New Political Roles for ASEAN,* in David Wurfel and Bruce Burton edited: *Southeast Asia in the New World Order: The Political Economy of a Dynamic Region, Macmillan,* 1996, p.36

References

Chia Siow Yue and Marcello Pacini (eds), *ASEAN in The New Asia, Issues & Trends,* Institute of Southeast Asian Studies, 1997.

Crone, Donald, "New Political Roles for ASEAN", in David Wurfel and Bruce Burton (eds), *Southeast Asia in the New World Order: The Political Economy of a Dynamic Region*, Macmillan, 1996.

Economy, Elizabeth and Michel Oksenberg (eds), *China Joins The World: Progress and Prospect*, Council on Foreign Relations, Inc., 1999.

Foreign Ministry of PRC (ed.), *China's Foreign Affairs*, World Knowledge Press, 2004.

Green, Michel and Patrick Crowning, *U.S.- Japan Alliance: Past, Present, and Future*, Council on Foreign Relations, Inc., 1999.

Khol, Tommy, *The United States and East Asia, Conflict and Co-operation*, Singapore The Institute of Policy Studies, 1995.

Lee Kuan Yew, "Why the China-US-Japan balance of power is so vital", speech, *The Straits Times*, Sept. 13, 1997.

Segal, Gerald, "How Insecure Is Pacific Asia?", *International Affairs* 73, 2, 1997, pp. 235-249.

Sheng Lijun, *China's Dilemma, the Taiwan Issue,* Institute of Southeast Asian Studies, 2001.

Teo Chu-cheow, Eric, *Solidifying China's Regional Partnerships,* in *China Daily,* May 15-16, 2004.

Wang Gungwu, "China Embraces Its Fourth Rise", in *Global Times*, Feb. 27, 2004.

Wang Hailiang, *The Role of ASEAN from China's Perspective,* in *Trends,* No.85, Sept. 27-28, 1997, *The business Times, Weekend Edition*, Singapore.

Wurfel, David and Bruce Burton (eds), *Southeast Asia in the New World Order: The Political Economy of a Dynamic Region*, Macmillan, 1996.

Zhang Youwen and Huang Renwei *et al., China's International Status Report 2004*, Beijing: Peoples Publishing House, 2004.

Chapter 9

China-ASEAN Political Relations: Post-Cold War Developments

Leo Suryadinata

China-ASEAN relations can roughly be divided into two periods: during and after the Cold War. During the Cold War (pre-1990), initially China appeared to be hostile, lukewarm and gradually friendly towards the non-Communist ASEAN states,[1] but after the end of the Cold War (post-1990), China-ASEAN relations improved tremendously. How do we explain China's changing attitude towards this region? What have been the responses of the ASEAN states towards China's policy? What are the problems and prospects? These are some of the questions that this chapter attempts to answer.

To understand China-ASEAN relations, one way is to examine China's foreign policy goals and its means to achieve them vis-à-vis the ASEAN states.

China's Foreign Policy During the Cold War: To put China-ASEAN Relations in Context

China has foreign policy goals and there are various means to achieve them.[2] High in its goals are national security, territorial integrity (including the unification with Taiwan), survival of the government, economic development, to be leader of the Third World and eventually, to achieve the status of great power. With regard to the political ideology and the interest of the so-called Chinese overseas (i.e. ethnic Chinese), they were not very high in its priority. The promotion of these interests only takes place whenever they coincide with high priority of the foreign policy. Otherwise, the ideology and ethnic Chinese are conveniently or quietly abandoned.

How does China achieve the above foreign policy goals? There are several ways: diplomacy and economic aids are most common measures used for conducting foreign policy. However, the PRC also had a unique means of conducting diplomacy: the so-called people-to-people diplomacy (also known as Ping Pong Diplomacy) and the dual policy or the two level policy: while establishing diplomatic ties with the country concerned, China also maintained its ties with local communist parties. When the state-to-state relations were cordial, it downgraded the party-to-party relations; when the state-to-state relations deteriorated, the party-to-party relations were promoted.

The last resort is to go to war. This is the most extreme means and has not been often applied by Beijing. So far, since its establishment in 1949, the PRC has only engaged in three wars: the Korean War (1950-53), The Sino-Indian War (1962) and the Sino-Vietnamese War (1978-79). If we examine these wars, all were waged along the borders of the PRC and they were closely linked to the perception of Chinese leaders regarding China's national security, territorial integrity and regime survival. Until today, China has not engaged in any war beyond its immediate boundaries.

In the first 30 years of the PRC history, Beijing was always concerned with its national security and regime survival. Initially, it faced the American "containment" policy, and later, the Soviet "encirclement" policy. It appears that these policies to "destroy" the PRC encountered failure. China emerged as a victor and was gradually free from this "be seized" mentality, especially after the reemergence of Deng Xiaoping in the political arena in 1977 and the introduction of four modernization programs. China began to be more confident in the international environment.

Early Relations between ASEAN and China: Suspicion and Animosity

At the peak of the Cold War, there was confrontation between the two camps: the communist and non-communist states. Southeast Asian non-communist states were suspicious of China. Indeed, China then supported local communist parties, destabilizing the political situation. The formation of ASEAN in August 1967 can be seen as a response to promote political solidarity against the communist threat.[3] It was a loose association, which was friendly with the West. Because of its non-communist and sometimes anti-communist stand, ASEAN was considered as a potential threat to the communist world, especially China. Not surprisingly, ASEAN in Mainland China was called (and still called) *Dongnanya Guojia Lianmeng* (The Alliance of Southeast Asian States) rather than *Dongnanya Guojia Xiehui* (The Association of Southeast Asian States/Nations). The term *lianmeng* refers to an alliance with military connotation while the correct translation should be *xiehui*. This reflects the perception of Beijing towards ASEAN: a form of military alliance, which targeted at the communist world, especially China.[4] It is interesting to note that Chinese scholars and Chinese language media in Singapore use the term *Yaxian* to refer to ASEAN to avoid incorrect connotation.

Animosity between the communist and non-communist countries continued for decades. Both China and some ASEAN states established diplomatic ties in the mid-1970s, and both sides attempted to adjust to each other, but the real improvement of diplomatic relations only took place after the Cold War. All of the six ASEAN countries eventually established or normalized diplomatic ties with the PRC. The PRC began to accept ASEAN as it is rather than a "military alliance" hostile to Beijing. ASEAN states too no longer considered China as being subversive as the PRC severed all its support for local communist parties. In fact, after the disintegration of the Soviet Union in 1990, Communism both as a form of organization and as a political system no longer posed any challenge to Southeast Asia. Islamic Radicalism has now replaced Communism as a new challenge, if not a threat, to the region.

Improved ASEAN-China Relations: From Animosity to Cooperation

In fact, improved ASEAN-China relations had started prior to the end of the Cold War.

The turning point of ASEAN-China relations was the Vietnam's invasion of Cambodia. Some ASEAN Six countries saw this as an aggressive act of Vietnam, which jeopardized national securities of small states; others were not too concerned with this. Despite internal division, ASEAN Six was able to put forward a united stand on the Cambodian issue, urging Vietnam to pull out from Cambodia. The six ASEAN states felt that Vietnam's action set a bad precedence and would negatively affect regional stability.

This common stand, which was unintended to favour China, appeared to have coincided with China's interests, as it viewed Vietnam as the proxy of the Soviet Union, which attempted to "encircle" China. With the efforts of ASEAN as a group, Jakarta Informal Meeting I and II (JIM I and II) were held.[5] The US was also quite happy with the ASEAN attitude as it was meant to reduce the Soviet influence in the region. The ASEAN efforts eventually bore fruits as the Cambodian issue was kept alive and Vietnam, after the diminishing support from the troubled Soviet Union, finally withdrew from Cambodia. The Cambodian issue was officially resolved in 1991.

Equally important was the political development in China. In June 1989 there was the Tian An Men incident during which the democracy movement was suppressed by the authority. The Tian An Men incident pushed Beijing in a defensive position and the West began to deplore Chinese leaders' behaviour. As China was being isolated by the West, it turned to the ASEAN states for support, as ASEAN, as a group, was not too critical towards Beijing compared to their Western counterparts.

The improvement of ASEAN-China relations can also be seen in the proposal of Dr Mahathir Mohamad regarding the East Asian Economic Grouping (EAEG) in 1990. The EAEG was later changed to EAEC (East Asian Economic Caucus) because of the Indonesian insistence. Suharto who felt that Mahathir had made the proposal before consulting Indonesia in advance was considered to be disrespectful to Indonesia. Suharto would also like to have the grouping to include the West, as the term "caucus" could not be independent and could only exist under the umbrella of the Asia-Pacific Economic Community (APEC).[6] In retrospect, one can see that EAEG/EAEC was an early ASEAN effort to build abridge with China.

There was no doubt that ASEAN-China relations had improved towards the end of the Cold War. It is understandable that China began to participate in the Indonesian /ASEAN initiated South China Sea Workshop since the 1990s. China showed its willingness to have dialogues with ASEAN with regard to the disputed territories. In fact, since the reemergence of Deng Xiaoping, China already offered ASEAN to put aside the sovereignty issue regarding the South China Sea and was prepared to develop the area jointly. Initially China wanted to conduct bi-lateral talks rather than multi-lateral talks with the ASEAN states, but later it was prepared to deal with ASEAN states at both levels.[7] This maybe due to the reason that ASEAN-6 was no longer perceived as the "allies" of the United States following the end of the Cold War; China no longer felt that her security was under threat.

Nevertheless, it does not mean that the South China Sea issue was resolved. On the contrary, there were some minor conflicts between China and some ASEAN countries over the Spratly islands after the Cold War. The conflict, however, did not escalate to a full-fledge armed conflicts, thanks to the confident-building initiated by ASEAN.

ASEAN Regional Forum and China: Common Security Concern

In July 1993, during the post-ASEAN Ministerial Meeting in Singapore, a proposal on the ASEAN Regional Forum (ARF) was put up. It meant to build "mutual confidence, preserve stability and enhance growth in the Asia-Pacific by creating a network of constructive relationship."[8] In the following year, ARF was officially launched. It is obvious that ASEAN would like to engage China in the regional security forum, as without its participation, it is not likely that regional security problems can be resolved. China was also aware of the usefulness of the ARF and was ready to participate. Nevertheless, ASEAN was cautious in assessing the role of the forum. Ali Alatas, then Indonesian foreign minister, stated that, "it is not meant as the instrument to solve problems. It's meant as a consultative forum. Its utility, its success should be judged from that angle."[9]

To further promote peace and stability regarding the South China Sea, ASEAN initiated the Code of Conduct of Parties in the South China Sea, which was later changed to the Declaration of Conduct of Parties in the South China Sea, emphasizing the peaceful solution to the issue. China also accepted the declaration. In other words, China was willing to discuss political and security issues in the multi-lateral forum rather than its earlier stand on the bi-lateral forum.

It should be noted that the ARF consists of 24 members. Apart from ASEAN and China, there are 13 other non-ASEAN members such as the US, Russia and Japan.[10] It was more a consultative forum rather than an instrument to solve problems.[11] Nevertheless, with this forum, ASEAN was able to engage China in dialogues, making the solution of problem easier. The response of China was favourable to ARF. One decade later, the ARF was hailed by a Chinese scholar as "the most important governmental forum for multilateral security dialogue and cooperation in the Asia-Pacific region."[12] He also said that "China has valued ARF and became its dialogue partner at the time of its founding. China has worked hard to strengthen its cooperation with the ASEAN countries within the ARF framework for regional security and stability."[13] Apparently, ARF has achieved much more than it was originally envisioned by some of its founders.

It should be noted that China has become more active in courting some ASEAN states, particularly Indonesia and Malaysia. This may be derived from Chinese strategic concern and some ASEAN states' eagerness to balance the presence of the US in the region. In April 2005 during the 50th anniversary of the Afro-Asian Conference (known also as the Bandung Conference), Chinese president, Hu Jintao, visited Indonesia and on 25 April he and President Susilo Bambang Yudhoyono issued the "Joint Declaration between the Republic of Indonesia and the People's Republic of China on Strategic Partnership".[14] This was hailed as the most significant strategic partnership ever offered by Beijing to any Southeast Asian country. In July 2005, Yudhoyono visited China and concluded more deals with Beijing. Although there are economic contents in the agreements, its strategic and security aspect is most interesting. One analyst maintains that,

"Beijing's strategic partnerships appear aimed at breaking out of what it deems as the 'strategic containment of China' by Washington on both the Pacific Coast and its western and eastern hinterland. After sealing a strategic partnership with Russia in October 2004, China signed a strategic partnership with India and then this latest one with Indonesia; it has now 'neutralized' (at least on paper) its big Asian neighbors from adhering an 'American anti-China coalition.' In so doing, Beijing seeks to ensure that a neutral Jakarta would not block Pacific and Indian Ocean access for Chinese exports and energy imports." (Teo, 2005).

In early September 2005, Malaysian Deputy Prime Minister, Najib Tun Razak, also visited China and signed an economic partnership agreement and an "MOU on Bilateral Defence Cooperation" with Beijing to boost trade and defence co-operation.[15]

China-ASEAN FTA and the East Asian FTA: Closer Relations?

China's keen interest in ASEAN in recent years can be seen in its proposal to establish the China-ASEAN FTA (CAFTA) six years ago. Zhu Rongji, Prime Minister of the PRC, proposed the concept of CAFTA at the ASEAN leaders informal meeting in 1999 in Singapore, but there was no agreement on the matter. Some ASEAN states, including Indonesia, did not support the concept. However, when Zhu attended the 7th ASEAN Summit in Brunei Darussalam and proposed the idea again in early November 2001, the concept was accepted fully by the member-states, including Indonesia, despite its earlier position of maintaining its distance from open approval. The readiness of ASEAN to accept this concept was partly due to the rise of China as an economic power and partly due to a rather poor economic condition in many ASEAN countries after the economic crisis. A lot of direct foreign investment went to China instead of ASEAN.

The CAFTA concept was supposed to be realized within 10 years and it can be implemented by stages, depending on the economic condition of the ASEAN states, as some new members of ASEAN were behind in their economic development.

What have been the motivations of China to propose CAFTA? There were many interpretations. One of the possible reasons was China's concern with her image in the Southeast Asian region. One Chinese scholar argues that "China's economic competition with ASEAN that could intensify following the entry into the World Trade Organization in January 2002. The competition itself can be manageable, but Beijing is concerned that some 'international forces' would exaggerate and play it politically to prove a 'China Threat'" (Sheng, 2003:6). But perhaps more importantly was its strategic motivation, the same scholar mentions that "The CAFTA is an application of China's New Security Concept that advocates a multi-polar world and multilateralism to dilute U.S unilateralism in world and regional affairs" (*ibid.*:7).

China accepted ASEAN as an organization that it could work with. On

8 October 2003 at the end of after the 9th ASEAN Summit, China signed the Instrument of Accession to the Treaty of Amity and Co-operation in Southeast Asia,16 acknowledging the leading role of ASEAN in the region. There is no doubt that China increasingly feels that ASEAN is important for economic, political and security interest of Beijing. Not only for the raw materials and investment but also the South China Sea and the Straits of Malacca which have been the major concern of the PRC. The American presence in the region, which is often seen as balancing, if not undermining China's interest, also presents a security issue for Beijing. The US is often seen as a force attempting to hinder the growth of other powers in the world, including in Southeast Asia. As usual, the ASEAN states would like to adopt a policy that encourages multiple presence of the major powers as their "national interests" are not always the same with those of major powers.

Some East Asian and ASEAN states, especially South Korea and Malaysia, felt that East Asia FTA rather than CAFTA will be a better concept since this would include South Korea and Japan as well. In fact, before the official announcement of the CAFTA, at the ASEAN-Post Ministerial Conference in 1997 with China, Japan and Korea, the idea of ASEAN 10+3 was developed.[17] The three East Asian countries, China, Japan and South Korea, are ASEAN dialogue partners. Unlike ARF, which has a larger membership, ASEAN 10+3 is a smaller forum and the role of China is more conspicuous than in the ARF. ASEAN+3 in December 1998 established the East Asian Vision Group (EAVG), which later (November 2000) developed into the East Asian Study Group (EASG). It was this group which proposed the East Asia FTA. China welcomed the proposal, but the progress of the East Asia FTA was extremely slow, unlike the CAFTA.

In my view, the concept of East Asia FTA can be linked to the concept of the EAEG/EAEC first proposed by Malaysia/Indonesia in the early 1990s. However, the concept failed to develop as Japan did not agree with the proposal, China was lukewarm and Indonesia was not serious. One observer maintained that the concept of EAEG/EAEC died together with the removal of President Suharto in Indonesia. No one talked about the concept anymore. I don't share the view, I would argue that the EAEG/EAEC concept was "revived" in the form of East Asia FTA. Nevertheless, it does not mean that it would be successful.

ASEAN-Ethnic Chinese Relations: Sensitive Issue in China-ASEAN Relations[18]

From the beginning, the ASEAN states have been concerned with the PRC policy towards the ethnic Chinese, as 80% of the Chinese outside China live in Southeast Asia. When the PRC was established in October 1949, it inherited the policy of Kuomintang that all Chinese overseas were Chinese nationals. However, once the PRC moved into the international community, it discovered that this policy was unpopular among the ASEAN states.

To win over the cooperation of Southeast Asian governments, the PRC offered the dual nationality treaty to solve the problem of the Chinese overseas. However, this ad hoc arrangement was not very successful as only Indonesia signed the treaty. But after General Suharto came to power in 1965, Jakarta unilaterally abrogated the treaty. The overseas Chinese issue was only officially resolved after the re-emergence of Deng Xiaoping. Deng visited Southeast Asia in 1978 and discovered the nationality issue was an issue which hindered China-ASEAN relations. In 1980 the PRC promulgated the first nationality law, which only recognizes one nationality. Chinese who were born or live overseas ceased to be Chinese nationals if they hold foreign country's citizenship. It abandoned the *jus sanguinis* principle for its Chinese overseas population and favored the "individual will" principle. In the past, in theory it was almost impossible for an ethnic Chinese outside China to repudiate his/her Chinese national status unless the country concerned had a dual nationality treaty agreement with China, or the ethnic Chinese obtained an approval from the Chinese Internal Affairs Ministry. With the promulgation of the new law, the nationality issue of the ethnic Chinese is resolved.

Nevertheless, there is a clause in the new nationality law that should an ethnic Chinese become a foreign national, it should be based on his/her own free will. With this nationality law, ethnic Chinese in Southeast Asia who have adopted local citizenship willingly are no longer under the jurisdiction of the PRC.

The test case was the Chinese in Indonesia in May 1998 during the anti-Chinese riots. Towards the end of Suharto's rule, anti-Chinese incidents intensified and some foreign journalists asked the Chinese authorities whether they would protect Chinese Indonesians. The Chinese ministry spokesman stated that China strongly believed that Indonesia could handle the situation and refused to intervene. During the last days of Suharto's rule, there were large-scale anti-Chinese (but not anti-PRC) riots in various Indonesian cities. Many Chinese Indonesians were attacked, looted, raped and killed. The systematic raping of Chinese women and girls was a new development as this never took place in the past; the anti-Chinese riots in May appeared to be organized.

The plight of Chinese Indonesians received worldwide attention. Nevertheless, Beijing did not protest. Only in July and August 1998 Beijing made statements to show its "concern" with the sufferings of the Chinese Indonesians. Beijing urged the Indonesian authorities to protect all of her citizens, including the ethnic Chinese. Apparently, China was concerned with cultivating friendly relations with local Southeast Asian countries and that the ethnic Chinese interest did not coincide with China's national interest. Also, there was no valid reason for China to protect "Chinese Indonesians" as they were Indonesian citizens and beyond the jurisdiction of China.

However, discussion of citizenship for the ethnic Chinese outside China was revived in 2002, following the wave of new Chinese migrants (*xinyimin*) to the West. A group of Chinese overseas, mainly from the United States, Europe and Canada where dual citizenship status is recognized, proposed the restoration of the dual nationality status for the "Overseas Chinese". The idea was echoed by some Chinese officials in the China's Political Consultative Council and Overseas Chinese Office (*qiaoban*). It resulted in several debates; some officials and scholars who were connected with the *xinyimin* supported the revival of the dual citizenship status, while those scholars who were formerly from Southeast Asia or familiar with the political condition of the ethnic Chinese in the region opposed it.[19] At the moment, the Chinese government continues to observe the "single citizenship/nationality" principle, and it is unlikely that Beijing will change this practice in the near future as it served the purpose well. But should Beijing decide to change, the impact on the ethnic Chinese and non-Chinese relations in Southeast Asia would be negative.

ASEAN-China Relations and the Taiwan Issue: An Important Factor

Taiwan has always been a sensitive issue in ASEAN-China relations. When the ASEAN countries established ties with the PRC, there was always a clause in their joint communiqué that the ASEAN state concerned did indeed acknowledge the "One China policy" and that Taiwan was part of China. In fact, many non-communist ASEAN states had good relations, even diplomatic relations, with Taiwan before establishing ties with the PRC. But all of them had to sever official ties with Taiwan once they established diplomatic relations with Beijing. Nevertheless, economic and other "non-political ties" have been allowed.

During the Suharto era when diplomatic ties between Jakarta and Beijing were severed, Jakarta showed some ambiguity towards Taiwan. Adam Malik, for instance, was accused of attempting to create "one China and one Taiwan" policy. Nevertheless, when Suharto normalized relations with Beijing in 1990, it became clear that Jakarta had to pursue the "One China policy". The Philippines prior to establishing ties with the PRC was a close "ally" of Taiwan, but when President Ferdinand Marcos decided to normalize ties with Beijing, it too followed the "One China policy". Singapore used Taiwan for combat training for its national servicemen for years, and continued even after the formal establishment of Singapore-China diplomatic relations. At one time Singapore's Senior Minister Lee Kuan Yew also played a mediator role between Beijing and Taipei, but such a role has ceased. All ASEAN states have had a common stand on the Taiwan issue.

However, Taiwan has not been a passive actor. It has sought every opportunity to approach the ASEAN states. Often, it has used economic means to achieve some political objectives. Nevertheless, the ASEAN countries were aware of the sensitivity of the Taiwan issue and attempted to deal with the matter cautiously.

The ASEAN states have been concerned with PRC-Taiwan relations and hope to have a peaceful resolution, as any conflict between China and Taiwan would affect the stability of the ASEAN region. Many ASEAN states wanted to contribute to the peaceful settlement of the Sino-Taiwanese problem, but the PRC continued to consider the Taiwan issue as an internal problem of China. ASEAN states should not "intervene", yet at the same time Taiwan has been very active in internationalizing the issue. As a result, the ASEAN states have been unable to do much as it has not been given the space or a role by the PRC to play.

There may be tension between the PRC and the ASEAN states over the Taiwan issue as many ASEAN states repeatedly stated that they pursued the "One China policy" and opposed Taiwan's independence, but they wanted to maintain economic and other political ties with Taiwan. The economic ties are tolerated by the PRC but other contacts often irritated, if not irked the PRC. The most recent example was the private visit of Singapore Deputy PM Lee Hsien Loong. China's MFA protested to Singapore over DPM Lee's private visit as it was "a serious violation on the One China Policy" and warned Singapore to "face all consequences" of his visit, while Singapore's MFA restated that Singapore valued the friendship of China and continued to pursue the "One China Policy" and opposed Taiwan's independence.[20] In fact, Singapore informed China in advance about the trip "as a courtesy" and China requested the trip to be cancelled. DPM Lee replied: "Singapore is a good friend of China. But to call off the trip at China's request would have undermined our right to make independent decisions, and damaged our international standing. As a small country, this is a vital consideration in our dealings with all countries."[21]

After Lee Hsien Loong's visit to Taiwan, relations between Singapore and Beijing were at the all time low. Visit of Chinese officials was halted. During the National Day speech, the new PM Lee Hsien Loong talked about the visit and openly stated that Singapore was not in favour of the independence of Taiwan. Gradually, the relations between the two countries improved. In September 2005, Madam Wu Yi, China's Vice Premier, visited Singapore and signed many more agreements, signifying the improved relations between the two countries.[22] Wu Yi also visited Thailand and Brunei during her trip. While in Singapore, she hosted the second meeting of China-Singapore joint committee of bi-lateral cooperation, while in Bangkok she hosted the second meeting of China-Thailand Joint Committee of Economy and Trade.[23]

The Taiwan issue is likely to remain as a thorn in ASEAN-China relations in the foreseeable future. If it is not handled cautiously, it may have a negative impact for cordial relations.

Concluding Remarks

China-ASEAN relations have improved tremendously after the Cold War. There is no doubt that China has been eager to foster cooperation with its ASEAN neighbours. ASEAN states have been responding to China's overtures, as good China-ASEAN relations are perceived to be beneficial for ASEAN as well. Both China and ASEAN were trying to settle various issues in peaceful manners. China has been eager to promote economic ties with ASEAN and proposed the China-ASEAN FTA in 2000. ASEAN states responded to the proposal and realized that this might be for mutual benefits. However, due to the diversity of ASEAN, the progress of China-ASEAN FTA may not be as fast as expected.

It should be noted that China did not lose sight of its foreign policy goals, especially regarding national security and territorial integrity. Although China has shown that it is willing to make some compromises with the ASEAN states, yet on national security and territorial integrity issues, especially on the Taiwan issue, it is still stern. The Taiwan issue, if not handled properly, may be a stumbling bloc in the relations between China and ASEAN. China is not likely to compromise on the Taiwan issue, which may bring China into conflict with the US. Such a situation would also put the ASEAN states in a difficult position.

It is also worth noting that China and ASEAN do not share the same perception of regional order. While China wants eventually to be a dominant power in Southeast Asia, the ASEAN states like to have a balance of power in the region.

China is conscious of its new emerging power status. For its future development, China is likely to need more raw materials (including oil and gas) and foreign investment from overseas. It also needs the overseas market for Chinese goods. The Straits of Malacca is also becoming strategically more important for China as its oil comes to China through the straits. China does not want the straits to be controlled by another major power or small powers not friendly with China.

It is clear that China as an emerging economic and political power, if not yet a military power, has strong influence over the ASEAN states. The states of ASEAN have felt the impact of China and they have responded to China's needs, provided that it would not be detrimental to their "national" and "regional" interests. Meanwhile, both China and ASEAN are developing their respective economy and a peaceful environment is needed to achieve this goal. It appears that regional stability is the common interest of both China and the ASEAN states.

Notes

1   Please note that during the Cold War, ASEAN consisted of only six member-states: Indonesia, Malaysia, Singapore, the Philippines, Brunei Darussalam and Thailand. The three Indochinese states and Myanmar only became members of ASEAN in the 1990s after the end of the Cold War. For a general view of the origin and development of ASEAN, see Chin Kin Wah, "ASEAN: The Long Road to 'One Southeast Asia'", *Asian Journal of Political Science*, vol. 5, no.1 (June 1997), pp.1-19.

2 For an analytical framework of China's foreign policy in general and towards Southeast Asia in particular, see Suryadinata (1985).

3 When ASEAN was first formed in 1967, there were five non-communist states: Indonesia, Malaysia, Singapore, the Philippines and Thailand. Brunei joined ASEAN in 1981. For the next 14 years it remained as ASEAN-6. Only after the mid-1990s Vietnam (1995), Laos and Myanmar (1997) and Cambodia (1999) joined the group. Prior to 1995 when speaking of ASEAN, we refer to ASEAN-6.

4 In fact, not only China perceived ASEAN as a "military alliance", North Vietnam/Vietnam also shared a similar view.

5 For a discussion on ASEAN and the Kampuchean issue, see Suryadinata (1996:112-137).

6 For a discussion on the EAEG and EAEC, see Suryadinata (1996:73-74).

7 For China-ASEAN relations in the 1990s, see Qingxi Ken Wang, "In Search of Stability and Multipolarity: China's changing policy towards Southeast Asia after the Cold War," *Asian Journal of Political Science*, Vol. 6, no. 2 (December 1998), pp. 57-78.

8 Lee Kim Chew, "ASEAN sees success at security discussions," *Straits Times*, 11 June 1994.

9 See Yang Razali's Interview with Ali Alatas in *Business Times* (Singapore), 27 July 1994.

10 The non-ASEAN members in the ARF are: Australia, Canada, China, European Union, Japan, New Zealand, Papua New Guinea, South Korea, Russia, US, India, Mongolia, North Korea and Pakistan. See "Japan and Pakistan set to sign TAC", *Jakarta Post*, 2 July 2004.

11 "Don't see ARF as a problem-solving tool: Alatas", *Straits Times*, 27 July 1994.

12 Liu Xuecheng, "Strengthening ASEAN-China Cooperation in the ASEAN Regional Forum", in Saw Swee Hock, Sheng Lijun and Chin Kin Wah, eds. *ASEAN-China Relations: Realities and Prospects*. Singapore: ISEAS, 2005, p.40.

13 Lee Xuecheng, *op.cit.*, p. 41.

14 For a full document, see *http://www.Indonesian-embassy.or.jp/menue/information/state/joint-decl...9/12/2005*.

15 "Najib Departs for Home After Seven-day Visit to China", Bernama.com,6 September 2005;
   http://www.bernama.com.my/bernama/v3/news-lite.php?id=153962.

16 See *http://www.aseansec.org/15272.htm*, 9/15/2005

17 According to the "Final Report of the East Asia Study Group", (See ASEAN Secretariat Website) ASEAN+3 was established after the 1997 crisis in order to promote better cooperation between Northeast and Southeast Asia.

18 This section is mainly derived from my earlier paper entitled: "ASEAN and Ethnic Chinese: Post-Cold War Developments", paper presented at the ASEAN-China Forum 2004, Institute of Southeast Asian Studies, 24 June 2004.

19 For a collection of papers and documents on the debate, see Zhou (ed.) (2005).

20 "Lee Xianloong shiren fang Tai, Zhongguo zhengfu qianglie buman", *Lianhe Zaobao*, 13 July 2004; "DPM in Taiwan: Beijing React", *Straits Times*, 14 July 2004.

21 "Taiwan trip 'doesn't change or contradict 'one China' policy", *Straits Times*, 17 July 2004.

22 "Singapore and China boost ties with Vice-Premier Wu Yi's visit", *http://www.channelnewsasia.com/stories/singaporelocalnews/print/169239...* 9/27/2005

23 Vice Premier Wu Yi to Visit Singapore, Thailand and Brunei, 2005/09/13", *http://www.fmprc.gov.cn/eng/xxxx/t211622.htm*

References

Chin Kin Wah, "ASEAN: The Long Road to 'One Southeast Asia'", *Asian Journal of Political Science*, Vol. 5, No.1, June, 1997.

Saw Swee Hock, Sheng Lijun and Chin Kin Wah (eds), *ASEAN-China Relations: Realities and Prospects*, Singapore: ISEAS, 2005.

Sheng Lijun, *China ASEAN Free Trade Area: Origins, Developments and Strategic Motivations*, ISEAS Working Paper: International Politics and Security Issues, Series No. 1, 2003.

Suryadinata, Leo, *China and the ASEAN States: The Ethnic Chinese Dimension,* Singapore University Press, 1985.

Suryadinata, Leo, *Indonesia's Foreign Policy under Suharto: Aspiring to International Leadership*, Singapore: Times Academic Press, 1996.

Suryadinata, Leo, "ASEAN and Ethnic Chinese: Post-Cold War Developments", paper presented at the ASEAN-China Forum 2004, Institute of Southeast Asian Studies, 24 June, 2004.

Teo Eric Cheow, "Assessing the Sino-Indonesian Strategic Partnership", *PacNet*, Number 25 (Pacific Forum CSIS, Honolulu, Hawaii), June 23, 2005.

Wang Qingxi, Ken, "In Search of Stability and Multipolarity: China's Changing Policy towards Southeast Asia after the Cold War", *Asian Journal of Political Science*, Vol. 6, No. 2, December, 1998.

Zhou Nanjing (ed.), *Jingwai huaren guoji wenti taolunji* (A collection of papers and documents on the nationality problem of the Chinese outside China), Hong Kong: Xianggang Shehui Kexue Chubanshe, June, 2005.

Chapter 10

On China's Sustained Economic Growth and Its Economic Relations with ASEAN

You Anshan

China is a country with a history of 5000 years and we're all proud of its splendid cultural and traditions. From what I know, China used to be a leading country in the world. China contributed 30% of world GDP in 1820, then things started to change, from 1850's China gradually lost its sovereignty and finally became a semi-colony. In 1949, when People's Republic of China was founded, China became an independent country. The past two decades witnessed amazing domestic economic development as well as great breakthroughs in regional economic cooperation. (Wu, 2001)

Sustained Economic Growth and Its Features

China's economy has been growing greatly since the open and reform policy was carried out, especially during 1990's and after that.

Firstly, the economy has grown remarkably in size. GDP has risen from RMB 300 billion in 1978 to RMB 10.2 trillion in 2002 at an average annual growth rate of 9.3%. Its relative place in the world economy has climbed from 2.2% in 1989 to 3.7% in 2002. As GDP approaches 10 trillion, China's overall national strength make great progress, the economic base becomes more solid. As Indicated in the Indexes of World Development issued by World Bank, in 2001, China is the sixth largest economy in the world.

Secondly, total export and import also grows rapidly, from $20.6 billion in 1978 to $620 billion in 2002, and about 1.5% of world total in 1978 to 4% in 2002, grows nearly 30 times in size. Accordingly, the place of China in world trade is from No.25 in 1978 to No.5 in 2002.

The third, foreign reserve is on the rise, increasing from $0.17 billion in 1978 to $280 billion in 2002. The number reached $403.25 billion in 2003, making China the second richest in foreign reserve in the world. (Zhang and Xu, 2004:299-301)

The fourth, the Annual Report of Global Competitive Ability during 2002-2003, issued by World Economic Forum in Geneva, showed that, China's competitive ability placed 33 globally, climbed two ranks compared with last year.

After China's entry into WTO, China's openness to the world market will be enhanced, and its great potential for economic development will be further explored. As indicated by such tendency, there is no doubt that China is capable of keeping an annual 8% growth of GDP in the next ten years.

However, great achievement cannot change the fact that, presently, China is still the largest developing country in the world. Comparing with those developed countries, China falls behind in various economic indexes, thus great space remains for economic development. The economic scale of China's mainland is only one quarter of that of Japan, while China's population is ten times larger than Japan's. The United States and European Union respectively have a total income of 10 trillion dollars, which is more than twice of Japan's total income and ten times of China's total income, furthermore, each of them enjoys a foreign trade which is as fourfold large as

China's foreign trade. Besides, with a population of one fifth of the world total, China's GDP and foreign trade is respectively only about 4% of the world total, and the capital market of China's mainland is as one sixth large as Japan's.

The fifth the hottest destination of foreign investment is emerging in China. Since early 1990's, China has attracted as much as $400 billion foreign investment. In 2002, China's FDI exceeded $50 billion and China surpassed US to become No. 1 in FDI. (Zhu, 2003)

The sixth, economic structure goes under great change. Inflow of foreign capital and technology, together with evolution of the economy itself, pushed China's economic structure from labor-intensive to transform more technology-intensive and capital-intensive, at the same time, more diversified. China's entry into WTO will further this structural change.

Last but not least, the establishment of CAFTA shows China's willingness and confidence in promoting regional economic cooperation and creating a fine future in Asia with neighboring countries. CAFTA along with China's entry into WTO features a foreign policy transform, which is to become a player, a responsible member of international communities rather than a looker-on. Chinese economic development gives a great room for regional economic cooperation, and also provides a suitable environment for attracting foreign capital and technology into China.

Bilateral Economic Relationship between China and ASEAN

Without doubt, a growing Chinese economy will have a significant impact on ASEAN countries and bring more opportunities for economic cooperation.

In a speech made at 2002 ASEAN-China Cooperation Forum, Long Yongtu, former Vice Minister of Foreign Trade and Economic Cooperation said that, China will contribute to the revival and further development of Asian economy, as well as world economy by providing more business opportunities to global investors. And ASEAN will be a major beneficiary due to the cultural and geographic relations.

Long Yongtu also pointed out, Chinese economy is expected to grow at an average rate of 7% according to the Tenth Five-Year Plan. Economic growth will increase demands for import and in 2005. Total import value is expected to reach $330 billion. In 5 years from 2001 to 2005, China will import $1400 billion worth of equipments, technology and goods. A sustaining domestic economic development accompanied by raising import demand can easily translates into a large market for foreign investors and surely presents more cooperation opportunities with both ASEAN and other regions. (Long, 2002)

In fact, ASEAN enjoys a continuous surplus in the recent rapid growth of bilateral trade, and it also attracts the largest part of Chinese tourist outside the borders. That means ASEAN has shared the fruit of China's rapid economic development. It also tell us that Chinese economic development poses no threat to neighboring countries, on the contrary, it brings along opportunities. Presently, the development of China-ASEAN bilateral economic relations is in good condition.

China's political relationship with ASEAN now is stable and developing. Visits between high-level officials take place frequently. China has signed the «Declaration on the Conduct of Parties in the South China Sea», the «Framework Agreement on Comprehensive Economic Cooperation between the Association of South East Asian Nations and the People's Republic of China, Treaty of Amity and Cooperation in Southeast Asia», which indicates that China-ASEAN relations had moved on to a new stage of political trust.

Economic cooperation between China and ASEAN is becoming closer and closer. Bilateral trade volume between the two parties increases from $7.96 billion in 1991 to $39.52 billion in 2000. Although the international trade growth dropped in 2001, bilateral trade between China and ASEAN was on the rise and reached $40 billion. Now ASEAN is the fifth largest trade partner with China while China is the sixth with ASEAN.

Investment going both ways is on the rise. From 1991 to 1998, ASEAN signed investment contract to China totaled $44.2 billion. ASEAN investment to China then decreased due to the Asian Financial Crisis and utilized investment was $18.4 billion. At the same time, Chinese companies increase their investment in ASEAN countries, though less than their counterparts' investment in China. In 2000 alone, Chinese companies signed 56 investment projects with a contract value of $170 million in ASEAN countries and utilized investment was $120 million. It's true that China's direct investment abroad has just started, after China's entry into WTO, the more and more Chinese companies has gone out of the country to invest and operate on a global base, thus giving incentive to world direct investment flow. ASEAN countries are Chinese investments' the first destination since ASEAN countries enjoy geographic advantage and are rich in natural resources.

Cooperation between China and ASEAN is all dimensional and successful. It includes communication and cooperation in trade, investment, technology, as well as in finance, air industry, traveling, postal service, transportation, shipping, and environment protection. (You, 2003)

Benefits from the China-ASEAN Free-Trade Area

The establishment of CAFTA is a great step forward for building a new type of relationship between China and ASEAN countries and signals a new phase for bilateral economic relations. This development is beneficial for both parties and will promote regional economic cooperation within East Asia, thus contributes to world economic development.

The establishment of CAFTA will deepen the trustful partnership between China and ASEAN countries, which is helpful for China to build a peaceful and stable neighboring environment, and also beneficial to the development of ASEAN countries. It is foreseeable that China and ASEAN countries will enjoy higher political status in the international communities.

As the development of domestic economy and the enhancing of anti-risk ability, China and ASEAN will also benefit a lot from the construction of CAFTA. According to a report issued by a China-ASEAN associated technical panel, the bilateral trade plays relatively small role in each part of export and import, therefore great potential exists in the future. Besides, China and ASEAN countries are mutual complementary in trade, both sides will benefit from the effect of trade creation as long as the Free-Trade Area is established. Backed up by a "Global Trade Analysis Model", the technical panel reaches a conclusion that the establishment of CAFTA will increase the export of ASEAN countries to China by 48% and China to ASEAN countries by 55%, the total GDP of ASEAN countries will also increase by 0.9 percentage points while GDP of China increase by 0.3 percentage points based on the data of 2000. (Lu, 2003)

As far as regional cooperation concerned, there is no doubt that the establishment of CAFTA will be propitious to the integration of East Asia. It is generally accepted that four parallel arrangements exist in the course of East Asia economic integration. The first is the integration inner ASEAN countries; the second is the cooperation between ASEAN countries and China, Japan, South Korea, respectively; the third is the cooperation among China, Japan and South Korea; finally, the cooperation of ASEAN and China, Japan, South Korea (10+3), which is supposed to be the aim of East Asia regional cooperation. The startup of CAFTA will enhance the cooperation inside the mechanism of 10+3, as well as the integration of East Asia. It can be predicted that a new economic pole will emerge in East Asia in the near future,

Last but not least, the establishment of CAFTA will tighten the economic relations between China and ASEAN, which will keep the region stable and secure, will probably soften the frontier collision, lead to more common interest and closer cooperation on anti-terrorism fight.

The Interactions of China-ASEAN Economic Relations

The Problems in China-ASEAN Economic Development and Cooperation

It is self-evident that the development of China and ASEAN needs much closer economic relations. However, the differences in economic condition and social system make the future of CAFTA full of uncertainty.

The 10 ASEAN countries differentiate a lot in economic development and trade relations. As some of them have stepped into highly developed countries whereas some remain underdeveloped, it is inevitable that difference in economic development and various national interests will become potential obstacle in the course of CAFTA.

Some Asian countries still regard the development of China as a threat to its neighbors. The inflow of Chinese goods arouses unnecessary worries about the losing of their domestic markets.

Besides the great mutual complementarities, fierce competitions also exist between the goods of China and those of ASEAN. Therefore, problems remain in many areas, such as trade protection, market opening, and so on. A win-win result is expectable if those problems are properly solved.

As the course of CAFTA is deeply affected by political environment, the conflict between China and ASEAN in the Islands of Southern Pacific Ocean must be treated with an attitude of realism as well as giving much respect to history. There is no doubt that the "The Conduct of Parties in the South China Sea" signed by China and ASEAN will play an important role in the settlement of the long existing conflict.

Furthermore, because of the enormous political, economic and military interests America owned in East Asia, its policy change will deeply influenced the establishment of CAFTA.

Related researches must be undertaken and all the problems above must be solved as soon as possible, or it must be the obstacle to the establishment of CAFTA.

The Economic Interaction between China and ASEAN Countries

A stable and friendly environment guarantees the healthy development of economic relations between China and ASEAN. The Free-Trade Area provides a platform for both parts to cooperate with each other and develop in the background of economic globalization and compartmentalization. The construction of that platform requires interaction and endeavor in economy, as well as sound knowledge and solutions to the problems that both parts concerned are confronted with.

Firstly, enhance the inter-government trust and support.

According to the principle of "reciprocal respect, equality, mutual benefit, openness, overall prosperity, and unanimity through consultation" for regional cooperation, high-level government officers of both China and ASEAN should maintain the mechanism of reciprocal visit as well as strengthen their frequent contact. The existing institutional arrangement for consultation and dialogue, such as the APEC, Meeting of the Leaders of East Asia, ASEAN Forum, should be well used to promote the inter-understanding and trust. Furthermore, the China's entry into "the Treaty of South-east Asia's Entente and Cooperation" should be taken as a new beginning to consolidate the political and juristic basis of the relationship between both sides, as well as create a sound atmosphere for the establishment of CAFTA.

Secondly, implement the policy of "good relations of neighborhood, peaceful existence between neighborhood and general prosperity in neighborhood".

On 7th, October, 2003, Premier Wen Jiabao came out with his lecture "the Development of China and the Revival of Asia" when attended the First Commercial and Investment Summit Conference of ASEAN in Bali Island, Indonesia. In that lecture, Premier Wen enunciated China's overall circumjacent foreign policy of "good relations of neighborhood, peaceful existence between neighborhood and general prosperity in neighborhood". According to that policy, to develop "good relations of neighborhood" is to follow the Chinese traditional philosophy of "make friends with the benevolent people, treat your neighbors kindly and pay much attention to harmony". The stable, harmonious relationship between various Asian countries can be achieved only if the principle of "peaceful co-existence" is well implemented. The policy of "peaceful co-existence between neighborhood" is aimed to provide a peaceful regional environment for the development of Asia. That means to maintain the regional stability and peace, enhance mutual trust by cooperation and dialogue, settle the difference with peaceful negotiations. To realize the "general prosperity in neighborhood" requires Asian countries to strengthen their mutual-beneficial cooperation with neighborhood countries, deepen regional and sub-regional cooperation, as well as enhance the regional economic integration.

Third, promote comprehensive communication and mutual-level cooperation on science and technology.

Both science and technology are vital factors in production. They play a more and more important role in China and ASEAN countries' industrial up-grade and economic development. Generally speaking, with a lack of human resources, the ASEAN countries suffer a relatively lower level on science and technology, whereas China has relative advantage on science, therefore great potential exists in scientific communication and cooperation between China and ASEAN. To establish the CAFTA, both parts should carry through various cooperation step by step, concentrate on generally concerned areas, such as biotechnology, information technology, and the research of tropic biological resources. According to the development of each country's science and economy, such cooperation can be undertaken through mutual negotiation and consultation. To meet the need of the communication in science & technology and realize the sustainable economic development of China and ASEAN, the construction of CAFTA should be accompanied with the establishment of the mechanism of science & technology cooperation, management cooperation and resources sharing.

Finally, cement the security cooperation and maintain the regional stability.

The cooperation on politics and security is essential to the successful establishment of China-ASEAN Free-Trade Area. Besides the establishment of Free-Trade Area, China always put much emphasis on the new views of security, of which the core is trust, mutual benefit, equality and cooperation, to try its best for the creation of a mutual-respect, tolerant, and peaceful atmosphere in Asia-Pacific region. Presently, some cooperation is undertaken in various areas, such as anti-terrorism, anti-illegal migration, prohibition of drugs and environment protection. A series of documents are published as the fruit of collective endeavor, for example, "The Plan of Cooperative Prohibition of Drugs between China and ASEAN", "The Conduct of Parties in the South China Sea" and "Joint Declaration of Cooperation in Non-traditional Security Field". In the future, China and ASEAN can establish direct cooperation in some departments as judicature, custom and intelligence to make the non-traditional security cooperation regular and institutionalized. The advancement in that field not only provides the assurance for China-ASEAN Free-Trade Area, but also benefit to the integrated development of regional cooperative mechanism.

All in all, the establishment of CAFTA will bring out not only a closer economic relationship but also a mutual benefit in politic and security. The Trade will be increased, the technical cooperation will be strengthened, the political relations will be enhanced, and the situation in home area will be more stable. Therefore, both China and ASEAN countries will enjoy a stable environment in their pursuit for economic development. All of us are looking forward to the great fortune brought by CAFTA.

References

Gu Xiaosong, "The Choice on the Form of China-ASEAN Free-Trade Area", *Around Southeast Asia*, May, 2002.

Kong Jian, "A Breakthrough in the Relations Between China and ASEAN", *China Review*, Hong Kong, January, 2002.

Liu Guangxi, *The Theory of Complementary Competition: Regional Group and Mutual Trade Mechanism*, The Publishing House of Economic Daily, September 9th, 1996.

Liu Jiayi, *The Trend of World Economic Regionalization*, Lixin Accounting Publishing House, November, 1996.

Long Yongtu, "ASEAN Will be the First to Benefit from the China's Development", www.xinhuanet.com, September 14th, 2002.

Lu Jianren, *The Today and Tomorrow of ASEAN*, The Publishing Company of Economic Management, September, 1999.

Lu Jianren, "Review of the Regional Economic Cooperation in East Asia during the Year of 2002", *World Economy*, Volume 3, 2003.

Wei Min, "The Conception and Prospect Belong to China-ASEAN Free-Trade Area", *Wen Wei Po*, Hong Kong, July 26th, 2002.

Wei Yanshen, *The Study of Triple Economic Cooperation in Asia's Growing up*, Chinese Price Publishing House, January, 1998.

Wu Fucheng, "A New Impact on Asia: The China-ASEAN Free-Trade Area", *Monthly Study of Taiwan Economy*, July, 2002.

Wu Yikang, Triple Power Poles? *The Characteristics and Trend of Development of EU, North America and Asia-Pacific Region*, Publishing House of Shanghai Academy of Social Science, 2001.

You Anshan, "On the Necessity and Prospect of the Establishment of China-ASEAN Free-Trade Area", *World Economy Study*, Volume 9, 2003.

Zhan Dong, "The Influence of China-ASEAN Free-Trade Area on Regional International Relations", *Around Southeast Asia*, May, 2002.

Zhang Yuwen and Xu Mingqi, *Economic Power: the Trend and Objective of China's Peaceful Rise*, People's Publishing House, March 2004.

Zhu Rongji, "Government Work Report", March 5th, 2003.

Chapter 11

China and ASEAN: A View from Northeast Asia

Yoshihide Soeya

Introduction

China is pretty much at the center of dynamic regional development in East Asia in recent years. Apparently, the economic strategy of China, premised on its ever increasing economic weight, has been creating the dominant regional trend toward greater regional integration and what eventually might turn out to be an East Asian community.

The flip side of the same coin, however, is the political and security dimension of development, which is often unseen partly because of Chinese conscious efforts to downplay elements of political and security competition. This, however, does not mean that political and security considerations are not important or have become irrelevant. Perhaps, the case is the other way around over the long run, if not in the foreseeable future.

This chapter will discuss place and role of China, as well as its initiatives toward ASEAN, in a larger regional context of post-911 security development in East Asia, and thus would attempt to provide a perspective to the discussion of the China factor in Northeast Asian security issues, as well as in the recent trend of regional integration driven by China-ASEAN FTA initiatives.

US-China Strategic Co-existence

The most fundamental and important aspect of a security system in the Asia-Pacific has been and will continue to be the strategic relationship between the United States and China, which is competitive in nature and over the long term but will remain cooperative in the foreseeable future.

The Bush administration in principle conceptualizes China as a "strategic competitor" (Rice, 2000). It, however, stopped calling her as such soon after its inauguration. Secretary of State Colin Powell for instance said in July 2001 on his way to Canberra from Beijing that " the relationship is so complex with so many different elements to it that it's probably wiser not to capture it with a single word or a single term or a single cliché." [1]

In fact, the Bush administration has endeavored to cultivate a relationship of strategic coexistence with China since soon after its inauguration. The 9.11 incident proved to create a firmer foundation for such relationship. China played a critical role in the passage of the UN Security Council Resolution 1368, legitimizing a war in Afghanistan. The United States does need a cooperative working relationship with China for the global war against terrorism.

China, on its part, stopped challenging the US predominance in the late 1990s. This has basically been the bottom-line of Chinese regional strategy since after the Taiwan crises in 1995 and 1996, when both Beijing and Washington sought to restore the relationship with the mutual visits by Jiang Zemin and Bill Clinton in 1997 and 1998.

In principle, Chinese regional and global strategy is founded upon its economy-centered orientation, making the most of its economic weight, both real and potential. As a consequence, the Chinese government has been keeping a low profile toward the US security presence in the region, including the Taiwan question and the US-Japan alliance.

There is reasonable evidence to believe that China has also readjusted its policy toward Japan with the same strategic considerations in the summer of 1999, perhaps upon re-examining the effect of Jiang Zemin's trip to Japan in 1998.

The strategic coexistence between Washington and Beijing, therefore, means the most critical great powers in the Asia-Pacific having different dreams in the same bed. They have different strategic orientations, and they need each other precisely for the pursuit of their own strategies.

Despite this strategic coexistence, however, the competitive nature of the US-China strategic relationship is unlikely to change easily. The way China engages itself in regional issues should be understood as reflecting both of these cooperative and competitive motives. At the official policy level, cooperative attitudes and thinking prevail and catch the eyes of observers, but their deep and long-term implications for a regional order could not be illuminated fully without taking into account the motivations of competition with the United States.

Taiwan Question

The Taiwan question is now an object of such strategic coexistence. Beijing basically maintained a low key against some of the initial provocative statements by President Bush, as well as the US policies of arms sale and allowing stopovers in the US by Taiwanese leaders including Chen Shui-bian himself. In order not to exacerbate the problem, the Bush administration has also re-committed itself to the principle of "one-China" and non-support of Taiwan "independence."[2]

In principle and over the long run, the Taiwan question still remains a wild card for U.S.-China relations, which could upset their strategic coexistence, but now, the Chinese economy-centered strategy appears to be working. Taiwan's economic dependence on China is ever deepening, which in turn gives confidence to Beijing advancing its "united front" policy toward "comrades" in Taiwan.

The Chen Shui-bian administration, however, has been taking mixed responses, legislating necessary measures for facilitating mutual trade, investment and travels, while increasing political concerns over the ever-deepening economic dependence on China. The prospect for stable cross-strait relations could be clouded over ever changing plans on the part of the Chen Shui-bian administration to exploit the timing of the Beijing Olympics schedules in 2008.

New US-Japan Alliance and China

Under the present Bush administration, the role of alliance has undergone a significant transformation in line with its new global strategy. The Bush strategy basically defines the U.S. national interests as the core, with the assumptions that the promotion of the U.S. national interests would lead to a better world and that the end of the Cold War has given the United States a unique opportunity to transform the world. The U.S. would carry out this mission with available and effective means including the unilateral use of its dominant power. This conceptualization of global strategy has not fundamentally changed since Condoleezza Rice presented the argument in her article in *Foreign Affairs*. Allies are expected to go along with such US global mission.

The initial attempt to conceptualize the US-Japan alliance in these terms by the core people in the Washington policy community, many of whom later assumed important positions in the Bush foreign policy team, was the so-called Armitage report, titled "The United States and Japan: Advancing Toward a Mature Partnership."[3] Although the reality fell far short of the American expectation, the message was explicit in calling for a U.S.-Japan alliance more closely modeled on the U.S.-U.K. relationship.

Implicit in the distinction by Rice between a strategic competitor (China) and an ally (Japan) was a frustration shared by the Bush foreign policy team about the Clinton administration's lack of conceptual clarity in its policy toward the two critical countries in Northeast Asia. Most problematically for the Bush team, the Clinton administration often confused a competitor for a partner, as exemplified by the declaration of a "strategic partnership" with China, at the cost of an alliance relationship with Japan.

This conceptual clarity in the US strategy under the Bush administration is an important source of the good state of the alliance between the United States and Japan, which is often called the best since the end of the World War II. Prime Minister Koizumi's performance with President Bush has been quite effective under this new U.S. definition of the alliance relationship. Koizumi in effect has been a cheerleader for the Bush global strategy.

This redefinition of the alliance for the Bush global strategy, however, has changed the modality of the U.S.-Japan alliance, from a traditional tight alliance relationship to a flexible, if only relatively, coalition of the willing. Even though there would be no fundamental shift in the ultimate choice of the alliance relationship with the United States for Japan, to the extent the alliance moves in the direction of a coalition of the willing, the management would become more political.

At the macro level, the recent Chinese "new thinking" toward Japan may well be interpreted as a Chinese strategic response to this shifting nature of the alliance. China may indeed have given up, or postponed for the time being, its efforts to challenge the US-Japan alliance. Instead, the new thinking toward Japan argues that China should not be preoccupied with the historical and security problems with Japan, but should cultivated economic and political grounds of mutual cooperation. In many of these arguments, the Chinese concern over the US predominance, globally and regionally, constitutes a key background element.

North Korean Problem

Just like many other issues, the state of the US-China strategic co-existence provides a general background for the evolution of the North Korean problem as well.

First and foremost, the policy of the Bush administration continues to set its baseline. At the time of the inauguration, the Bush foreign policy team already designated Iraq, North Korea and Iran as the three rogue regimes, but it argued that the leadership regime in Pyongyang was living on a "borrowed time" and the United States should not hurry. This was in sharp contrast to the case of Iraq, where it did stress the point that without removing Saddam Hussein nothing would change.

These different assumptions between Iraq and North Korea did not change, or even consolidated, after the three rogue regimes were upgraded to the "axis of evil" in the State of the Union Address on January 29, 2002 by President Bush[4]. In sharp contrast to the case of Iraq, Bush was explicitly pushing for a multilateral framework for the North Korean problem, and this eventually encouraged China to take the lead in the Six Party Talks under the general background of the US-China strategic co-existence.

Initially, however, the Bush policy toward North Korea should have frightened Pyongyang. In particular, missionary zeal often pronounced by Bush himself in denying the legitimacy of the North Korean leadership must have created an impression in Pyongyang that the Bush administration should be aiming at regime change. In fact, President Bush has often expressed his sympathy and the need of assistance toward the people of North Korea. This aspect of the Bush policy toward North Korea, compounded by the rhetoric of the "axis of evil," would have naturally aroused a strong sense of crisis for the leadership in Pyongyang.

This perceived deep crisis for the regime survival was a central factor motivating Kim Jong-il, the supreme leader of North Korea, to begin a surprising move to accept Japanese Prime Minister Junichiro Koizumi to Pyongyang in September 2002. The determination on the part of Kim Jong-il to seek helping hands from Japan was unmistakable in Kim himself confessing and apologizing for the abduction of Japanese citizens and the spy ships (Soeya, 2003).

When the gamble to normalize diplomatic relations with Japan stalled, however, Kim Jong-il once again faced, or did not have any other choice but to face the United States squarely and to employ unusually provocative measures, climbing up step by step the ladder of nuclear escalation.

Against these escalation tactics of Pyongyang, the Bush administration, pushed by the ever mounting domestic pressures from the Congress, considered seriously an option to go to the United Nations for sanctions in early 2003. Perhaps, this move alarmed China, which would account for the timing of Chinese shift in its diplomacy toward North Korea from the emphasis on bilateral talks between Washington and Pyongyang to taking an initiative to convince Pyongyang toward joining a multilateral framework.

As is often the case with its diplomacy, China initially moved very cautiously, which materialized into a de facto three-party talk in Beijing on April 23, 2003. At the time, China refused to call it a three-party talk, due to the felt necessity to deal with Pyongyang with care as well as because of its own previous insistence on the bilateral dealings between Pyongyang and Washington, but the Chinese strategic shift was obvious. China then upgraded its efforts to persuade Pyongyang, and hosted the first Six Party Talks in August.

It was against these new backgrounds that Koizumi decided to pay his second visit to Pyongyang in May 2004. This time, opportunity was ripe for Koizumi to relate the progress in Japan-North Korea diplomatic normalization talks to the development of the Six Party Talks. China has not only supported the Koizumi initiative but apparently encouraged Kim Jong-il to move forward with Japan. The innate logic here is that the progress in Japan-North Korean bilateral talks is a boost for the Six-Party Talks.

Critical behind these overt developments is none other than the strategic coexistence between the United States and China. It appears the United States has decided to give a leadership role to China for the time being, and will deal with North Korea without discrediting the Six Party Talk framework.

To what extent the Bush administration has trust in the multilateral framework, as an effective means to settle the North Korean nuclear problem with the CVID formula, however, is not certain. Perhaps not much. Here is s source of a strategic clash between the United States and China, which, however, would not surface in an interim period. And, there might be a different development if Mr. Kelly is should be elected as the next US president.

China-ASEAN FTA and an East Asian Community

In early 1997, anticipating the birth of ASEAN 10, Japanese Prime Minister Ryutaro Hashimoto proposed a Japan-ASEAN summit to further accelerate the integration of ASEAN as well as Japan's relations with the ASEAN countries. The realization of ASEAN 10, however, coincided with the Asian financial crisis, forcing ASEAN countries to go through a series of difficult efforts to restructure domestic economies and politics as well as regional arrangements. Also, at about the same time, China has shifted its main strategic focus from high politics to low politics. ASEAN, following its usual instinct to carefully balance relations with external powers, gave a benign neglect to the Hashimoto proposal and instead took its own initiative leading to the establishment of ASEAN+3 at the end of 1997.

The organization of ASEAN+3 has ushered in a new momentum toward deepening regional integration. Singapore took an important initiative to officially propose an FTA with Japan in December 1999 when Prime Minister Goh Chok Tong visited Japan. Japanese economic ministries, most notably the Ministry of Economy, Trade and Industry (METI), which had already started to study such arrangements with several countries including South Korea and Mexico, responded positively and the negotiations gained momentum.

In the meantime, observing the momentum of a series of bilateral FTA initiatives and having achieved the goal of joining the WTO, China also came up with its own FTA initiative, as most symbolically indicated by the Chinese proposal of a free trade agreement with ASEAN at the occasion of the ASEAN+3 summit meeting in November 2000. In the following year, Chinese and SEAN leaders reached a basic agreement that they would achieve a free trade area within the coming 10 years. This was quickly followed-up in November 2002, when the leaders signed a comprehensive framework agreement to carry out the plan.

Here, a sharp contrast between Japan and China was obvious. Japanese approach, initiated by several officials of METI, was essentially economic, reflecting their concerns about the failure of WTO negotiations and the fear of being left out in the FTA arrangements in North America and EU. South Korea shared the same concerns, motivating President Kim Daejung and Prime Minister Keizo Obuchi to agree on starting a study on a bilateral FTA agreement as early as 1998.

The necessity on the part of Japan to approach FTA economically was also conditioned by the fact that Japan is a developed country, and therefore would not be able to conclude a WTO-incompatible agreement. This most critically meant that Japan in principle should include all the commodities in an FTA agreement, which has the most important bearings on the agricultural products.

China, on its part, took advantage of the enabling close of WTO regulations, which allows a developing country to conclude an FTA agreement without fully complying with WTO rules. This has made it possible for China and ASEAN to focus on feasible agreements.

At any rate, these China-ASEAN initiatives have prompted the Koizumi administration to develop its won political strategy built upon the ongoing process of FTA negotiations. In Prime Minister Koizumi's policy speech delivered in Singapore in January 2002, Koizumi proposed an "Initiative for Japan-ASEAN Comprehensive Economic Partnership," built upon the "Japan-Singapore Economic Agreement for a New Age Partnership," the so-called Japan-Singapore FTA, which Koizumi signed prior to the speech[5].

More importantly, the Koizumi proposal included an ambitious reference to an East Asian community. Koizumi said to the audience in Singapore that "our goal should be the creation of a community that acts together and advances together." Koizumi expressed his expectation that, starting from Japan-ASEAN cooperation, "the countries of ASEAN, Japan, China, the Republic of Korea, Australia and New Zealand will be core members of such a community."

Reportedly, the Chinese government is now formulating its own concept of an East Asia Community. What is explicit in the arguments by many Chinese observers of the FTA development is the emphasis on the political and strategic utility of the Chinese FTA initiatives in breaking the US strategy of "encircling" China. One obvious strategic reference point in Chinese efforts toward promoting regional integration and eventually an East Asian community is the exclusion of the United States.

Seen in this light, it may well be the case that the inclusion of Australia and New Zealand in the Koizumi proposal has an element of competing with the Chinese vision of a regional community. Japanese position implied here is that an East Asian community may not extend the formal membership to the United States necessarily, but should not entail the logic of excluding the United States, either.

Conclusion

Elements of political and security competition among China, the United States and Japan should not be taken as ominous nor destructive necessarily. There are seeds of strategic clashes, which need to be managed carefully, but these seeds may turn out to grow in different shape if we deal with them prudently at this time of critical transition.

The US-China strategic rivalry is likely to remain only potential for many years to come, due to clear commitment to different strategic goals on the sides of the United States and China.

Equally, the arguments on Sino-Japanese rivalry are most unproductive and indeed counterproductive in many ways. True, there has developed an unfortunate emotional vicious cycle between the two peoples over the last decade. In reality, however, strengths of China and Japan are essentially complimentary from a broader regional point of view. Economically, this should be most obvious. If seen from a Southeast Asian point of view, for instance, benefits available for Southeast Asian nations through FTA arrangements with Japan and China are basically complimentary. There are no substantial elements of economic competition here between Japan and China.

Some tend to make an argument of an economic threat from China, which might apply to some of the economic sectors negatively affected by Chinese economic development. If seen from a macro regional perspective, however, present China is in fact what Japanese diplomacy toward China since the 1970s and the 1980s has aspired to achieve for regional stability and prosperity.

Politically, too, Japan and China could engage in positive competition. Competition over a vision of an East Asia community is a case in point relevant for our discussion here. Since the US factor is ultimately in question, the competition may not be smooth necessarily, but entails the most critical element in order for an East Asia community to become a substantial entity. ASEAN here is not a by-stander at all.

Notes

1   Secretary Colin L. Powell, "Remarks to the Press En route to Canberra, Australia," (July 29, 2001), *http://www.state.gov/secretary/rm/2001/4347.htm*
2   "President Bush, Chinese President Jiang Zemin Discuss Iraq, N. Korea," *http://www.whitehouse.gov/news/releases/2002/10/20021025.html*
3   "The United States and Japan: Advancing Toward A Mature Partnership," Institute for National Strategic Studies Special Report (October 2000).
4   "The President's State of the Union Address," *http://www.whitehouse.gov/news/releases/2002/01/20020129-11.html*
5   Speech by Prime Minister of Japan Junichiro Koizumi, "Japan and ASEAN in East Asia: A Sincere and Open Partnership," (January 14, 2002). Available at *http://www.mofa.go.jp/region/asia-paci/pmv0201/speech.html*

References

Rice, Condoleezza, "Promoting the National Interest," *Foreign Affairs,* January/February, 2000.

Soeya Yoshihide, "Japanese Diplomacy and the North Korean Problem," *Japan Review of International Affairs,* Vol. 17, No. 1, Spring, 2003.

"The United States and Japan: Advancing Toward A Mature Partnership," Institute for National Strategic Studies Special Report, October, 2000.

Chapter 12

Southeast Asia and China Studies

Tan Chee-Beng

Introduction

China has a long historical relationship with Southeast Asia. With the rise of China as a major economic and political player in the world since 1978, China Studies has assumed a crucial role for Southeast Asian nations. While some major universities in the West have a long history of studying China, China Studies in Southeast Asia, perhaps with the exception of Singapore, has been not only new and rather weak, but often confined only to the learning of Putonghua or Mandarin. There is a need to treat China Studies more seriously, and it should not be confined to economic and political aspects only. There is a need to have a broader understanding of history, culture and society of China. That a good Center of China Studies is of strategic interest to Malaysia is obvious, although ISIS has been providing some basic related functions for policy makers. From what we can learn from the West, national strategic interest is closely linked to comprehensive good academic studies. There should be an open attitude to encourage different kinds of study, which should not be evaluated from some short-term strategic concerns only.

I shall discuss some socio-cultural features that both Malaysia and China can learn from one another, namely (a) ethnic diversity, (b) religious diversity, (c) democracy, liberty and political stability, and (d) migration, China and Chinese overseas.

Ethnic Diversity

Both China and Malaysia have a diversity of ethnic groups, though China is so much bigger and even more diverse. Officially China has 56 *minzu* which can be loosely understood as *bangsa* though not necessarily ethnic groups. A *minzu* is a meta ethnic category, and is officially classified. The Han people (Chinese in Malaysia comprising Hokkien, Hakka, Cantonese, Teochiu, Hainanese, etc are overwhelmingly of Han origin) constitute one *minzu*, and the rest are 55 minorities. But minorities in China are minorities only in the national sense, for in a particular region a minority *minzu* may be the majority. In many parts of Guangxi, for example, the Zhuang "minority" people are actually the majority people, more numerous than the Han people there. The Zhuang are the largest minority in China, numbering slightly more than 15 million people in 1990 (cf. Schein, 2000:70), much more than half the population of Malaysia. What is interesting in China is that there are Han Chinese who prefer to belong to a minority group if there is an opportunity. It is common to meet a mixed marriage couple, such as a minority group person and a Han, who prefers their children to be listed as belonging to the minority *minzu*. This is because minorities in China are entitled to some socio-economic advantages, such as needing less points to enter university.

Contrary to the bash-China writers' portrayal, the minority policy of China is better than most countries, and in fact better than that of the U.S. (in relation to the American Indians) and Malaysia (in relation to the Orang Asli). China' s constitution requires minorities to be represented in the local government. Thus, in a Yi majority area the county head has to be a Yi, and a Tibetan in the Tibetan autonomous region. In the one- person one-vote system of democracy practiced in Malaysia that is still largely ethnically based, it is almost impossible for an Orang Asli to be elected in a state or national election. Even where positions are bureaucratically appointed, it is rare, if any, for an Orang Asli to be appointed to such a position. In fact, the main officials of the Department of Orang Asli Affairs are not Orang Asli. Whereas in China there are many nationalities affairs commissions, these are mostly run by cadres who are minorities themselves, although in sensitive regions, government-trusted Han officials may hold the real power. Of course, China has more security concerns over certain minorities in certain regions, especially Xinjiang and Tibet.

The recognition of minorities is seen in Chinese currency. On a Chinese currency note, the Bank of China is not only written in Chinese pinyin, that is, *zhongguo renmin yinhang*, it is also written in Mongolian, Tibetan, Uygur and Zhuang scripts, to represent the five minority autonomous regions of China, that is, including the Hui who use the same Chinese script as the Han. China has even introduced written scripts for some minorities who do not have a literary tradition. But education of minorities/indigenous minorities is a difficult issue for China and Malaysia, and for the minorities themselves. In theory, minorities in autonomous regions can study in their own schools, but in practice it is difficult even if the minorities want them. In fact many parents of minorities even insist that their children study in Zhongwen (Chinese) because this will provide the opportunities for upward mobility in China, as such children have a better chance of entering universities in future. Similarly in Malaysia, one has to study Malay so as to be able to participate at all levels of Malaysian society. In the 1980s the Kadazan in Sabah wanted to have Kadazan included in school syllabus, but there is problem of which Kadazan dialect to use and the shortages of Kadazan textbooks. Some *minzu* in China integrate themselves into the national Chinese language education better than others. For example, Hansen (1999) reports that the Naxi accepts the Chinese education better than the Dai (both in Yunnan). National education does not accommodate the teaching of Dai language and Buddhism in school and this accounts for the Dai seeing national education as being imposed, and many prefer to send their children to temple schools. This has to do with not just the government policy on education but also its policy on religion. Perhaps the incorporation of the teaching of Islam in national schools in Malaysia is a model China can consider for implementation for some minorities, but at present the communist ideology on religion makes this not possible.

Going back to education for minorities, both Malaysia and China have to cope with the educational achievement of minorities/indigenous peoples in remote regions. From my research in East Malaysia and visits to some remote regions of minorities in China, I am of the opinion that the Malaysian government has given better support to students in remote regions. The Malaysian government has given more attention to providing some basic needs for these students, including placing students of the interior in *asrama* (hostels) and providing basic food and textbooks (cf. Tan 1993). In China, students in similar situation do not get such support, and on top of that they have to pay fees – compulsory primary education in China does not mean free education. I am not saying that Malaysia has already done very well in rural education, what I want to emphasize is that there is much that Malaysia and China can learn from one another, and it is relevant to do research on, for example, minority education in China, and vice-versa.

Religious Diversity

Related to ethnic diversity is religious diversity. Like Malaysia, China also has to deal with religious diversity. The Dai case mentioned above shows that it is a tricky issue with regards to religious education. In Malaysia, Islamic education is incorporated into the national educational system for the Muslims. The majority of the people in China practice Chinese popular religion and Buddhism while many are agnostics and atheists, and a number of *minzu* are Muslims. The Chinese-speaking Hui (distributed in different parts of China) and the Turkic-speaking Uygur (mainly in Xinjiang) alone number about 9 million and 7 million respectively (Schein 2000: 70). Other smaller groups include Kazakh, Kyrgyz, Salar, Uzbek, Tatar, Tajik, Bao'an, and Dongxiang. There had been some protests by Muslims in different parts of China arising from events that the Muslims felt insulted. From my few contacts with Muslims in China, it is clear that there is a real need for religious dialogue and for the mainstream Chinese (who are not Muslims), especially the cadres dealing with Muslims, to be educated about basic teachings of Islam and be aware of the attitude of Muslims towards their religion. In August 2001 I visited Bole at the northwestern border of Xinjiang, and I was well received by some Uygur including an Ahong (Imam) because I told them that I was from Malaysia. They associated Malaysia with Islam, although I did say that I was not a Muslim and explained the religious diversity in Malaysia. From what they told me, it was clear that the ordinary Uygur view the Chinese government as not respecting their faith and their practice of the religion. There is distrust. While the government has been tough on the separatists, who are a minority, there is no obvious outright oppression to the practicing of Islam. It seems to me that the main problem is lack of dialogue and trust: the ordinary people not trusting the non-Muslim cadres while the latter generally see the Uygur as separatists or supporters of separatists, and many Han Chinese do look down on Muslims. The Chinese Communist ideology of seeing religion as superstitious no doubt hinders the promotion of religious dialogue and the education of cadres about Islam or other religions such as Theravada Buddhism with regards to the Dai people. It is quite obvious to me that the main religious problem with regards to the Muslims in China is the lack of understanding of and respect for Islam and Muslims. For example, a Uygur in a government office told me that his Han colleagues asked him not to attend Friday Prayer at the mosque since he was a cadre and therefore in theory should be a Communist and an atheist. He felt rather insulted and an incident like this no doubt sows the seed of distrust.

While visiting Guilin in Guangxi in May 2001, I learnt about a crisis that the Head of the local Nationalities Affairs Commission, herself a Muslim, had to attend to, cautiously and immediately. In his enthusiasm to promote tourism, a low-level cadre from a local government department had published in the party newspaper a proposal that touches on pigs and Muslims, and this infuriated the Muslims. I was able to learn how the Bureau played the crucial role of helping the government head off a local religious conflict which, if not handled quickly and with care, could have spread to other parts of China. Thus even with my limited observation in China, I am able to see the problem: the need to educate mainstream Chinese about the minorities and their religions, and to promote religious dialogue. Overall in Malaysia there is a greater understanding of the need of religious tolerance and mutual respect in Malaysia, but one cannot be complacent. Learning about diverse religions and respecting people of different faiths remain crucial for the stability and unity of the country. There is much that China and Malaysia can share and learn about religious diversity and national unity.

Dialogue between religious groups need not be confined to people within China or Malaysia only, but can involve both countries together. This will help to widen people's horizon about religion and ethnicity, to have a broader view of religious affiliation. There is already considerable educational contact between the Muslims of Malaysia and China. There are Muslims from China who study in Malaysia, including at the International Islamic University, while Malaysian Muslims who meet Muslims in China perhaps have become more open-minded about Chinese and Islam, for in Malaysia the Malay stereotype of Chinese is that they are non-Muslims while Chinese Malaysians tend to associate Islam with Malays. Even conversations between non-Muslim Chinese of China and Chinese of Malaysia can widen local Malaysian horizon. A few years ago a woman (not a Muslim) in Quanzhou, Fujian, told me of her tour experiences in Malaysia. What impressed her most was the National Mosque. I had to admit to her that I had not visited it. It then occurred to me that few Chinese Malaysians ever visit a mosque, nor do the Muslims visit Chinese religious sites. The only *surau* I had visited and joined in the Friday Prayer was when I visited the Bedeng

Kenyah of Long Busang in interior Sarawak in July 1992. Some of the Badeng there had embraced Islam. In Malaysia we tolerate each other's religion but we remain quite separate in matters religious.

Democracy, Liberty and Political Stability

Given the ethnic and religious diversity and potential conflicts, political stability is of utmost concern to both China and Southeast Asian countries. Despite the Communist rule, economic liberalization is expected to help bring about greater liberty and perhaps even democracy in China, especially with the growth of the middle class. A great concern, however, is the increasing economic gap between the better off urban people and the large number of rural poor. Both the political leaders and many ordinary people in China fear *luan* or social disorder, and this is often taken as an excuse that China cannot be expected to have western-style democracy. There is also the potential military conflict between Mainland China and Taiwan, and this is of concern not only to China, but also to the whole of East Asia and Southeast Asia. While some countries in Southeast Asia appear to have more democracy than China, they are not necessarily more liberal and stable than it. Malaysia today is quite a special case, for while it is not as liberal it is politically more stable than the Philippines, Thailand and Indonesia, with its democratically elected government, despite all its flaws.

There are debates about democracy, liberty and stability in Asia, but it is beyond the scope here to discuss them. Perhaps one can pay some attention to Hong Kong. Despite the vocal criticism of opposition politicians and democracy activists, Hong Kong remains a very liberal and stable society. I would even say it is the most liberal Chinese society in the world that is governed by the rule of law. There is much that a center of China Studies can study and compare the issues of democracy, liberty and stability. After all a strong and stable China, and hopefully a more liberal and democratic one too, is important to the stability and prosperity of Southeast Asia. Such a center of study should study not just Mainland China, but also Hong Kong, Macao and Taiwan.

Migration, China and Chinese Overseas

Migration, both within China and from China to other countries, is an important issue. The present-day large-scale rural to urban migration in China is unprecedented, as farmers from poorer regions move to cities, especially the more prosperous coastal cities and the special economic zones, for better economic opportunities. The fate of these people has lots of implication for the future of China and even Asia. An unstable China might lead to new waves of mass migration that will have serious consequences globally, especially East and Southeast Asia.

Chinese transnational migration is not new, and today there are Chinese all over the world. It is therefore relevant for a center of China Studies to include the study of Chinese overseas. After all Chinese overseas have significant impacts on both the development of China and their own countries of residence, as well as the economic and social relations between Southeast Asian countries and China. There are also new migrants from China, both legal and illegal ones, not only in the West but also in Southeast Asia. Singapore, for example, has attracted many new immigrants from China (cf. Liu 2003, *Yazhou Zhoukan*, 25 April 2004, pp. 14-21). Unlike in the Philippines where there are many illegal Chinese migrants, Malaysian control over migrants is tighter. Even then, it is a common sight to see young women from China peddling various kinds of goods from coffee shop to coffee shop in Kuala Lumpur and Penang. There are also transient sex workers. But there are well off economic migrants, too, and a recent report shows that many of the applicants for the "second home" project in Malaysia are Chinese from Mainland China and Taiwan (*Yazhou Zhoukan*, 25 July 2004, pp. 50-51). The point is, Chinese migration is a relevant topic for a center of China Studies.

Conclusion

Overall it is important to establish at least one center of China Studies in Malaysia, one that is comprehensive enough to cover a wide range of topics and involves different disciplines, especially anthropology, economics, history, political science, and sociology. Such a center should cover Mainland China, Hong Kong, Macao and Taiwan, as well as Chinese overseas. I thus congratulate the University of Malaya for establishing this Institute of China Studies (ICS), in the words of the Vice-Chancellor in his invitation letter to this conference, "to advance scholarship and research on politics, economics and social developments of China and the 'Chinese World'."

Other than research, it is also important to train local China specialists. For a new center to be successful, it is necessary to have exchange programs that facilitate bringing not only scholars from China but also from institutions in the west and in the region, as well as sending local scholars to China and elsewhere. Cooperation with similar institutions in Southeast Asia is important too, and perhaps we can begin with cooperation with the East Asian Institute of the National University of Singapore, which Prof. Wang Gungwu now heads.

References

Hansen, Mette Halskov, *Lessons in Being Chinese: Minority Education and Ethnic Identity in Southwest China*, Hong Kong: Hong Kong University Press, 1999.

Liu Hong, *The Transformation of Chinese Society in Postwar Singapore: Localization Process, Regional Networking, and Global Perspective* (in Chinese), Xiamen: Xiamen University Press, 2003.

Schein, Louisa, *Minorities Rules: The Miao and the Feminine in China's Cultural Politics*, Durham and London: Duke University Press, 2000.

Tan Chee-Beng, "Education in Rural Sarawak", *Borneo Review* 4(2):128-141, 1993.

Editors

Dr **Hou** Kok Chung is the director of the Institute of China Studies, University of Malaya, Kuala Lumpur, Malaysia. Email: *houkc@um.edu.my*

Dr Émile Kok-Kheng **Yeoh** is an academic at the Institute of China Studies, University of Malaya, and the Department of Economics, Faculty of Economics and Administration, University of Malaya, Kuala Lumpur, Malaysia. Email: *emileyeo@correo.nu*